# A MANY-VALUED APPROACH TO DEDUCTION AND REASONING FOR ARTIFICIAL INTELLIGENCE

THE KLUWER INTERNATIONAL SERIES
IN ENGINEERING AND COMPUTER SCIENCE

# A MANY-VALUED APPROACH TO DEDUCTION AND REASONING FOR ARTIFICIAL INTELLIGENCE

by

**Cary G. deBessonet**

*AI Project, Louisiana State Law Institute*

*and*

*Southern University*

KLUWER ACADEMIC PUBLISHERS

**Boston/Dordrecht/London**

**Distributors for North America:**
Kluwer Academic Publishers
101 Philip Drive
Assinippi Park
Norwell, Massachusetts 02061 USA

**Distributors for all other countries:**
Kluwer Academic Publishers Group
Distribution Centre
Post Office Box 322
3300 AH Dordrecht, THE NETHERLANDS

**Library of Congress Cataloging-in-Publication Data**

DeBessonet, Cary G.
A many-valued approach to deduction and reasoning for artificial intelligence / by Cary G. deBessonet.
p. cm. — (The Kluwer international series in engineering and computer science ; SECS 129)
Includes bibliographical references and index.
ISBN 0-7923-9138-1 (acid-free)
1. Artificial intelligence. 2. Computational linguistics.
3. Cognition. I. Title. II. Series.
Q335.D42 1991
006.3—dc20 90-22194
CIP



*Printed on acid-free paper.*

Printed in the United States of America

Dedicated to my Mother, **Doris Virginia Cary deBessonet**

# Table of Contents

## List of Figures

# PREFACE

This book introduces an approach that can be used to ground a variety of intelligent systems, ranging from simple fact-based systems to highly sophisticated reasoning systems. As the popularity of AI-related fields has grown over the last decade, the number of persons interested in building intelligent systems has increased exponentially. Some of these people are highly skilled and experienced in the use of AI techniques, but many lack that kind of expertise. Much of the literature that might otherwise interest those in the latter category is not appreciated by them because the material is too technical, often needlessly so. The so-called logicists see logic as a primary tool and favor a formal approach to AI, whereas others are more content to rely on informal methods. This polarity has resulted in different styles of writing and reporting, and people entering the field from other disciplines often find themselves hard pressed to keep abreast of current differences in style. This book attempts to strike a balance between these approaches by covering points from both technical and nontechnical perspectives and by doing so in a way that is designed to hold the interest of readers of each persuasion.

During recent years, a somewhat overwhelming number of books that present general overviews of AI-related subjects have been placed on the market. These books serve an important function by providing researchers and others entering the field with progress reports and new developments. What they lack is coverage of a wide range of problems within the context of a unified approach. A researcher must now consult a number of sources to cover the problem domain of a particular approach, and incongruities in the source materials often make the endeavor unproductive. The kind of book that seems to be missing from the literature is one that devotes itself to a single approach while addressing a variety of problems. An exception to this is is the book that touts logic, particularly the predicate calculus, as the primary AI tool. A sea of literature exists on this subject, and much of it describes how a logic-based approach can be used in diverse domains, although there appear to be problems with employing it in areas such as modal, epistemic and nonmonotonic reasoning. Some of the books are highly technical (e.g. Wojcicki, *Theory of Logical Calculi*, Kluwer Academic Publishers), whereas others are more pedagogically oriented (e.g. Genesereth and Nilsson, *The Logical Foundations of Artificial Intelligence*, Morgan Kaufmann Publishers). It would be difficult for one to remain ignorant of the potential that standard logic has for use in AI systems in view of the fact that the market has been flooded with literature on logic for over a decade. One might recall that books such as Kowalski's *Logic for Problem Solving* (North Holland) ushered in a mass of literature on the use of the clausal form of logic in AI systems. Those who have attempted to employ logic-based representations on a broad scale have run into representation problems in the areas mentioned previously. Until those problems are resolved, there is much room for viable alternatives.

Nonstandard logics seem to be logical candidates for bringing new ideas into the field of AI, and indeed one sees more frequent reference to them in the literature. Books on the use of nonstandard logics are also becoming available (e.g. Smets, Mamdani, Dubois and Prade, *Non-Standard Logics for Automated Reasoning*, Academic Press). One deficiency that books on standard or nonstandard logics seem to have is that although they purport to describe unified approaches, one is sometimes hard pressed to appreciate the approaches in that way. Often such a book consists of a collection of papers, each describing a different formal style, and the reader becomes lost during the process of making simultaneous attempts to understand the formal details and to grasp the overall approach. In contrast, the proposed book maintains the same style throughout its discussion of various problem domains, and it keeps considerations pertaining to the implementation of the theory in view for the reader during most of that discussion. This is why the book might be of particular interest to those who are looking for an approach that can be used creatively to build AI systems in multiple domains.

The book addresses several needs in the field of AI. Besides helping to fulfill the need for literature on a unified approach that can be used to solve typical AI problems, it introduces methodologies that are sorely needed in AI to overcome some of the limitations that accompany the use of two-valued first-order logic. It might be especially appreciated by persons coming into AI from other fields because it begins at the basic level and proceeds step by step to higher levels. The basic points are made in the context of delimiting the philosophical foundations of the system, and during that process, challenges are made to the traditional ways of doing things. The hope is that this will hold the interest of both types of readers.

The general thesis of the book is that the theoretical foundation of an AI system should be specially tailored to fit the requirements of the automated environment in which the system is to be implemented. Since AI systems usually employ the marking and recognitive capabilities of automated technologies within environments of addressable spaces, the formal systems upon which they rest should be defined specifically with reference to those capabilities and environments. Such a formal system need not be defined as a first-order logic. By adopting the approach described in the book, a researcher achieves freedom to abandon some of the troublesome constraints that might be imposed by the use of a first-order language and freedom to extend traditional notions in ways that make them more appropriate for use in AI systems. The approach recommended employs an English-like representation language and an accompanying many-valued system. A case is made for the position that a many-valued approach is better suited than two-valued logic for simulating the kind of reasoning and other cognitive processes that take place in human conversation. The hope is that the book will motivate readers to employ the approach creatively in their areas of interest so that the underlying theory can be developed and implemented to its full potential more rapidly.

Readers who are not interested in the formal details of the theory presented in this book should skip any portion that becomes too technical for their taste. An attempt has been made to introduce the theory in segments, and each segment is given an informal description prior to giving it a more formal description. Thus, if a technical segment is encountered, the reader can simply move forward to the next nontechnical segment.

## ACKNOWLEDGEMENTS

This book describes some of the results of my research over the years. I am grateful for the support of: the Louisiana State Law Institute [Jack Caldwell (President), William Crawford (Director)]; the Southern University Law Center [B. K. Agnihotri, Chancellor]; the LSU Law Center [Winston Day, Chancellor]; the Center of Civil Law Studies of the LSU Law Center [Saul Litvinoff, Director]; and the LSU Computer Science Department [Donald Kraft, Chairman]. I thank the indicated officers and department heads of these institutions for their past and continuing support. I would also like to thank the State of Louisiana, including its Board of Regents, for the LEQSF funding (86-87)-UNEXP-1 and (86-87)-UNEXP-3 that was used to create the research environment within which I work and to sponsor a significant part of the work that has led to these results.

I extend special thanks to Saul Litvinoff and the Center of Civil Law Studies for being the first to sponsor my work in this field; to William Hawkland (Chancellor Emeritus, LSU Law Center), T. Haller Jackson (Past President, Louisiana State Law Institute), and William Crawford for their special efforts in helping create research opportunities for me and a research environment within which to take advantage of those opportunities; to William Arceneaux (President, Louisiana Association of Independent Colleges and Universities) for his helpful suggestions pertaining to the creation of a suitable research environment; to Peter Maggs (Professor of Law, University of Illinois) for introducing me to the field of AI and Law while I was his graduate assistant; and to Jason Xenakis (deceased), my logic teacher, for introducing me to logic and related fields.

Special thanks are also extended to George Cross (Contel Technology Center), with whom I have collaborated over the years on many matters and articles, and to John Martin (Department of Philosophy, University of Cincinnati) for his insightful suggestions pertaining to the theory presented. I also thank the following people for their critiques and comments on some of the theory underlying this work: Sukhamay Kundu (LSU); Leslie Jones (IMSL); Charles Delzell (LSU); Andrew McCafferty (LSU); Robert A. Pascal (Law, LSU); John Baker (Philosophy,LSU); Ja-Song Leu (LSU); Jerry Draayer (LSU); Layman Allen (Michigan); Michael Dyer(UCLA); Carole Hafner (Northeastern); Thorne McCarty (Rutgers); and Doris Carver (LSU). I am particularly grateful for the help and support of my assistants Satyanarayana Amaravenkata, Steve Gant, and Bill Lynch in preparing the camera-ready version of this manuscript and for the help of Leslie Jones and Karen Westphal in creating some of the figures. Thanks also go to the following graduate students who assisted in proofing the text: Pam Langley, Denise Groene, and Patti Foster. I apologize to anyone whom I should have mentioned but forgot to do so. Naturally, I thank my wonderful wife and family for their encouragement and support through it all. Most of all I thank the good Lord for allowing this all to come about.

# A MANY-VALUED APPROACH TO DEDUCTION AND REASONING FOR ARTIFICIAL INTELLIGENCE

## CHAPTER 1

# OBSERVATIONS AND ISSUES

### 1.1 Frames, Nets, FOL and SL

Over the years a number of schemes of knowledge representation (KR) have been developed that purportedly possess expressive power comparable to first-order logic (hereafter 'FOL'). Frames (Minsky, 1975) and semantic networks (e.g. Schubert, 1976; Hendrix, 1979; Shapiro, 1979) have been employed successfully in a number of systems and are well known in AI circles. Whether or not these systems are merely notational variants of FOL has been the subject of much debate (e.g. Israel and Brachman, 1984). Tenacious loyalty to the predicate calculus by some AI researchers is no doubt the result of its deductive strength and familiarity (e.g. Nilsson, 1971, 1980; McDermott, 1987). It has become popular to employ the linear notation of the predicate calculus to build databases that become intelligent through implementation of rules of inference and proof strategies (e.g. Robinson, 1965; Bundy, 1983; Wos *et al*, 1984; Genesereth and Nilsson, 1987). The viability of first-order languages as KR systems is being increased by the development of methods to handle quantification over events, say through individuation of those events (see e.g. Davidson, 1967), and to handle knowledge and belief, say by allowing possible worlds to be admitted into the domain of quantification (see e.g. Moore, 1984). At the other end of the spectrum is the view that logic is inadequate from both psychological and linguistic perspectives. Some researchers who hold this view have concentrated their efforts on the development of what has been described as informal methods for commonsense reasoning (e.g. see Schank and Nash-Webber, 1975). The polarized views on the role of logic in AI have prompted notable efforts to produce a common core of principles that would have a unifying effect on AI (e.g. Sowa, 1984). As yet, these efforts have failed to unify the field, and the aforementioned polarity in AI is still quite appreciable.

An important point of contention between the proponents of these views seems to be whether one should specify a formal theory of semantics for a given representation scheme prior to using it to build systems. The well known claim of the logicists is that to fail to specify such a formal theory in advance is to proceed in an *ad hoc* manner. The opposite view maintains that the better approach is to first develop a scheme, say to represent the content of natural language unambiguously, and then try to find a way to manipulate its contents in a manner that would simulate commonsense and other forms of reasoning. The idea is that if this works, why worry about the specification of some underlying formal theory, if indeed one exists. The logicists question whether a system built in this way can ever achieve the generality it needs to be employed usefully in practice. Their view seems to be that only by specifying an adequate formal theory and then building the system to fit the theory can one cover the problems that must be addressed to achieve generality.

It is interesting to note that the proponents of each view seemingly would agree with the observation reported by Levesque (1986) that thinking can be usefully understood as mechanical operations over symbolic representations. The divisive issue seems to be whether a formally specified theory should accompany the notation that is to be used in a system that is to simulate thinking. This book describes a nonstandard, many-valued approach that combines the strengths of both formal and informal approaches to produce a more powerful means of handling certain aspects of the knowledge representation problem. The proper balance seems to have been struck, and the resulting approach seems to hold important advantages over its predecessors. From the informal view, the approach borrows the independent goal of developing a language that can be used to represent the content of natural language unambiguously (see e.g. Schank and Abelson, 1977). From the logicist view, it borrows the goal of grounding the language in a specified formal theory. The approach is described as being many-valued because its underlying formal theory is specified with reference to a many-valued system of evaluation. The approach has been used to implement a system called SMS (*S*ymbolic *M*anipulation *S*ystem) and will be referred to in this book as the SMS approach. The version of SMS described herein is a 7-valued system (see section 3.3), but the approach may be modified to accommodate additional values. The justification for distinguishing SMS from the typical many-valued logistic system is discussed in Chapter 6.

Mention should be made here of the view, discussed in [Gaines, 1977], that linguistic precision should grow *ad hoc* to meet the demands of whatever problem is at hand. Under this view, clarity of explanation is thought to be rooted in the naturalness and simplicity of the concepts and vocabulary used, and emphasis is to be placed on the primacy of natural, *fuzzy* concepts. Any increase in linguistic precision should be justified (Gaines, 1977). This view is held by the adherents of fuzzy set theory. Doubts about whether Tarski's criterion of truth should be applied to a statement such as, "the number of trees in Canada is even" (Putnam, 1976), due to the effects that the 'fuzziness' of the Canadian boundaries and the nature of a tree would have upon the determination of eveness, are typical of the doubts that have led to the use of fuzzy set theory in reasoning (e.g. Zadeh, 1965, 1979, 1985; Prade, 1982; Farreny and Prade, 1986 ). The theory rejects the assumption that only a "yes" or "no" answer is proper for the question whether an element of a space belongs to a particular subset of that space. The fuzzy theorists claim that almost everything that relates to natural language (e.g. ordinary English) is a matter of degree (Zadeh, 1986). This points to a theory of meaning that is based on fuzzy sets and infinite-valued logic instead of ordinary sets and two-valued logic.

In opposition to the view of the fuzzy theorists, it can be argued that although there may be aspects of the world that are continuous (e.g. time, temperature and distance), natural language rarely makes use of the kind of distinctions that a calculus of fuzzy values provides. Natural languages have 'fuzzy' words like *almost, very,* and *more or less* that are used as *hedges* to handle cases in which conceptual standards are not quite satisfied, and rarely does one need a vocabulary to describe a continuous range of variability. By employing hedges, one can describe discrete states that bear recognized relations to the states that satisfy whatever conceptual standard is at hand. Human beings readily understand, for example, that *almost grown* describes a different state than *completely grown.* Thus, although the world itself may be fuzzy, human thought and reasoning may not be fuzzy (Sowa, 1984).

In an effort to avoid the quibbling over the relevance of fuzzy set theory for human thought and reasoning, the many-valued approach described in this book has been defined without reference to a calculus of fuzzy values of the sort employed by the fuzzy theorists. Instead, the system is oriented toward the use of discrete descriptions and natural language hedges. This is not to say that the fine gradations recognized in fuzzy systems cannot be usefully employed within the system. Section 3.3 describes how certain problems of imprecision can be addressed without resorting to finely graded values, but section 4.10 describes how representational devices very similar to 'fuzzy' mechanisms (e.g. possibility distributions; see section 6.1) can be incorporated into the scheme if one wishes to do so. These mechanisms are given special interpretations in the environments into which they are introduced. In this respect it may be said that the SMS approach is compatible with the fuzzy approach. The same may be said to hold between the SMS approach and the probabilistic approach (see section 4.10). In preparation for a demonstration of compatibility between these approaches, some aspects of fuzzy set theory and fuzzy logic (FL) will be discussed from time to time in the sections that follow. It has been assumed that the reader is already familiar with FOL, so preparatory discussions about FOL have been minimized. Chapter 7 compares and contrasts the many-valued approach with FOL.

The attempt to combine the aforementioned approaches has produced some pleasant surprises. One might think that the representations over which such a formal theory would be defined would have to look like logic notation. Logic programming languages, for example, bear resemblance to standard logic notation. It was found, however, that as a result of independently attempting to invent an unambiguous way of expressing the content of English, an easy and somewhat direct mapping to and from English was maintained, and the resulting notation turned out to be more English-like than logic notation. In this respect, the notation seems to hold an advantage over logic-oriented languages. Another surprise was that the notation allows a powerfully broad and free specification of mechanical operations to be defined over it in a way that can be employed to simulate human reasoning. This broadness and freedom of specification makes the language an attractive alternative to first-order notation. It was discovered, for example, that the concept of derivability can be extended to include relations between nonsentential linguistic objects, which means that derivability need not be defined solely as a relation between propositions as it is in FOL. This to some extent allows derivability at the propositional level to be defined in terms of derivability at the nonpropositional level, a matter discussed in section 4.6.

The remaining sections of this book describe a language and an accompanying many-valued system that can be used to simulate some aspects of human reasoning. The following simple examples are offered to set the scope of the discussions that follow. Given the sentence:

A large white block is heavy. (1)

(where the article 'A' is to be interpreted in a particular rather than universal sense so that reference is being made to some unspecified block), the statement could be cast into the following first-order form:

$$E(x)\ (\ Bx \bullet Wx \bullet Lx \bullet Hx\ ) \qquad (2)$$

where 'E' is the existential quantifier, '•' represents logical conjunction, 'B' means 'is a block', 'W' means 'is white', 'L' means 'is large', and 'H' means 'is heavy'. By giving the block a name (e.g. 'block-1'), the same sentence could be represented as a frame, as in:

```
(block-1 (isa block)                (3)
         (size large)
         (color white)
         (weight heavy))
```

or in the linear predicate calculus modified for the Lisp environment, as in:

(inst block-1 block) (4)
(size block-1 large)
(color block-1 white)
(weight block-1 heavy)

where 'inst' is a 2-place predicate that identifies its first argument as an 'instance of' its second argument. It can also be represented as a simple net as follows:

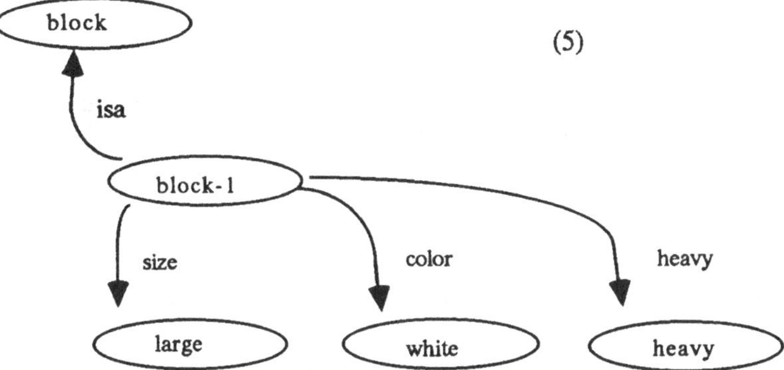


These simple representation schemes are transformable into one another, as any AI researcher familiar with the basic schemes knows. This is not to say that they are semantically identical in all respects. Example (2), for instance, employs the existential quantifier and thus has existential import provided the quantifier is given its common interpretation, whereas examples (3), (4) and (5) require special interpretations to incorporate that meaning. It should also be noted that information about the classification of predicates would have to added to example (2) for it to capture meaning on par with the other examples (e.g. 'large' would have to be classified as a measure of size). It is beyond the scope of this book to show that these notations are more or less equivalent or that they can be made so without difficulty. It is well known, for example, that quantification can be incorporated into a net (e.g. Hendrix, 1979), and in that respect example (5) could easily be made equivalent to example (2).

It has been pointed out that some KR languages appear to be nothing more than parenthesized English or natural language (Charniak and McDermott, 1985). A similar claim can be made about the each of the notations above, including the FOL example. Each representation consists of parenthesized or demarcated English (or abbreviations thereof), plus necessary punctuation marks, connectors and arcs. It is of course the interpretation of these representations that allows them to capture the meaning of the original sentence. The approach advocated in this book employs a language referred to herein as SL (*S*ymbolic *L*anguage). The trivial example below is offered to introduce the reader to the syntax of SL. The reader should assume that SL has a lexicon that appropriately categorizes the terms used in the example (e.g 'large' would be categorized as a measure of size, 'white' as a color, and 'heavy' as a measure of weight). It should also be assumed that particularization of the term 'block' would be accomplished by a default scheme of individuation, a matter discussed in section 2.3.2. Sentence (1) would be expressed in SL as follows:

< <block<large><white>> is heavy >. (6)

This somewhat unsophisticated representation is essentially a sequence consisting of the subject, verb and object of the given sentence. The two adjectives that modify the subject are set within wedges immediately following the subject. At this point it seems fair to say that each of these examples consists merely of assortments of English words and symbols fixed in particular syntax. It seems that SL is every bit as expressive as the other notations and that it contains the formal rigor necessary for it to be employed successfully in a reasoning system. Unfortunately, it is not convenient to make detailed comparisons between SL and each of the notations mentioned in this section. However, since FOL has been frequently compared and contrasted with these other notations, perhaps some appreciation of the merits of SL can be gleaned from a comparison of SL to FOL. Such a comparison is made in Chapter 7.

In the way of general comparison, it appears that a couple of favorable features of SL can be discerned at this point. The first is that the SL is more English-like than the other notations. Although perhaps only faintly appreciable to the reader at this juncture, this observation will become clearer as more examples are given. SL has been designed to be expressed in much the same way as one expresses sentences in ordinary English, that is, with subjects, verbs, objects and indirect objects cast into a typical active voice ordering with modifiers appearing immediately after the words modified. This, combined with the fact that this English-like notation and the mechanical operations defined over it qualify as a formal system with features comparable to a logic, makes it particularly suitable for use in AI systems. This too will be made clear in the pages that follow.

The goal in creating SL was to produce a language that would have expressive power comparable to ordinary English yet which would bear sufficient formal structure to be processed intelligently by computer. The idea was for SL to be used like logic notation to capture a sufficient segment of the essential structures and logical relationships that seem to underlie English discourse so that it could be used effectively in knowledge representation. The hope was that it could be made as readable and easy to use as ordinary English. Symbolic logic has well known drawbacks in this regard, as any teacher of the subject knows. Unfortunately, the goals set out for SL have not been achieved completely. SL is not as readable as English, and it is more difficult to use than English. Nonetheless, some success has been realized. SL is more readable and easier to use than FOL because one comprehends SL text in much the same way as one comprehends English text. To be able to use the current version of SL, about all that is required is that one become familiar with the punctuation and special operators of SL and become accustomed to having modifiers follow terms rather than precede them.

One can immediately see that SL shares an advantage with the techniques exemplified in (3) and (4) above in that they each employ Lisp-like notation, an advantage not held by the techniques exemplified in (2) and (5). For the most part, all one need do to the SL examples in this book to convert them into LISP data structures is to replace the wedges with parentheses. In fact, the only reason why wedges are used instead of parentheses in the examples in this book is to stress the importance of *sequence* for SL. The formal methods by which sequences are manipulated in SMS are described in later chapters.

Proponents of FOL are quick to rely on the assertion that the syntax of FOL is well understood and precise (e.g. McDermott, 1987). Although some (e.g Wang, 1967; Sowa, 1984) have questioned whether FOL is as well understood as some logicists would have one believe, it may be granted that FOL notation is generally recognized, but perhaps too much importance is being placed on this factor. This point is discussed in more depth in Chapters 3 and 6. One might question why anyone would want to use a system like SMS in preference to FOL, which has evolved through a host of representation problems. The answer is much the same as that which has been given in defense of conceptual graph notation, to wit:

1) SMS supports a more direct mapping to and from natural language;

2) SMS has direct extensions into the modal realm, a realm that has caused problems for FOL;

3) the theoretical developments that have gone into FOL can be transferred to SMS;

4) proofs in most cases are easier in SMS than in FOL; and

5) SL is easier to learn and read than a first-order language (cf. Sowa, 1984, at pages 149-150).

An important additional reason for preferring SMS over some other systems is:

6) SMS can handle certain semantical and syntactical imprecisions that might pose considerable difficulties for FOL-based systems ( e.g. see example 24 in section 4.2.2).

It has been maintained that conceptual graph notation can easily coexist with other logical notation. The same may be true of SMS, at least to some extent, but this is not being touted as an advantage because it may not be worth the trouble to map SMS to and from FOL, which incidently is something that has been done for graphical notation (Sowa, 1984).

Although this book describes a particular system, the goal is to demonstrate the usefulness of a general approach. For this reason, the discussions for the most part avoid narrow representation issues and concentrate on more general ones to prove the viability of the overall approach. Although the theory is introduced in the context of describing a system that allows one to build a database of assertions and then query that database, which causes less emphasis to be placed on matters that would be stressed for rule-based systems, the theory can be extended to cover complex rule-based applications. Current plans call for the extension of the theory to meet the rule-based requirements of the legal domain, which calls for the optimization of unification and resolution methodologies. The development of these methodologies is well under way, but since the goal of this book is to demonstrate the general potential of the theory, the discussions will not focus on those techniques. Instead, a framework will be established for a unified approach that can incorporate already established methods.

This way of doing things differs from the way some others have attempted to achieve similar goals. It is common for discussions to focus on narrow representation issues when new schemes are introduced, but this often loses the reader in details with the result that the general methodology fails to be appreciated. In the way of an alternative approach, this book will touch upon a number of problem areas in an attempt to outline a set of representation techniques that can be used to address a variety of problems at more refined levels. The hope is that the reader will become sufficiently acquainted with the techniques to employ them creatively at those levels.

## 1.2 Automating SMS

The features of SMS described in this book can be coordinated and implemented as an automated system capable of responding to queries about information in its database. Chapter 12 describes a simple prototype that allows a user to enter statements in SL to form a database of assertions. A useful comparison can be made between this system and one that would allow the user to enter statements in FOL to build a knowledge base. The comparison is useful because it brings to the fore some questions about how one should go about comparing schemes for use in AI systems. The notation employed in a system should be distinguished from the methodologies or programs that manipulate the notation in carrying out proof procedures. Students of FOL are familiar with how proofs are constructed by hand. The given premises are transformed or manipulated in accordance with the inference and instantiation rules of the system. Often the premises are reduced to other forms and then combined to produce the desired conclusion. The point is that unless the conclusion to be proved is given outright in the premises, it must be derived through transformation and manipulation of the premises. This raises what might be called the first criterion for usefulness of a representation language (or formal system that can serve in that capacity) in an automated system, and that is, the notation should be usable directly in the automated environment. SL meets this criterion. One can enter SL statements directly into SMS to build a database and can query that database using SL statements. SMS automatically converts the database into a massively optimized frame-based representation. A diagram of the general structure of SMS is given in Figure 1. Any SL statement that is presented as a query is treated as a conclusion to be proved, and SMS takes care of all the manipulations and transformations needed to prove the conclusion, or else determine that it is not derivable from the database under the derivation procedures employed by the system.

The resolution principle (Robinson, 1965) is one of the most popular proof tools employed in logic-oriented systems. It has been used effectively on clausal databases constructed from predicate calculus notation (see e.g. Stickel, 1988; Genesereth and Nilsson, 1987; Charniak and McDermott, 1985) and has also been used in fuzzy logic (e.g. Giles, 1985; Liu and Xiao, 1985; and Shen *et al*, 1988). Section 11.8 describes the use of the resolution principle in SMS. In using the principle, a resolution theorem-proving system ordinarily does not maintain the distinction between antecedents and goals (i.e. what is sought to be proved). Nonresolution (or natural deduction) theorem-proving systems, on the other hand, do maintain such a distinction because it facilitates man-machine, interactive theorem-proving (Bledsoe, 1977). Because of the clarity that nonresolution techniques bring to the proof process for human beings, a nonresolution-like style has been employed in this book to describe some aspects of the proof process; however, in the actual implementation some of the proof procedures are more resolution-based than not. The discussions in Chapter 11 help clarify this point.

---

SMS SYSTEM

{ SL Database} ◄─► { Optimized Representation } ◄─► {SMS Interface }

---

Figure 1. General Structure of SMS

## 1.3 Semantics

In the discussions about SL and SMS, a distinction will be drawn between objects that are *sentences* and those that are *statements* or *assertions*. The term 'sentence' will be used to describe sentential objects that are not to be considered as part of the assertive component of an SMS database. Once a sentence enters such a database, the sentence becomes becomes a *statement*. Unless otherwise indicated, reference to an SMS database is to be taken to be a reference to the assertive component of that database. Statements in the database are taken as *given*, and once they are transformed into an optimized frame-based representation, that representation is taken to constitute the world as far as the system is concerned. From this perspective, it may be said that the system is grounded in a semantic theory known as *knowledge-base semantics* (*see generally* Hirst, 1987). Under this theory, a knowledge base might consist of assertions written in some logic notation, each assertion in the knowledge base being taken as true, or of data objects cast onto a knowledge structure denoting relationships between the objects (Hirst, 1987). A distinction can drawn between *knowledge semantics* (Tarnawsky, 1982), in which sentences but not their components are interpreted, that is, assigned meaning, and *object-oriented semantics*, in which interpretation is extended to components of sentences. Hirst (1987) reports the use of the latter approach in his work on a natural language understanding system that employs a parser to parse language text into a parse tree, which is then given to a semantic interpreter. The semantic interpreter replaces words with pointers to appropriate segments of the knowledge structure, and the text is 'understood' by combining the appropriate segments. The result is that the original text is 'interpreted' with reference to the knowledge structure. A rough yet useful comparison can be made between SMS and the system described by Hirst, although at present SMS is not a natural language understanding system. SL sentences are encoded by hand and correspond roughly to the parse trees produced in the system described by Hirst. SMS contains a component that functions as a semantic interpreter by interpreting SL statements with reference to a database of frame-based structures.

Hirst (1987) claims that a knowledge base can be thought of as a model of the world in the sense used in model-theoretic semantics. In the model-theoretic approach, a formal model of the world is used to test the truth or falsity of statements. A statement is true if it conforms to the model. If *On* is a predicate of two arguments such that its first argument is said to be *On* its second argument, and *a* and *b* are constant symbols, each of which has an object in the model as its denotation, the first-order sentence *On(a b)* is true only if it is true that the object that is the denotation of *a* is on the object that is the denotation of *b*. A more formal way of saying this is to say that the sentence is true if the ordered pair <*a,b*> is a member of the extension of *On*, that is, the set of all ordered pairs for which the predicate *On* holds in the model. In like manner, a knowledge base can be taken to be a model of the world, and a statement can be considered to be true or false depending on whether it conforms to the information in the knowledge base. In this sense of conformity, a statement conforms to the knowledge base if it is represented in the knowledge base or is provable from it.

Most systems that use knowledge-base semantics employ only two values in assigning values to sentences. Typically, a sentence is assigned 'T' (for true) if it conforms to the knowledge base and 'F' (for false) if it does not. SMS differs from those systems in that it employs a many-valued scheme to evaluate statements, but it is like those systems in that it assigns values to statements based on whether the statements conform to the database. The ways in which a statement can conform to the database are specially defined and graded (see section 3.3). The database of SMS is taken to define the entities and relations in the world of SMS. If the statement to be evaluated is found to be represented in the database without any associated qualification, it is assigned the value 'IPR' (for *i*s *pr*esent). If a statement is not found in the database, it is assigned another value depending on whether it bears one or more specially recognized relations to other statements that are present. If, for example, the statement to be evaluated almost matches (in a precisely defined way) a database statement, it might receive the value 'APR' (for *a*lmost *pr*esent). The justification for the adoption of this approach is presented in Chapter 3.

If one considers the database of SMS to be a world model, then to some extent the semantics of SMS can be defined formally in a model-theoretic mode. The vocabulary of SL has mappings into the model (database). The constants of SL (referred to herein as *markers*) have denotations in the model, and the predicates (referred to herein as *links*) have extensions in that model, although some of those links do not have a neat mapping to familiar terms and concepts of natural language. This is not to say that a complete formal semantics can be specified for the system in this way. Indeed SMS suffers from some of the same difficulties that plague truth-functional systems in modal and epistemic realms (see section 4.7 for relevant discussion). On that score, Chapter 4 describes the general approach being employed in these areas. Chapter 6 provides an overview of the philosophical foundations of the system, including a discussion of semantics and reasons for avoiding the truth predicate.

The fact that SMS does not make the familiar semantic ascent to the truth predicate, opting instead for a semantic ascent to a many-valued set, may cause some people to be particularly inquisitive about the meanings of the values it does employ. Similar concerns may result from the fact that SMS employs some terms that do not have familiar mappings to logic or natural language. This is especially true of certain *links*, which correspond to verbs of English. A broad and powerful conception of *link* or *connective* has been adopted for SMS. The idea is that a connective should be able to connect any objects that may be used as subjects or objects of SL sentences. On this count, SL has a more direct mapping into English than does FOL. The point to be made here is that SL provides one with a broader choice of connectives than does FOL. In standard logic, connectives for conjunction and disjunction are defined truth-functionally by truth tables. A theory of predication allows one to form atomic statements by joining one or more constants or variables, as appropriate, to a predicate. Compound statements are created by using logical connectives to connect sentences. One of the primary benefits that results from the truth-functional approach is that the truth-value of a compound statement is a function of the truth-values of its constituent sentences. Although this feature of compositionality of meaning is nice to have around, the truth-functional approach has its limitations. The primary one, and the one that prompted the avoidance of a truth-functional-based semantics for SL, is that the truth-functional connectives of standard logic are not suitable for convenient representation of some commonly recognized connections. For example, the English sentence:

'Mary was delighted by the fact that Ben bought a home'

describes a causal connection between two sententially expressible situations:

1) Ben's purchase of a home; and

2) Mary's state of delightment.

[Note: For the sake of simplicity, temporal and other precising information is not represented in this example.]

For expository convenience, these situations will be represented in abbreviated SL form as:

1) <ben bought home>; and

2) <mary is delighted>.

SL would allow one to represent the causal connection between the two situations as follows:

<<ben bought home> caused <mary is delighted>>

where 'caused' functions as a non-truth-functional connective (link). It would not make much sense to give this link a truth-functional definition because it is obvious that the truth-value of this causal sentence is not a function of the truth-values of its constituent sentences, yet the semantics of standard logic take the truth-value of the compound sentence to be the truth-value assigned to the main connective by operation of the truth function on the truth-values of the constituent sentences. In this example the connective 'caused' is clearly the main connective. Although FOL does not treat 'caused' as a connective, SMS does treat it as such. One might be reluctant to recognize the term 'caused' as a connective on the basis that it does not have a truth-functional definition, but this seems to beg the main issue. Should the use of a 'connective' be disallowed simply because the connection it represents is not immediately appreciable in a truth-functional way? If the connection exists, it would seem that the best representational approach would be to allow the connection to be *represented* directly by a connective and to define validity of inference in a way that accommodates that connective. This is the approach that has been adopted in SMS. SL provides a number of links that can be used to represent causation, and SMS provides rules for inferencing over those links. Thus, representational flexibility is achieved, and validity of inference is preserved, all without recourse to truth-functional definitions of causal links. An inference rule based on transitivity principles, for instance, can be specified for inferencing over causal links (see section 11.4). Causality in SMS is to be understood with reference to the causal model described in section 2.5.

It is also worthy of note that the links of SL are not constrained by the FOL rule to the effect that connectives may be used only to connect sentences. In SL, links may be used to connect nonsentential objects as well as any combination of sentential and nonsentential objects. The expression:

<john caused <mary is delighted>>

connects the nonsentential object 'john' with the sentential object '<mary is delighted>' just to give an example. SL and SMS are being developed on the general belief that as long as validity of inference can be preserved over the links recognized by a language, that language should strive to recognize as many connectives as are needed for the representation of the connections entailed in the states and events that the language is supposed to represent.

Perhaps the best way to address concerns about the semantics of SL is to describe how one might go about making a total valuation on SL. Any statement that is present in the database without qualification is assigned the value 'IPR', which represents the maximal degree of presence recognized by the system. The system also recognizes lesser degrees of presence for certain statements and assigns them values that are indicative of the differences in degree. Presence in a degree less than IPR is considered to be tainted (see section 3.3). In SMS, any nondeductive inference is assigned a degree of presence less than IPR. For example, given the truth of the statement:

David saw a tree in the yard

the inference 'David was in the yard' does not follow as a deductive inference because it is not necessarily true that David would have had to have been in the yard to have seen the tree, at least under one plausible interpretation of the statement. Thus, the SL counterpart of this inference would be assigned a value indicative of its nondeductive status. Each statement entered into the database of SMS is assigned a *penumbra* consisting of a limited set of nondeductive inferences that are generated in accordance with a set of special inference rules. Section 4.2.2 on penumbral inferencing describes this kind of inference and gives reasons why statement penumbras are recognized. Besides having the ability to generate a penumbra for each SL statement, SMS has a set of inference rules by which inferences can be generated in more conventional ways (see section 11.4). It has, for example, an inference rule that corresponds to the familiar *modus ponens* of standard logic.

A total valuation on SL can be made based on an SMS database that has been inflated to serve as a model of the world. A sequence of statements can be entered to produce an initial database, and this database can be given inflated presence through recognition of the presence of statement penumbras and inferences generated to a fixed point* by the inference rules of the system. A transformation can be made on this inflated database by using a function $v$ that would take a statement as its argument and would return an ordered pair, the first element of which would be a new statement consisting of the components of the original statement maximized to reflect a full degree of presence. The second element of the ordered pair would be a value indicative of the degree of presence of the components of the original statement, that value being no higher than the *weakest* degree of presence found among the original components. Using the statement form '<$\Phi_1$ mcause $\Phi_2$>' as an example, where $\Phi$ ranges over the nouns, noun phrases and sentences of SL and where the link 'mcause' is slightly weaker than the maximally strong link 'cause', the function $v$ might return the pair '<<$\Phi_1$ cause $\Phi_2$>, APR>'. The link 'mcause' has been maximized to 'cause', but the weakness implied by the term 'mcause' has been retained in the assigned value 'APR', which indicates slightly tainted presence. Given that $v$ could be made to perform this operation on each and every statement present in the inflated database, a function $v_t$ can be defined to produce a total valuation on SL statements. The inflated database would function as a world model with reference to which the total valuation would be made. Any SL statement $\Phi_i$ could be assigned a value by $v_t$ in accordance with the following rules:

1) if $\Phi_i$ matches any statement $\Phi_j$ of the inflated database, $v_t(\Phi_i)$ is equal to the value previously assigned to $\Phi_j$ by $v$.

2) if $\sim\Phi_i$ matches any database statement $\Phi_j$, and if the value previously assigned to $\Phi_j$ by $v$ is either 'IPR' or 'APR', then $v_t(\Phi_i)$ = NPR-IC;

3) otherwise $v_t(\Phi_i)$ = NPR, where 'NPR' signifies that $\Phi_i$ is simply *n*ot *pr*esent in the database.

---

* The term *fixed point* as used here refers to a point in inference generation at which no new inferences can be generated by the recursive application of the inference rules. The rules and the database would have to be limited so that the fixed point could be reached. The rule of addition, for example, would not be used because of the problem of infinite recursion, and all database functions would have to be defined to terminate automatically.

If a database statement has a degree of presence of either IPR or APR, the consistency rules of the system will not allow the negation of the statement to enter the database (section 11.7). Under rule 2 above, the value 'NPR-IC' would signify that $\Phi_i$ is inconsistent with the world described by the inflated database. For a discussion about how a total valuation might be made on SL for a slightly different perspective, see section 4.2. The rules of inference specified for SMS are designed to recognize the values assigned to the statements over which they operate and to reflect the effects of those values in the conclusions drawn.

## 1.4 Immediate Goals

The immediate goal is to develop SMS to a point at which it can be used to describe world phenomena in sufficient detail to enable one to build what would correspond to a commonsense database of world knowledge, and to do so by way of conversation with the system. This means that sufficient expressive power must be built into the system to enable it to describe human and physical phenomena. It has been pointed out on frequent occasion that a scheme for handling commonsense reasoning must be able to deal with a variety of human cognitive processes and emotions, including those that are employed in planning, understanding, and evaluation (e.g. Schank and Ableson, 1977; Dyer, 1983; and Wilensky, 1983). The representation problems presented by the physical domain, including those pertaining to time (e.g. Allen, 1981, 1984; Hafner, 1985), are also quite formidable (see generally Hobbs and Moore, 1985). It seems that concurrent processing will have to be brought to bear on processing tasks to achieve the overall goal. SMS has been designed with parallel processing in mind (cf. Fahlman, 1979).

## 1.5 Relationship Between SL and SMS

It is not feasible to attempt to describe all the operations of SMS in this book because of their number and complexity. Although many of its features are still being developed, the theoretical structure of the system is sufficiently appreciable at this point to warrant a description of some of its key aspects. With the intent of acquainting the reader with the general approach being recommended, the remaining sections of this book describe a select group of features that constitute the heart of the system. Each feature in itself could be the subject of an entire book, and because so many aspects of the system had to be covered, depth was sacrificed for breadth of coverage in many areas.

The operations of SMS are most often described in this book as if the system itself is carrying out the marking and inferencing operations over the SL notation. This is because the description is written with the automated version of the system in view. Confusion about the relationship between SL and SMS can be avoided if the reader keeps in mind that SMS processes SL notation in a way that corresponds to the way human beings construct proofs by hand from first-order notation. When human beings use FOL, processes of instantiation, transformation, and inferencing are carried out mentally and manually in attempts to derive conclusions. In the automated version of SMS, the user enters SL statements to form a database and then presents the system with the conclusions (queries written in SL) to be proved. All the required marking, instantiation and inferencing is done automatically by the system over the SL notation. This is not to say that these procedures cannot be done manually by human beings. Proofs can be done manually in SMS just as can be done in FOL. The reader can compare a manually driven version of SMS to FOL by simply imagining that it is a human being instead of the system that is performing the described operations over SL notation.

### 1.6 Language Used to Describe SMS

For the most part, English, FOL and set-theoretic notation will be used to describe SL and SMS. The following notation from FOL will be used in the metalanguage:

1) '•' will represent conjunction;
2) 'v' will represent nonexclusive disjunction;
3) '→' will represent material implication; and
4) '∀' will be used as the universal quantifier; and
5) 'E' will be used as the existential quantifier.

In addition, the italicized letters *f*, *g* and *h* . . . will represent functions (in mathematical sense).

At times it will be appropriate to emphasize that a given expression is to be taken *as is*. In such a case the pair '⌈ ⌉' will be used to enclose the expression that is not to be evaluated. The expression FW, for example, stands for a set of linguistic objects that constitute what will be referred to herein as the 'fictitious world' (FW), but ⌈FW⌉ refers to the expression 'FW'. Chapter 8 introduces some special symbols into the metalanguage.

## CHAPTER 2

# INTRODUCTION TO SMS AND SL

## 2.1 SMS as a Formal System That Employs Sequences, Signs and Tokens

SMS is a formal system that employs SL, a notation built upon a set of formation rules and a depository of symbols set in a partitioned space. For those who appreciate a distinction between a first-order language and a first-order logic, SL corresponds to the former and SMS to the latter. SMS in some ways resembles restricted FOL, yet it has special features that appear to be extensions of FOL. The syntactical format of SL is similar to infix notation, and as in FOL, well formed formulas (wffs) can be constructed (see section 2.4) and treated as premises from which conclusions can be drawn (see sections 11.3 and 11.4). Derivations in SMS correspond to derivations in FOL but are distinguished by the fact that they are not founded on truth-functional notions of validity. It is in this sense that SMS may be said to fail to achieve status as a logistic system since many people consider the notion of truth to be a necessary component of a logistic system, although some appear to believe otherwise (e.g. Hogger, 1984; Wojcicki, 1988). Perhaps it could be said that SMS is a logistic system in a mere syntactical sense. It is well known that within a formal logical system, validity can be defined both syntactically and semantically (e.g. Gallaire, Minker and Nicolas, 1977; Haack, 1978; and Levesque, 1986). Given a formal language L and a set of wffs $F_1, ..., F_{n-1}, F_n$ $(n \geq 1)$, the validity of $F_n$ as a derivation from the axioms of L and $F_1, ..., F_{n-1}$ can be defined syntactically in terms of whether $F_n$ is derivable by the rules of inference of L. The semantic validity of $F_n$ as a derivation can be defined as follows: $F_n$ is valid in L if it is true in all interpretations in which $F_1, ..., F_{n-1}$ are true. Semantic validity is thus defined in terms of the truth predicate, whereas syntactic validity need not be understood with reference to the truth predicate. Validity is defined in SMS from both syntactical and semantical points of view; however, the semantics of the system are specified with reference to a many-valued set instead of the truth-predicate. The philosophical justification for adopting this approach is given in section 3.5 and in Chapter 6.

The legitimacy of the SMS approach will be defended in much the same way that one might go about defending a non-truth-functional, probabilistic approach to many-valued logic (see Rescher, 1969, at pages 184-88). An attempt will be made to show that inference patterns of classical two-valued logic map into inference patterns of SMS [cf. Rescher, 1969, at pages 186-88, on comparing the tautologies of **PL** ("probability logic') with the tautologies of the classical two-valued propositional calculus]. Section 11.4 attempts to show that such a mapping exists and that the SMS patterns which have no counterpart in the propositional calculus constitute an extension of those that do. A corresponding attempt to demonstrate the utility of fuzzy logic can be found in [Zadeh, 1985; and Bellman and Zadeh, 1977].

Before proceeding further, more should be said about the basic representational device employed in SL - the *sequence*. It was chosen because position is of crucial importance both to the derivation process and to a host of other relations that are specified with reference to location. The sequence serves well in the system because it is defined in terms of ordered locations or positions. It is defined in SL to be an ordered tuple of n-positions enclosed by the pair '< >'. Each position in the sequence is separated by a space and may be occupied by an individual term or by another sequence; however, in the interest of spatial economy, the requirement that there be a space between elements is not always honored in the notation in this book. A sequence containing just one element will be referred to as a *unit* sequence. Nesting is allowed to whatever depth desired as long as syntactical constraints are met. Section 2.4 sets forth the formation rules of SL. For example, to represent the idea that any logician loves logic, the following sequence could be employed:

< <logician <any>> loves <logic <some> > (7)

[Note: Perhaps a more accurate representation would make reference to logic in general. Such a reference was not used in this example to avoid a lengthly explanation of the qualifier 'cl*', a term used to create that kind of reference (see section 2.3.3).]

Here the term 'any' serves as a universal quantifier and the term 'some' serves as a particular but not existential quantifier (see section 10.1). This sequence consists of three positions (blank spaces are ignored), the first of which is occupied by the sequence '<logician <any>>', which itself is a sequence of two positions with the term 'logician' in the first position and the unit sequence '<any>' in the second position. The expressions 'loves' and '<logic <some>>' occupy the second and third top level positions in the given sequence. Sequence (7) is a sentential sequence, that is, a sequence that serves as a sentence in SL. The second position in sentential sequences is reserved for linguistic objects that function like verbs or verb phrases of ordinary English. Objects of SL that correspond to verbs of English will be called *links* throughout this book. Individual terms, including links, will be called *atoms*. In the sequence given in example here, the atom 'loves' functions as a link.

Since sequences (ordered tuples) will be referred to often, the following conventions have been adopted for them. The letters 's, $s_1$, ..., $s_n$' will be used to refer to sequences in general. Sequences that correspond to sentences of ordinary English or FOL are called *sentence-sequences* and form a subclass of the more general class of sequences. The letters '$ss_1$, $ss_2$, ..., $ss_n$', where $n > 2$, will be used to refer to sentence-sequences. Throughout this book, the letters 'i', 'j' and 'k' will be attached to symbols to represent arbitrarily selected members of the particular set or class under consideration. Thus the symbol '$s_i$' represents an arbitrarily selected sequence, and the symbol '$ss_j$' represents an arbitrarily selected sentence-sequence. Since sequences are used as the basic mode of expression in SL, the expressions *wfs* and *wfss* will be used as abbreviations for 'well formed sequence' and 'well formed sentence-sequence' respectively. As a notational convention, numbers will be attached to letters to differentiate variables. Each letter will be described as having a range, and distinct variables will be created by attaching different numbers to the letter. Thus, if the Greek letter β is chosen to range over atoms, $\beta_1$ and $\beta_2$ would constitute distinct variables.

In talking about SL, it will be useful to recognize distinctions between *signs* and their *tokens*. *Signs* are linguistic objects that form the vocabulary of SL. In conformity with the formal approach being adopted, signs are distinguished from other linguistic objects based solely on their locations within the system. A schematic representation of the lexicon as a family of sequences is given in Figure 2.

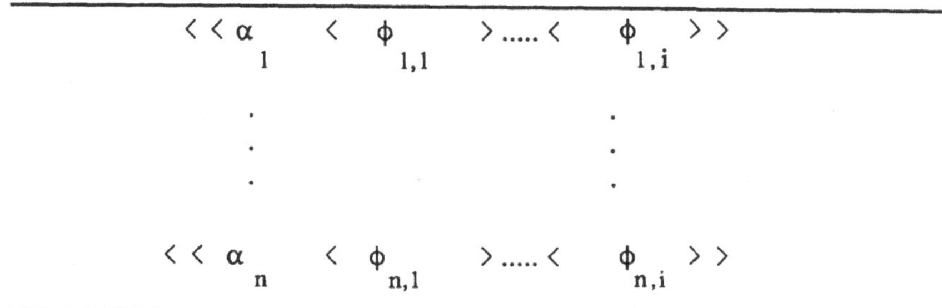

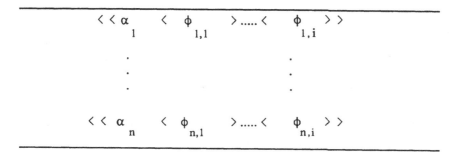

Figure 2. Schematic Representation of Lexicon

In this figure, $\alpha$ ranges over signs, $\phi$ ranges over properties and constraints, $i > 1$, and $1 < n > i$. The lexicon of SMS is an ordered sequence of sequences, and the first position in each subsequence is reserved for a sign. It is the occupation of this position that identifies an object as a sign. Signs are assigned properties and constraints and correspond to entries in a lexicon. For that reason the terms 'sign' and 'entry' are used synonymously in this book. Objects that are syntactically identical with a given sign will be referred to as *tokens* of that sign. SMS presupposes an alphabet of characters that are employed uniformly in terms of shape and size. Syntactical identity is defined in terms of an exact match in terms of shape and size. Section 4.3 has more to say about syntactical identity.

Signs are subcategorized into *labels*, *markers* and *particles*, each of which is also subcategorized. Section 2.3 describes the scheme of categorization. Labels correspond to words of ordinary English, whereas markers are linguistic objects used to mark labels, thereby setting the denotations of the labels within the system. Each noun or link label is marked, that is, assigned a marker, as it enters the system, and the label and the marker are from that point bound to one another for future operations. The label adds specificity to the marker by inheriting properties from its corresponding sign in the lexicon. The properties are thereafter associated with the marker. Any linguistic object that is not a label or a marker is a *particle*. Particles correspond to syncategorematic objects of FOL such as punctuation marks. The particles '<' and '>' of SL, for example, are used respectively to mark the beginning and the end of *sequences*. Sections 2.3.1 - 2.3.3 provide more information about labels, markers and particles.

## 2.2 Use of SL in SMS

SL consists of a vocabulary and a set of construction rules. One represents English sentences in SL by using the vocabulary and the rules to form well formed sentential expressions. The process is done by hand in a manner that roughly corresponds to the way one manually represents English sentences in a first-order language. This section gives examples of how SL is used to represent English sentences. Section 2.3 gives an overview of the vocabulary of SL, and section 2.4 summarizes the rules for forming well formed phrases and sentences. The term 'phrase' will be used collectively to refer to what corresponds to subordinate clauses and phrases of ordinary English. Thus, it will only be necessary to speak of individual terms, phrases and sentential expressions when describing SL.

The reader should keep in mind that one of the major goals of this book is to show that it is easier to represent English sentences in SL than in FOL because of the somewhat direct mapping that SL notation has into English expressed in the active voice. The plan is to convince the reader that this more English-like notation should be preferred over typical first-order notation because of its expressive correspondence with English; however, to establish this preference, it must also be shown that inferencing can be defined over SL notation as effectively as can be done over first-order notation. This last point will be dealt with as a major theme in this book.

It should be mentioned here that representing English sentences in SL does not solve all problems of ambiguity and indefinite reference. A sentence in SL may be just as ambiguous as its English counterpart. One of the motivations for adopting a many-valued approach in SMS was to bring about a means of dealing with these problems. Human beings are able to use imprecision effectively in ordinary conversation and reasoning, and a system that is to simulate these phenomena must have some means of dealing with inferencing that involves imprecise concepts and reference. Chapter 3 will show how a many-valued approach can be used effectively in this area.

Thus far SL has been described as a language that has direct correspondence with ordinary English in that its terms are used like the parts of speech of English. As will be described in section 2.3, special punctuation marks and operators are used to establish desired relations and effects. The following examples illustrate the use of SL and concomitantly introduce some special terms used in the language to produce special effects. Suppose one were given the English sentences below.

John, Mary and Jim are persons. (8)

Any person who saw the play on Saturday saw John during that time. (9)

Mary, who saw the play on Saturday, loves Jim. (10)

Any person who saw John on Saturday is happy. (11)

Assuming that all the references to 'Saturday' are to the same day and that present tense verbs are construed in the normal sense of 'now', it would not require much reasoning power to be able to answer the following questions:

Is Mary happy? (12)

Is Jim loved by a happy person? (13)

Did Mary see the play? (14)

The average human being handles reasoning problems of this kind on a daily basis. Human cognitive processes are able to combine, analyze, and make deductions from this kind of information almost effortlessly. SL is being designed to cause one to invoke similar if not the same cognitive processes. An SL sentence (sequence) begins with a subject and is followed by a verb (link). If a direct object is present, it follows the verb. An indirect object is placed between the verb and the direct object. If any subject, verb, indirect object or direct object is anything other than a single term, it is enclosed by an independent pair of wedges. Modifying terms, phrases or clauses are also enclosed by wedges and are placed after the terms they modify. English sentences (8), (9), (10) and (11) could be represented in SL as follows:

<<person <any> (15)
<who <saw <t-on saturday>> <play <the>>>>

<saw <t-on <saturday <the>>>>

<person <n=i john>>>

In the automated version of SMS, SL serves as a programming language. Sequence (15) amounts to a series of commands to the system to individuate the labels appearing in the sequence and to identify and mark the relations that hold between the markers. The terms 'saw', 'saturday', 'play' and 'john' would be assigned individual markers, whereas the term 'person', being within the scope of the universal quantifier 'any', would be assigned a special kind of marker that would function as a variable. In this example the variable could be instantiated by any marker that: 1) is bound to the label 'person'; and 2) is related to the markers for 'saturday' and 'play' through the marker for 'saw' in the way that would be called for by the expression '<who <saw <t-on saturday>> <play <the>>>>' if the instantial marker were to replace the term 'who' in that expression. These markers constitute the denotations of the labels to which they are bound. Relations are marked with reference to constituent denotata. The results are then cast into a scheme over which inferencing is defined. The term 'n=i' is used to introduce proper names. Once introduced in a given context, a name may continue to be used in that context without further use of the term 'n=i' (see section 2.3.4 for examples of how proper names are used in SMS). SMS would handle sequences (16) and (17) below in a manner similar to the way it handles sequence 15. The process is explained in more detail in later sections.

<<person <n=i mary> (16)
<who <saw <t-on <saturday <the>>>> <play <the>>>>

<loves <now>>

<person <n=i jim>>>

<<person <any> (17)
<who <saw <t-on <saturday <the>>>> john>>

<is <now>>

happy>

Sentential sequences (15), (16) and (17) entail sentence (8) and bear respective correspondence to sentences (9), (10) and (11). Each sentential sequence has been broken down into what amounts to a listing of the subject, verb and object of the corresponding English sentence. The term 't-on' is a temporal preposition that is used to introduce references to time (in this case the term 'saturday' is the primary reference). The term 'the' serves as a pointer just as it does in English to refer back to some previous occurrence of a term. The reader should note that the expression '<play <the>>' in sentence-sequence (15) lacks a referent just as does the expression 'the play' in sentence (9).

In SMS, one asks questions much as one does in English. For example, one might ask:

<mary is happy>? (18)

<<person <some><happy>> (19)
loves
jim>?

<mary saw <play <the>>>? (20)

These queries, written in SL, bear respective correspondence to English queries (12), (13) and (14). The claim being made is that mechanical operations that simulate thinking can be defined over SL statements as effectively as can be done over a first-order language. SL sequences are to be read as one reads English, making appropriate adjustments for the positions of modifiers and the presence of wedges, and with a little practice one can spot answers to queries almost as effectively as can be done when using English. The answer to question (20) is contained in sequence (16), mostly in what amounts to a parenthetical expression, and processes very similar to the ones used the derive the answer to the corresponding English question are used to answer the SL query. The point is that both the English and SL versions present similar problems of interpretation and reasoning, and similar processes are used to solve them. This seems to be a favorable feature of SL and, it appears that ensuing benefits become more appreciable the more English-like SL becomes. One such benefit is that it becomes easier to develop new features to handle some of the more difficult inferencing problems, such as those in the modal realm. Being able to think about and express solutions to those problems as one does in English makes the life of a system designer a little more enjoyable.

Although SL is to be read in a way very similar to English, the question remains whether it is able to capture meaning that corresponds to the meaning of the English sentences. Answering this question would drive the discussions into a detailed descriptions of how SMS handles quantification; the individuation of linguistic objects that correspond to descriptions of persons, things and events; time; and inferencing, just to name some. These topics will be covered in due course in subsequent chapters. The point to be made here is that inferences based on SL representations of English descriptions are drawn as rigorously as would be inferences based on first-order representations of those English descriptions. This point is easy to state but difficult to prove. The task of proving the point is given high, even tedious, priority in this book.

An additional point worthy of note is that SMS treats SL statements in sequence. The order in which sequences are entered makes a difference, just as the order in which one writes sentences in English text makes a difference. SMS employs special individuation processes that depend on a precise ordering of statements. The term 'the', for example, is used to refer to previous uses of terms so that proper marker assignments can be made. The processes by which SMS draws conclusions takes advantage of this sequential ordering not only by keeping track of marker bindings, but also by incorporating *position* (e.g. of each statement and of each term contained therein) into the scheme of inferencing. The position of statements (recorded as numbers assigned to them as they enter the database in sequence) and of the components of those statements (recorded as structural codes for the position of the components in the statements) are as much a part of the formal system as are the contents of the statements. The derivation process is crucially dependent on the proper use of these indices, codes and markers. Section 11.5 on querying brings this dependency clearly into focus.

## 2.3 Description of SL

Now that examples of how SL is to be used have been presented, the discussion will turn to a description of SL as a language. The vocabulary of SL consists of three basic categories of linguistic objects. The categories are:

1) labels;

2) markers;

3) particles.

The following subsections briefly discuss these categorizations.

### 2.3.1 Labels

This category for the most part contains linguistic objects that correspond to nouns, verbs, adjectives, prepositions and the like of ordinary English, but in SMS the objects are uninterpreted and have roles defined solely in terms of positions in sequences and other spaces. Based on how the expressions of SL are used in SMS, the following subcategorizations of labels can be specified for SL (described here in familiar metadescriptions for the convenience of the reader):

1) nouns (e.g 'person', 'house');

2) noun forms of adjectives or adverbs (e.g. 'happiness', 'quickness');

3) noun forms of verbs (e.g. 'loving', 'running');

4) adjectives (e.g. 'faithful', 'virtuous');

5) adverbs and auxiliaries (e.g. 'very', 'completely', 'can', 'cannot');

6) links (cf predicates and connectives):
   a) one-place links (e.g. 'occur', 'happen');
   b) two-place links (e.g. 'love', 'help');
   . . .
   n) n-place links (e.g. 'and', 'or')

7) restricted links:
   a) for mental objects (MOs) (e.g. 'believe', 'think');
   b) communicative links (e.g. 'assert', 'speak');
   . . .

8) prepositions
   a) temporal (e.g. 't-at', 't-for' where 't' for 'time' flags temporality);
   b) spatial (e.g. 'l-at', 'l-by' where 'l' for 'location' flags spatial meaning);
   . . .
   n) special
      i) for name introduction (e.g. 'n=i', 'n=b');
      ii) introductory words (e.g. 'bmo', 'iaw')
      [Note: 'bmo' stands for 'by means of' and 'iaw' stands for 'in accordance with']

9) special modifiers (e.g. 'blk', 'nm')
   [Note: 'blk' indicates solidarity and 'nm' means 'is a name'.]

Noun and link labels function as typed variables. The label 'person', for example, may be instantiated only by an individual object that qualifies as a 'person' in the system or by another label that is a subtype of the label 'person'. Labels are instantiated as they enter the system. The only exception is when a label is used to represent a general classification (see discussion on the use of the 'cl*' operator in section 2.3.3). Unless a noun or link label is accompanied by a quantifier, it is concretely individuated, that is, bound to a ground literal.

### 2.3.2 Markers

Markers are special linguistic objects used to mark labels as they enter the system. A singular form of a label is taken to be a unary entity. Any marker assigned to a unary entity consists of a newly generated number concatenated to the letters 'ue' (*u*nary *e*ntity) by a hyphen, as in 'ue-5'. A plural form of a label is taken to be a cluster (group) of entities, and any marker assigned to a cluster-entity consists of a newly generated number concatenated to the letters 'ce' (*c*luster *e*ntity) by a hyphen, as in 'ce-16'. Only noun and link labels are marked in the system. Once a marker is assigned to an instance of a label, the marker is bound to the label. The relationship between the marker and label is represented by the *isa* link. If the marker 'ue-5' were to be assigned to the label 'person' in the sequence '<person exists>' the effect would be to make information of the following sort available to the system:

< <ue-5 exists>
and
<ue-5 isa person> >.

Markers represent the ground level of distinguishment in the system. A ground literal statement in SL is a *wfss* of concrete markers. The 'markers' category is subcategorized into:

1) markers for quantifier-free nouns;
2) markers for quantified nouns;
3) markers for quantifier-free links;
4) markers for quantified links;
5) markers for quantifier-free sentence-sequences; and
6) markers for quantified sentence-sequences.

The reader need not be troubled by the fact that mention here is made of quantified links and sentence-sequences. SMS specially defines quantification in a way that distinguishes it from the quantification recognized in FOL. In SMS, nouns, links and sequences may be quantified (see Chapter 10 on quantification), and *quantifier-markers* are assigned to quantified entities, thereby enabling the markers to be treated as *variables* for use in instantiation and in cross referencing (see discussion below on limited individuation). Throughout this book, universal quantifier-markers will consist of newly generated numbers concatenated to the letters 'uqe' (for '*u*niversally *q*uantified *e*ntity'), as in 'uqe-77', and particular quantifier-markers will consist of newly generated numbers concatenated to the letters 'pqe' (for '*p*articularly *q*uantified *e*ntity'), as in 'pqe-24'. It should be noted that subcategories 5) and 6) above presuppose an ability to individuate sentence-sequences. Individuation is the process of assigning markers to labels or sentence-sequences. Two types of individuation are employed in SMS:

1) *concrete* individuation; and
2) *limited* individuation.

Concrete individuation corresponds to instantiation of a variable by a constant in FOL. In SMS, the variable would be a label or quantifier-marker. Syntactic identity between markers of labels (tokens) implies semantic identity between those labels since individuation produces meaning. In other words, the marker that results from the individuation process is the meaning. The assignment of a quantifier-marker to a linguistic object does not produce a *concrete* individuation as does the assignment of a concrete marker. The object is individuated only in a limited sense. Limited individuation is merely a way of giving a variable a description so that it can be recognized and instantiated uniformly in the system. It corresponds to instantiating variables with flagged variables that can be followed from the moment the instantiation takes place. The effect of creating a quantifier-marker is that the system sets up a test for membership in the class associated with the marker. It does this by using the *ism* (for '*is m*ember-of') link. The marking of the linguistic object '<logician <any>>' in sequence (7) by the marker 'uqe-77' would have the effect of making information of the following sort available to the system:

< <uqe-77 loves logic>
and
<if < β isa logician > then < β ism uqe-77 >> >

where β is a variable that ranges over concrete markers and quantifier markers. The variable β has been employed here for expository convenience. The system need not actually create such a variable but may use an an abstract label (e.g. 'something') in its place. The information above indicates that if a marker bears an 'isa' relation to the label 'logician', that marker is a member of the class marked by 'uqe-77'. As will be discussed later, the effect is that the marker may be used to instantiate 'uqe-77' in the expression '<uqe-77 loves logic>'. It is in this sense that quantifier-markers (in this case 'uqe-77') are said to serve as variables that may be instantiated in the system.

Individuation is an extremely important process in SMS because the derivation process depends on it. For the derivation process to function properly, both individual labels and events (sentence-sequences) must be marked. Event individuation has proven to be a tough problem for logicians, some of them questioning whether a satisfactory approach can be worked out in FOL (e.g. Quine, 1986). SMS employs its own scheme to mark events, and the scheme is described in section 10.5, *infra*.

SMS employs a default marking scheme by which every new token of a noun or link sign that enters the system is assigned a new marker unless the system is explicitly told otherwise. The marking process proceeds from left to right in the sequence in which the markers are being assigned. Examples of the process are given in the following subsection.

### 2.3.3 Particles

There are two types of particles in SMS: those that set the scope of either expressions or quantifiers and those that invoke special procedures when they are encountered. The latter are referred to collectively as *operators*. Section 2.3.2 mentions the fact that quantifiers are employed in the marking process to produce quantifier-markers which, in turn, function as variables. Chapter 10 gives details about this process. What this amounts to is that special procedures are called when quantifiers are encountered. The effects produced by the activated procedures correspond to the uses of quantification in ordinary English. Terms such as 'all,' 'any,' 'some,' 'none,' 'few,' and 'several' are thus employed in a way that corresponds to the way the terms are used in English. They are classified as particles because of the special procedures they invoke in SMS. An example of such a particle is the operator 'some*', which is used as a quantifier of the nonuniversal sort. A term modified by this operator is taken to be quantified in a special sense that enables the system to achieve results similar to that produced by Skolemization* in other systems. This perhaps can be best illustrated by example. The sentence:

Any person has a father

can be represented in first-order logic as:

$$\forall(x)\ [\ Px \rightarrow E(y)\ (Fyx)\ ]$$

where 'P' means 'is a person', 'F' means 'is the father of' and $\rightarrow$ is the connective for material implication. The reader should note that advantages are achieved

---

* Readers not familiar with Skolemization may ignore this remark for the present since the purpose served by the 'some*' operator can be understood independently of any knowledge of Skolemization.

by employing the scoping conventions set for the universal quantifier. The 'x' in the expression 'Fyx' inherits the other predications of 'x' that are made within the scope of the universal quantifier. In SL, the English sentence given above could be expressed as follows:

1. < <person <any>> has-rel <father <some*>> >

[Note: The sequences in this example will be numbered to illustrate the automated numbering scheme used in the system. Consecutive numbers are assigned to inferences as they are generated.]

The term 'has-rel' is a special link used to describe the *rel*ation (hence the use of 'rel' in 'has-rel') that the direct object of the link holds to the subject of the link. The nature of that relation is identified by the label of the direct object of the link, which in this case is the label 'father'. This sequence means that any object that conforms to the label 'person' has a 'father'. It would not suffice to use the modifier 'some' here instead of 'some*' because 'some' would cause the label 'father' to be marked and bound to some unspecified individual in the system, which would make the sequence imply that all objects that conform to the label 'person' are related to the same 'father'. The 'some*' operator helps capture the intended meaning. It is most often used to modify a label when that label is cast into relation with another universally quantified label (in this example 'person'). The effect of using the terms 'any' and 'some*' in the current example is that the sequence would be allowed to become part of the assertive component of the database of SMS. As an assertion, it could be employed in its current form in inferencing and querying. Thus, if a query matches the assertion, an affirmative response could be given to the query. The sequence could also be used in the inference generation process. There it would be used to create an open sequence that could be instantiated to produce inferences. An open sequence in SMS corresponds to an open sentence in FOL, that is, a sentence that contains a free variable (see section 10.2 for more details). The expression '<person <any>>', for instance, could be individuated by a quantifier-marker, say by the marker 'uqe-50', and would function as a variable that could be instantiated by any marker that might conform to the label 'person'. The open sequence might take the form:

2. < uqe-50 has-rel <father <some*>> >.

This sequence would be considered to be part of the nonassertive component of SMS and would be used to generate additional inferences. The inferences would be generated based on instantiations of uqe-50 by another marker. If, for example, the instantial marker happened to be 'ue-15', the inference produced would be:

3. < ue-15 has-rel <father <some*>> >

At this point, the 'some*' modifier would complete its task as an operator, that is, as a term that invokes special procedures when it is encountered in expression. The 'some*' operator would cause a newly generated concrete marker, say 'pqe*-1', to be assigned to the label 'father' and would generate appropriately numbered sequences to describe the relation between the subject and object of inference 3. The result would be:

4. < pqe*-1 isa <father <cl*>> >

5. < pqe*-1 is-father-of ue-15 > >

The term 'cl*' (for *cla*ss reference), which appears in the subsequence '<father <cl*>>', is itself an operator that is used to make abstract or general reference to a class. Its presence as a modifier of a label tells the system to retain the label instead of instantiating it with a concrete marker. The sequence '<john loves <animals <cl*>>>' corresponds to the English sentence 'John loves animals in general', just to give another example.

The effects produced by individuating the label 'father' in inference 3 are similar to those produced by Skolemization in FOL. One can see that since the quantifier-marker 'uqe-50' in inference 2 may be instantiated by any marker that conforms to the label 'person', numerous instantiations of that quantifier-marker might occur, and for each instantial marker, inference 2 implies that the marker has a 'father' who might not be the same 'father' that might have been associated with another instantial marker for 'uqe-50'. In other words, the system must provide for the possibility that a different 'father' will have to be recognized for each instantial marker. In a first-order setting, one might handle this kind of problem by using a Skolem expression to replace the existentially quantified variable (which would be y in the first-order logic representation given above) and by dropping the existential quantifier altogether. In other words, the existentially quantified variable would be replaced with a function of the universally quantified variable. If $f$ is the Skolem function used for this purpose, the resulting first-order representation might read:

$$\forall(x)\ [\ Px \rightarrow Ff(x)x\ ].$$

[Note: In Skolemization, after the removal of existential quantifiers, the universal quantifiers may be dropped on the assumption that all remaining variables are universally quantified.]

In SMS, this problem is handled by employing the operator 'some*', which invokes the process described above. The result of the process is that the 'father' referred to in inference 3 is 'pqe*-1', which is the marker that resulted from individuating the label 'father' in that sequence. Since inference 3 does not contain a universal quantifier-marker, the individuation of the label 'father' in that inference corresponds to the technique employed when an existential quantifier is not within the scope of a universal quantifier. In such a case, the existentially quantified variable can be replaced with a Skolem constant and the existential quantifier can be dropped (see e.g. Charniak and McDermott, 1985). Although some other marker, say 'ue-250', might also be a 'father' in the system, the conclusion that 'ue-250' is the father of 'ue-15' does not follow from inference 3 unless the marker 'ue-250' is cast into an appropriate relationship with 'pqe*-1' (see section 10.2 for details). One reason for this is that the 'some*' operator normally prevents the instantiation of its label with a previously created marker (in this case 'ue-250' is assumed to be such a marker). Only in special cases would such an instantiation be allowed (see section 10.2). Another reason is that a special relation would be created between inferences 3 and 5 that would bind the direct object of inference 3 to the subject of inference 5. The relation is such that the only marker that would be recognized as an instantiation of the label of the direct object of inference 3 would be the marker that occupies the subject position in inference 5.

A couple of points are worth noting in this example. First, the 'some*' operator controls the instantiation of its associated label in a special way. The operator serves as a particular quantifier and thus would block any attempt to instantiate the label with a preexisting marker. This corresponds to the well known restriction on existential instantiation in FOL. Second, each sequence bears a number, and since each component within a sequence has an assigned structure code that describes its position within that sequence, a unique address can be assigned to any component of any sequence simply by combining the appropriate position code with the number of the sequence in which the component appears. Components can then be related to one another through their addresses, an important result enabled by the adoption of the sequence as a basic representational device. In this example, the direct object of inference 3 has been cast into a special relation with the subject of inference 5. A more formal, set-theoretic description of the operator 'some*' is given in section 10.2.

SL has a number of other operators that invoke special procedures. One of the most important operators is the symbol 'd*'. This symbol is used as a modifier and causes the system to set up a means of testing other expressions to see whether they are semantically identical to the expression in which the symbol appears. Assuming that the system knows how to precisely identify 'james', the sequence:

<brother <of james> <d*>>

would cause the system to assign a marker to 'brother' and to set up a test to determine when reference is being made to a 'brother' of 'james'. If such a reference occurs, the system makes a marker assignment that is consistent with the one made for 'brother' in the sequence. In general, any object that fits a description given in a phrase that contains the modifier '<d*>' will be assigned a marker that is syntactically identical to the one assigned to the root (first term in the phrase) of the phrase. Thus, in this example, any object that is a member of the set {x | x isa <brother <of james>>} would receive the same marker assigned to 'brother' in the sequence. If the modifier '<d*>' had been omitted, a member of the set {x | x isa <brother <of james>>} would not necessarily be the 'brother' that would have been marked in the sequence, and hence a new marker would be assigned to the new occurrence of 'brother'.

As mentioned in the previous section, SMS employs a default marking scheme by which any new instance of a label is assigned a new marker unless the system is told otherwise. The 'cl*' operator discussed previously in this section, for example, can be used to prevent the assignment of a new marker to a label. There are two other operators that can be used to avoid the default procedure. The first is the term 'the'. When 'the' is used as a modifier of a label, it causes the system to retrieve the marker of the immediately preceding instance of the label and to assign that marker to the new label. If the label has no previous occurrence, it is assigned a new marker. The other device that can be used to avoid the default procedure is the 'c*' operator used for *c*ross referencing. It is used in conjunction with a number to mark an object so that it can serve as the referent of subsequent expressions. The general form for using this operator is:

< Φ ... <c* #> >

where Φ ranges over any SL expression that may receive a marker and where # ranges over numbers. When this operator appears in expression, the associated number is joined to the 'c*' by a hyphen to create a unique reference symbol which, in turn, is bound to whatever marker is assigned to Φ. If, for example, the marker 'ue-6' is assigned to the term 'brother' in the expression '<brother <of james><c* 3>>', the expression '<c* 3>' would be used to create a unique reference symbol (because of the presence of the operator 'c*') that would be bound to 'ue-6'. Any subsequent use of the sequence '<c* 3>' would cause the system to assign the marker 'ue-6' to the root of the sequence in which '<c* 3>' appears.

It should be noted that the operator 'the' causes the system to retrieve the marker of a label that is *syntactically identical* to the label that is modified by the operator. As illustrated in Figure 3, the 'c*' operator does not operate under such a constraint.

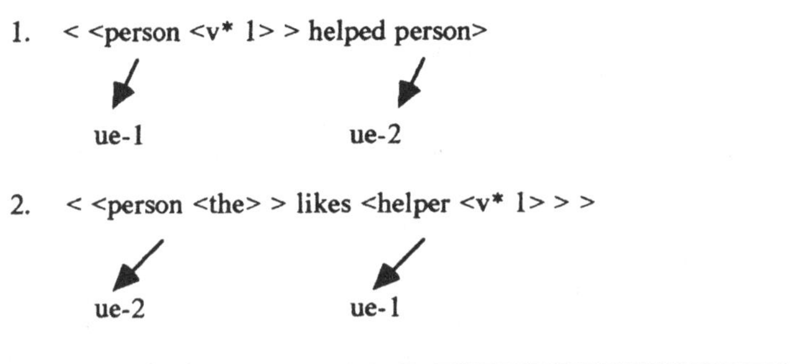
1. < <person <v* 1> > helped person>
ue-1
ue-2
2. < <person <the> > likes <helper <v* 1> > >
ue-2
ue-1

Figure 3. Illustration of Marking Scheme

In reading Figure 3, one should assume that sequence 1 was entered into the database of SMS prior to sequence 2. The arrows in the figure point to the markers that would have been assigned to the instances of the labels 'person' and 'helper' that appear in the two sequences. The marking process proceeds from left to right in each sequence. The marker 'ue-1' would have been assigned to the first instance of 'person' in sequence 1. The presence of '<c* 1>' in the subject of that sequence would have caused the system to create the reference symbol 'c*-1', which would have been bound to the marker 'ue-1'. The second instance of the label 'person' in sequence 1 would have been assigned a new marker (i. e. 'ue-2') under the default scheme. The first instance of 'person' in sequence 2 would have been assigned the marker 'ue-2' because of the presence of the operator 'the'. The presence of 'the' would have caused the system to retrieve the last marker that had been assigned to the label 'person', (which in this case would have been the marker that was assigned to the direct object of sequence 1) and to assign that marker to the current instance of the label. The label 'helper' in sequence 2 is modified by '<c* 1>' and thus would have received the same marker (i.e. 'ue-1') that had already been bound to 'c*-1'. It should be observed that the expression '<c* 1>' functions to bind different labels (i.e. 'person' and 'helper') to the same marker, whereas the 'the' operator functions to bind identical labels (i.e. 'person' and 'person') to the same marker.

The operators described in this section do not constitute the total set of SL operators. This is not to say that the set is unmanageably large. The prototype was implemented with less than twenty operators, and it seems that it will not be necessary to go much beyond that number to achieve an acceptable amount of generality. The operators and links defined in this book are given in boldface print in the index. Instead of bogging discussion down at this point with detailed descriptions of operators and their use, the discussion will turn to a description of how names are used in SMS. Any time a new operator is introduced into the SL notation in later sections, a brief description of the procedures invoked by the operator will accompany the introduction. It is particularly important for the reader to note that operators play a significant role in enabling SL to capture the expressive power and rigor of first-order and higher-order languages. This will become more apparent as quantifiers and the inferencing mechanisms of SMS are introduced and described.

### 2.3.4 Proper Names

The reader may have noticed that proper names were not included as examples in the listing of noun labels given in section 2.3.1. The reason for the omission is that names are specially treated in SMS. Proper names are not included in the base vocabulary of SL; however, they may be introduced into the system at pleasure by using one of the special prepositions (e.g. 'n=i' for *n*ame of an individual object) set aside for the introduction of names. The only restriction is that the phrase that introduces the name must be associated with a label so that the marker assigned to the label can also be bound to the name. The concomitant effect is that the name is associated with whatever properties and constraints are associated with the label since the marker of the label inherits those properties and constraints and since the name is bound to that marker. The properties and constraints may be specified in the lexicon of SMS, or they may be explicitly written into the database. The sequence:

1) <<person <n=i paul>> is happy>

introduces the name 'paul'. The sequence is well formed because the phrase containing the preposition 'n=i' and the name 'paul' modifies a label (i.e. 'person'). The system marks the label and assigns the same marker to the name. Thereafter the name is treated as a label that is bound to the assigned marker. Names differ from other labels in one important respect. The convention that every new instance of a label is to receive a new marker unless otherwise provided is reversed for names. A new marker will not be assigned to a new instance of a name unless the system is explicitly told to do so. Thus, the default scheme is for the name to be bound to the same marker to which the last instance of the name was bound. The operator 'm*' is used to cause the system to assign a new marker to a name. This convention was adopted because in ordinary human conversation it seems that names are most often introduced in a given context to be used repeatedly to refer to the same individual. Thus, if the marker 'ue-3' had been assigned to 'paul' in the sequence above, and the sequences:

2) <paul has wisdom>

3) <<person <n=i <paul <m*>>>> has <hair <black>>>

were then entered into the system in the order indicated by the numbers, the 'paul' of sequence 2) would be bound to the marker 'ue-3', whereas the 'paul' of sequence 3) would receive a new marker because of the presence of the operator 'm*'. This way of doing things avoids the problem of having to specify in advance what names may be assigned to objects. Names may be introduced as they are needed in expression. The sequence:

< <person <n=i aurel>> and <city <n=i jerusalem>> and <dog <n=i fido>> >

introduces three names, one for a person, one for a city and one for a dog. Once introduced, the names may be used in new expressions without any accompanying modifiers of the special type reserved for names.

## 2.4 Formation Rules

This section gives the general specifications for well formed formulas (wffs) in SL. The formation rules will be described using the following notation:

1) the letters p, $p_1$, $p_2$, ..., $p_n$ will stand for labels classified as nouns;

2) the letters q, $q_1$, $q_2$, ..., $q_n$ will stand for labels classified as noun forms of adjectives, adverbs or verbs;

3) the letters v, $v_1$, $v_2$, ..., $v_n$ will stand for links (superscripts will indicate the appropriate number of arguments);

4) the letters aj, $aj_1$ $aj_2$, ..., $aj_n$ will stand for labels classified as adjectives;

5) the letters av, $av_1$, $av_2$, ..., $av_n$ will stand for labels classified as adverbs;

6) the letters pr, $pr_1$, $pr_2$, ..., $pr_n$ will stand for labels classified as prepositions;

7) the letters sp, $sp_1$, $sp_2$, ..., $sp_n$ will stand for the special modifiers of SL; and

8) the letters op, $op_1$, $op_2$, ..., $op_n$ will stand for particles that are operators.

A single label, marker, or quantifier will be referred to as an *atom*. The notation described in 1) through 8) above is used to represent atoms. It will also be necessary to speak of sentence-sequences and phrase-sequences when describing wffs. Sentential sequences are formed through recursive use of wedges to enclose atoms or *wfs*s, or both, in accordance with the formation rules described below. The Greek letters Φ and θ will be used to represent sentence-sequences and phrase-sequences respectively. If it is important to note how a given sequence is used, one or more letters of the English alphabet will be attached to the Greek letter to indicate the particular use, the term 'use' here being defined in terms of position in the sequence in relation to other components. The letter 'n' will be employed to indicate use as a noun, the letter 'v' to indicate use as a link, the letters 'aj' to indicate adjectival use, the letters 'av' to indicate adverbial use, the letters 'pr' to indicate prepositional use, and the letters 'sp' to indicate use as one of the special modifiers of SL (see section 2.3.1). Adjectival, adverbial and prepositional phrase-sequences, as well as sequences that serve as as special modifiers, are all *modifying* phrase-sequences. The letters 'md' will be used to indicate the use of a phrase-sequence as a modifier without indicating the precise nature of the use. A sequence of one element that is an operator (e.g. a quantifier; see section 2.3.3) is called an *operative* phrase-sequence.

The pair ‘< >’ is employed to represent sequences in SL, where ‘<’ marks the beginning of a given sequence and ‘>’ marks the end. A sequence is defined to consist of 1, ..., n positions (where n ≥ 1) enclosed by the pair of wedges. Two basic types of sequences are used in making statements in SL: the phrase-sequence and the sentence-sequence. Phrase-sequences and atoms are used to form *simple* sentence-sequences, that is, sentence-sequences that do not contain any other sentence-sequence as a component. To qualify as a *wfs*, each position in the sequence must be occupied by:

1) an atom; or

2) a *wfs*.

Any sequence that has a link or link phrase in the second position in the sequence must qualify as a sentence-sequence under the rules given below or else it will fail the test for a *wfs*. Any sequence that does not have such an expression in the second position will be classified as a phrase-sequence, provided it passes the test for a well formed phrase-sequence (hereafter abbreviated as *wfps*). The first position in any phrase-sequence is referred to as the *root* position of the sequence.

### 2.4.1 WFPSs

For an expression to qualify as a *wfps*, an atom must occupy the root position in the sequence. The only exception allowed is the case in which the second, top-level position in the sequence is occupied by a unit sequence that contains a *sentential* quantifier. In that case the first position may be occupied by a sequence. This convention allows for quantification over sentential expressions (see Chapter 10 on quantification for details). The following are not well formed schemata for phrase or sentential sequences:

1) aj ; and

2) < < aj > av >.

The first schema is not enclosed by the pair ‘< >’ and hence is not a sequence. The second schema is not well formed because its first element is a sequence and no link, link phrase, or sentential quantifier phrase appears in the second position in the sequence, a condition that must be fulfilled whenever a sequence occupies the first position. The following are well formed schemata:

1) < aj >;

2) < aj < av > >; and

3) < <<p<op>> $v^2$ <q<sp>>> <∇Ψ> >

where 3) is a schema that has a sentence-sequence as its first element (i.e. ‘<<p<op>> $v^2$ <q<sp>>>’) and a unit sequence containing the sentential quantifier ‘∇Ψ’ as its second element. Here Ψ represents a quantifier and the symbol

$<\nabla\Psi>$ is used to indicate that the quantifier is to operate as a sentential one.

Phrase-sequences are categorized based on the roles they serve in *wfsss*. For a sequence to qualify as a *wfss*, the second position at the top level of the sequence must be occupied by a link or by a phrase the root of which is a link. Each link has a specified number of arguments that must appear in the sequence in specified locations. Each such argument is said to occupy a *noun position* in the sequence and is referred to as a 'noun phrase-sequence'. To qualify as a noun phrase-sequence, the root position must be occupied by a marker or by a label that is either a noun or a noun form, and the rest of the sequence must qualify under the rules for *wfpss*. The reader should be warned, however, that SL classifies some terms as nouns that might not be so classified in English. The term 'happy', for example, is classified both as a noun and as an adjective. At the top level of a noun phrase-sequence, every position other than the first position must be occupied by a *modifying phrase-sequence* sequence. Each type of modifying phrase-sequence has a set of rules that govern its formation. A well formed prepositional phrase-sequence, for example, takes one of the following forms:

1) $<\ \mathrm{pr}\ \theta_n\ >$; or

2) $<\ \mathrm{pr}\ \theta_{md_1}, \ldots, \theta_{md_n}\ \theta_n\ >$.

[Note: Here the expression '$\theta_n$'is allowed to range over phrase-sequences and atoms classified as noun labels or noun markers.]

Adjectival phrase-sequences may occur in any of the following forms:

1) $<\ \mathrm{aj}\ >$; or

2) $<\mathrm{aj}\ \theta_{av}>$.

Although not described here, the syntax for phrase-sequences can be extended to include boolean combinations of objects in the modifying positions. The syntax for the adjective phrase-sequence, for example, can be extended to allow more than one adverbial phrase-sequence to be used to modify the root of the phrase.

Adverbial phrase-sequences may occur in any of the following forms:

1) $<\ \mathrm{av}\ >$; or

2)$<\ \mathrm{av}\ \theta_{av}\ >$.

The general form for the noun phrase-sequence can be represented as follows:

$<\ \mathrm{p}\ \theta_{md_1}, \ldots, \theta_{md_n}\ >$.

where 'md' is used in a restricted sense here to exclude adverbial phrase-sequences. An adverbial phrase-sequence may be used to modify a label that is classified as an adjective, a link, or another adverb.

Link phrases are similar to noun phrases except that a link must occupy the root position in the phrase. An adverbial phrase must be used in place of an adjective phrase to modify the root of a link phrase.

### 2.4.2 WFSSs

Given these general specifications, the formation rules for a *wfss* can be defined. The Greek letter $\beta$ will employed as a variable to range over noun phrase-sequences and over atoms that are classified as noun labels. The Greek letter $\delta$ will used as a variable to range over links (other than 'and' and 'or') and over link phrase-sequences. The letter $\alpha$ will range over the links 'and' and 'or'. SL has been developed for use in SMS to build databases and to query those databases. Since the database of a particular implementation is to be taken as the world as far as the system is concerned, entering sentences are required to meet specifications designed to produce order within the system before those sentences are allowed to become assertions. These specifications impose restrictions on links and their associated terms (arguments). For each link, there is a specified range of object types that may be associted with the link as arguments in a well formed sentential object. The link 'has-emot' (for *has emot*ion), for instance, has associated with it a set of constraints that require the subject of the link to be something that may have an 'emotion' and the object to be something that is an 'emotion'. Thus, the expression '<john has-emot popcorn>' would not qualify as a wfss unless 'popcorn' somehow would be recognized as an 'emotion'.

Generalizing these ideas, the specifications for an n-place link of type 'tj', where 'tj' represents a type description, may require arguments to meet certain specifications. Given, for example, that the link is a 2-place link, the specifications might require that the subject of the link be of the form $\beta_{ti}$ and that the object be of the form $\beta_{tk}$, where $\beta$ ranges over labels and '$_{ti}$' and '$_{tk}$' represent type descriptions to which the labels must conform. In such a case, only an expression of the form $<\beta_{ti}\ \delta_{tj}\ \beta_{tk}>$ would qualify as a wfss. Rather than complicate the notation, representations of restrictions on type will be omitted from the listing of schemata for well formed expressions in SL as well as from most of the remaining notation in this book. The reader should assume that the type requirements are implicitly present and that each instantial expression for a given schema meets those requirements. With these qualifications in view, the schemata for *wfsss* can now be specified. The following are proper schemata for *wfsss*:

1) $< \beta\ \delta >$ (where the root of $\delta$ is a 1-place link);

2) $< \beta_1\ \delta\ \beta_2 >$ (where the root of $\delta$ is a 2-place link);

3) $< \beta_1\ \delta\ \beta_2, \ldots, \beta_n >$ (where the root of $\delta$ is an n-place link);

4) $< \beta_1\ \alpha\ \beta_2 >$; and

5) $< \beta_1\ \alpha_1\ \beta_2\ \alpha_1\ \ldots\ \beta_n >$.

The closure of well formed schemata for sentence-sequences can be completed as follows using the variable $\Phi$ to range over well formed sentence-sequence schemata:

6) $< \Phi \; \delta >$ (where the root of $\delta$ is a 1-place link);

7) $< \Phi_1 \; \delta \; \Phi_2 >$ (where the root of $\delta$ is a 2-place link)

8) $< \Phi_1 \; \delta \; \Phi_2, \ldots, \Phi_n >$ (where $\delta$ is an n-place link);

9) $< \Phi_1 \; \alpha \; \Phi_2 >$;

10) $< \Phi_1 \; \alpha_1 \; \Phi_2 \; \alpha_1 \; \ldots \; \alpha_1 \; \Phi_n >$; and

11) any combination formed through recursive use of one or more of the schemata above.

The following 'if ... then ....' schema is allowed as a special construction:

$< \text{if } \Phi_1 \text{ then } \Phi_2 >$.

Conjunctive or alternative sequences of 'if ... then ....' schemata are also permitted, as in:

$< < \text{if } \Phi_1 \text{ then } \Phi_2 > \alpha < \text{if } \Phi_3 \text{ then } \Phi_4 > >$.

## 2.5 The Expressive Power of SL

The expressive power of SL results from a number of contributing features of the language. By using the operators of SL, one can quantify and make reference both to specific objects and to classes of objects. The use of the sequence as a basic representational device allows statements and their components to be assigned addresses (e.g. position codes) that can be used to help drive the inferencing process (see sections 2.3.3 and 11.5 for examples). These features, coupled with the fact that structures of sentential objects are first classified and then related to one another on that basis, provides an environment in which the notation can, at the very least, capture the expressive power of a first-order language. The punctuation in each sentential expression is taken as a structure that performs a scoping function over the components of the expression. In a first-order language, a quantifier is assigned a scope within which the appropriate, quantified variable is bound. Meaning is captured through predication, that is, by joining a predicate to the variable. Some of the complexity in meaning can be represented by using logical connectives to relate multiple predications of the same variable. The scoping conventions employed to capture meaning are allowed to operate over all the logical connectives of FOL. Using the existential quantifier and the variable x, for example, one can represent the idea that something large and heavy exists by joining the variable to the predicates 'LARGE' and 'HEAVY' and then conjoining the results using the logical connective for conjunction. The result would be:

$$E(x)(\text{ LARGE}x \bullet \text{HEAVY}x \text{ })$$

The expressive advantage achieved by using this notation is that x can be used in multiple predications to capture complex meaning. In this example, the scope of the existential quantifier extends beyond the connective for conjunction, and thus the multiple predications of x constitute a proposition since x is bound in all instances by that quantifier. In SL, the same kind of complexity in meaning is easily captured by a more English-like notation:

< <something <large><heavy>> exists >

The language is defined so that the syntax of this sequence identifies the terms 'large' and 'heavy' as adjectives and associates them with the label 'something'. The syntax also identifies the term 'exists' as a link. Section 2.3.3 gave an example of how the scoping conventions of FOL are allowed to capture meaning over the connective for material implication. It was shown in that example that the same meaning can be realized in SMS by employing SL. The process described in that example produces results that are at least as beneficial as those produced by Skolemization in a first-order setting. Section 7.4 gives an example of how SMS can recognize effects similar to those that would be recognized in FOL through scoping over the connective for disjunction.

When one writes in SL notation, in effect what one is doing is specifying what *inferences* are to follow from the statements being asserted. If one quantifies a label with a universal quantifier, for example, one is making reference to all the proper instantial terms for that label. The encoder controls the meaning of statements by controlling how the inferences drawn from components of the statements are to be related to one another. The relations are specified in terms of links, and quantifiers are used to control which members of one set of inferences are to be related to one or more members of another set. Chapter 10 describes in detail how one controls meaning in this way.

These simple examples are offered to suggest that SL has the potential to be able to capture meaning through its syntax at least as effectively as can be done by the syntax of a first-order language. The fact that sentence-sequences and their components have assigned position codes in the system allows marking and other operations to be performed on them to produce results over which inferencing can be defined. Later chapters will describe this process in detail.

One of the primary goals being pursued in the development of SL is to make available a sufficient number basic links that can be employed to define a sufficient set of higher-level relations that will be adequate for particular representation tasks. Some links will not have definitions or subtypes within SMS and thus will function as undefined primitives. The amount of expressive power that will be realizable in any implementation of SMS will depend on the adequacy of the links available for use in defining higher-level links. The link 'has-possess' might be chosen, for example, as a primitive to be used to represent the idea of something having possession of something else. As a primitive, it would have no subtypes, so one might have difficulty in representing distinctions between situations in which something has physical possession of a thing as opposed to mere constructive possession of it. Even if a link were to be introduced to represent physical possession, say the link 'has-possess-phys', this alone would not suffice to enable one to represent the distinction between the concept of immediate physical possession and the concept of possession that is not immediate in the physical sense.

SL is being developed so that undefined primitive concepts can be related to other terms to produce effects similar to those that would be produced by having subtypes of links available to make fine distinctions. Instead of introducing a link like 'has-possess-phys', for instance, one might produce desired results by retaining the link 'has-possess' as a primitive and by allowing it to be modified with the term 'physical', as in '<has-possess<physical>>'. The adequacy of this approach will depend upon the ability of the system to integrate the meanings of the terms cast into relationships with one another in this way. The goal in this regard is to enable the user to define terms as needed as a database is being built. Work is still in progress on this aspect of the system, but it seems that definitions of this type could be introduced into the database through special 'if* ... then* ....' constructions that would be interpreted by the system in a definitional way. One might, for example, add some specificity to the concept of 'physical possession' by associating it with the concept of 'physical contact' in an 'if* ... then* ....' construction as follows:

<If* <<something<c* 1>> <has-possess<physical>> <something<c* 2>>>
then* <<something<c* 1>> <contacts<physically>> <something<c* 2>>>>

Even if this capability is available, it appears that primitives and type/subtype relationships among links will have to be established to achieve the best results.

Before concluding this section, something should be said about how SMS allows concepts to be defined in terms of one another. This can be illustrated by schematic example. First, a general concept of *change* will be defined, and then it will be used to define the meaning of a particular type of causal link. To enable individuals, states and events to 'change' in the world of SMS, some model or representation of what it means to 'change' must be provided unless 'change' is to represent an undefined concept within the system. The idea here is to define 'change' in terms of information already given and to use the result to build a more complex concept. In doing so, it will be useful to employ the concept of a situation. In these discussions, a situation is to be taken to be a set of relations that hold, usually at or for (abbreviated herein as 'at/for') some given point or interval of time. For simplicity, a point will be considered to be an interval so that it will only be necessary to speak of intervals in the discussion. Under this conception, the following would qualify as a schematic example of a situation:

<<$\theta_1$ <is<t-at tr-1>> $\theta_2$>
and
<$\theta_1$ <has<t-at tr-1>> $\theta_3$>>

where θ ranges over labels. A *change* in a *situation* can be represented schematically as:

<$\Phi_i$ <changes<t-over tr-i>>>

where Φ ranges over situations. In this representation, $\Phi_i$ represents an abstract set of relations, abstract in the sense that although they are to be understood to hold, they are not bound to any particular time interval. The relation '<$\theta_1$ loves $\theta_4$>' would qualify as a schema for such a relation since it does not bear temporal information. The negation of a situation, represented schematically as $\sim\Phi_i$, is to be taken to mean that at least one of the relations in $\Phi_i$ does not hold. A situation may be bound to a time interval, in which case all relations in the situation are taken to hold at/for that interval. In the schematic notation, this will be represented by subscripting a description of the interval to the symbol that represents the situation, as in $\Phi_{i<t\text{-}at\ tr\text{-}i>}$. This symbol indicates that all the relations described in $\Phi_i$ hold at/for time interval 'tr-i'. The negation of a situation may also be bound to an interval, as in $\sim\Phi_{i<t\text{-}at\ tr\text{-}j>}$, which is to be taken to mean that at least one of the relations described in $\Phi_i$ does not hold at/for 'tr-j'. Using this notation, the meaning of '<$\Phi_i$ <changes<t-over tr-i>>>' can be defined with reference to the following basic pattern for *change* in a *situation* over time:

$\Phi_{i<t\text{-}at\ tr\text{-}j>}$

and

$\sim\Phi_{i<t\text{-}at\ tr\text{-}k>}$

and

<tr-j is-prior-to tr-k>

and

<<tr-j within tr-i> and <tr-k within tr-i>>

where the link 'is-prior-to' indicates that its first argument is prior in time to its second argument and where the link 'within' indicates that the interval referred to by its first argument is within the interval referred to by its second argument. An inclusive model of what has been described thus far can be represented as:

<<$\Phi_i$ <changes <t-over tr-i>> from <$\Phi_{i<t\text{-}at\ tr\text{-}j>}$> to <$\sim\Phi_{i<t\text{-}at\ tr\text{-}k>}$>>

and

<tr-j is-prior-to tr-k>

and

<<tr-j within tr-i> and <tr-k within tr-i>>>

Now that a basic model for *change* in a *situation* over time has been specified, some causal links that imply *change* can be defined with reference to that model. *Causation*, like *change*, is defined with reference to time intervals. States and events in the world of SMS occur over time, and to assert (here schematically) that one state or event $\Phi_i$ has *caused* another is to say that some initial state(s) or event(s) has changed over time to become what will be referred to as the *result* of the causal event, and that $\Phi_i$, by act or omission, or both, bears a special relationship to the change. $\Phi_i$ will be referred to as the *agent* of the causal event. The link 'cause', which is used to define various types of causal relations, is one of the most basic causal links recognized in the system. It, or one of its alternate forms or derivatives, may be associated with a modifying phrase introduced by the special term 'bmo' (*by means of*) to indicate what was done or omitted to bring about the result, but beyond that, about all it does is link the *agent* to the *result* of the causal event. The causal sequence '<$\Phi_i$ <caused <bmo $\Phi_j$>> $\Phi_{result}$>' expresses the idea that the agent $\Phi_i$ caused the result $\Phi_{result}$ by the means $\Phi_j$. It also asserts that there was some sequence of time intervals in which some initial state(s) or event(s), say $\Phi_{initial}$, held for the first interval in the sequence and that $\Phi_{result}$ held for the last interval in the sequence. The way the model for *change* enters the picture is through a binding of $\Phi_{i\text{-}<t\text{-}at\ tr\text{-}i>}$ in the model to $\Phi_{initial}$ of the causal event and $\sim\Phi_{i\text{-}<t\text{-}at\ tr\text{-}j>}$ in the model to $\Phi_{result}$ of the event, so that the relation between $\Phi_{initial}$ and $\Phi_{result}$ is understood as one of 'change'.

Generalizing these ideas, a theoretical sense of causality involving change can be understood as a 7-tuple:

$$<\delta_1, \delta_2, \delta_3, \delta_4, \delta_5, \alpha_6, \alpha_7>$$

where $\delta$ ranges over sets of objects and ordered pairs, and $\alpha$ ranges over temporal markers. $\delta_1$ represents an ordered pair, the first element of which is a set that contains the object(s) that qualifies as the agent(s) for the causal event. The second element of the pair contains a set of sentential objects that describe what was done by the agent(s) to bring about the *result*. If that information is not available in a given situation, the second element of the pair will be the null set. $\delta_2$ represents a set that contains one or more sentential objects that describe some initial state(s) or event(s). $\delta_3$ represents an ordered pair. The first element of the pair consists of a set of abstract objects, each object being an abstraction of an object entailed in the *result*. The second element of the pair is a set of sentential objects that describe the *result* in an abstract way. The idea is for the abstractions to function like variables that may be instantiated. The following pictorial examples are given to shed light on what might be contained in $\delta_3$. If the pictorial version of the *result* of the event is '[•]', the objects in that result might be taken to be '[ ]' and '•'. The first element of the ordered pair contains abstractions of these objects, and taking '{ }' and '0' to be abstractions of '[ ]' and '•'

respectively, the first element of the pair would contain the objects '{ }' and '0'. Under these specifications, the abstraction for the *result* could be represented as '{0}', which would be a member of the set that constitutes the second element of the pair. Thus, the ordered pair $\delta_3$ abstractly represents the objects that will be involved in the *result* and the types of relationships they will bear to one another in that *result*. In this example, it abstractly represents the dot ending up inside the brackets. $\delta_4$ represents the set of objects that are involved in the *result*, and $\delta_5$ is a set of sentential objects that describe the *result*. $\alpha_6$ represents the interval in which the initial state holds, and $\alpha_7$ represents the interval in which the *result* holds. Part of the meaning of the causal event can be understood with reference to the instantiation of the abstractions with more concrete information. The set of abstractions function as a model of what is to take place, and instantiation of the model with the objects in $\delta_4$ produces the result given in $\delta_5$.

Default values can be set up for the model so that, for example, if information about the initial situation is omitted, which would make $\delta_2$ be the null set, the negation(s) of the sentence(s) in the result can be taken to be the initial set $\delta_2$; however, the time reference given in the model for the initial state or event, or else the default value for that reference, must be substituted for the appropriate time reference in the negated result before the negated result can become the initial state by default. Also, any other time indicators entailed in the result statements would have to be replaced by appropriate time indicators. The model can be extended to include information about how that is to be done, perhaps through use of one or more special operators. It should be noted that this causal model can be used to represent causality that does not involve the kind of *change* defined in this section. An agent might be the cause of the *preservation* of a situation over time. To capture this idea, the initial situation and the result in the causal model would be made identical except for time references.

The causal model described in the foregoing discussions can be employed to define higher-level causal links. The link 'acquire-possess', for example, might be defined as follows to accommodate a general concept of self-caused acquisition of possession of a thing. The following sentential formalism could be employed in defining the link:

$$<\Phi_i <\text{acquires-possess} <\text{t-at tr-j}>> \Delta_i>$$

This formalism can be defined in terms of the causal model described above and the link 'has-possess' (for 'has possession of') and its negation 'has-possess-not'. The causal model is delineated below vertically with numbers assigned by arrows to components of the model according to position for convenient reference. Identifying comments for components have been placed after the numbers. The model could be instantiated to produce:

$< <\{\Phi_i\}$ ------------------------------------------> 1. First Element of Ordered Pair

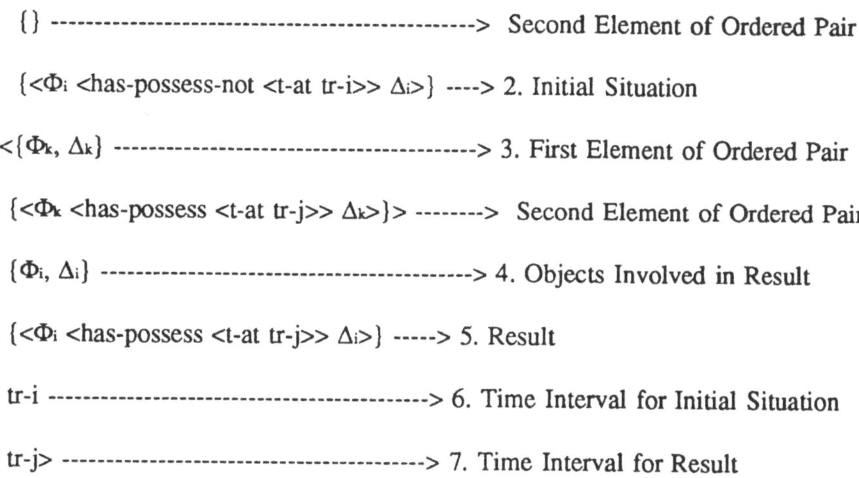


Implicit in the model are the following relations: (1) $\Phi_i$ and $\Delta_i$ are, in respective order, proper instantial items for $\Phi_k$ and $\Delta_k$ since the latter two items are the respective generalizations of the former; and (2) tr-i is before tr-j in the sequence of time. The original expression '<$\Phi_i$ <acquires-possess <t-at tr-j>> $\Delta_i$>' has thus been defined in terms of the expressions:

<<$\Phi_i$ <has-possess-not <t-at tr-i>> $\Delta_i$>

and

<$\Phi_i$ causes <$\Phi_i$ <has-possess <t-at tr-j>> $\Delta_i$>>

and

<tr-i is-prior-to tr-j>>

These expressions indicate that $\Phi_i$ did not have possession of $\Delta_i$ at one point in time, and that $\Phi_i$ caused itself to have possession of $\Delta_i$ at another and subsequent point in time. These expressions conform to the causal model as shown above, and that is sufficient to identify the 'acquire-possess' link as a causal link. Lower-level expressions such as these that have been used to define a higher-level expression constitute what will be referred to as an *expansion* of the higher-level expression. The expansion is derivable from the higher-level expression and the reverse also holds.

Taking another example, the link 'shorten', as in '<$\Phi_i$ shortens $\Delta_i$>>', can be defined by sentences that conform to the same basic causal model. An abstract definition of *shorten* can be given, in terms of what it means to decrease the length of something. The link 'has-dimension', which is used to relate an object to a term that qualifies as a 'dimension', can be employed to construct this definition. An obvious component sentence of the *result* of the shortening process could be represented as '<$\Delta_i$ has-dimension $\text{length}_j$>, which means that $\Delta_i$ has $\text{length}_j$ at the result stage in the shortening process. Common sense tells one that the length of $\Delta_i$ would have had to have been longer in the initial stage of the process. Hence, the definitional expansion for '<$\Phi_i$ <shortens<t-over tr-k>> $\Delta_i$>' might read something like:

<<$\Delta_i$ <has-dimension <t-at tr-i>> <$\text{length}_i$ <c* 1>>>

and

<$\Phi_i$ causes <<$\Delta_i$ <the>> <has-dimension <t-at tr-j>> <$\text{length}_j$ <c* 2>>>>

and

<<$\text{length}_j$ <c* 2>> is-less-than <$\text{length}_i$ <c* 1 >>>

and

<tr-i is-prior-to tr-j>

and

<<tr-i within tr-k> and <tr-j within tr-k>>>

[Note: The presence of the 'c*' and 'the' modifiers may be ignored for the moment. They are included so they can be used when these expressions are instantiated and then individuated as part of an interpretive process done by SMS. A later example will demonstrate that process.]

It should be noted that the initial state is not the negation of the result in this example. However, if the system knows that $\Delta_i$ cannot have more than one length in this context, it could deduce that '<$\Delta_i$ <has-dimension-not <t-at tr-i>> $\text{length}_j$>' because it would know that $\Delta_i$ has '$\text{length}_i$' at that time, and it could deduce that '$\text{length}_j$' is not equal to '$\text{length}_i$' based on it knowledge that '<$\text{length}_j$ is-less-than $\text{length}_i$>', which is given in the result. In other words, negation of part of the result is implicitly present in the initial state.

A point to be made here is that these abstract sentences and expansions can be instantiated to produce SL assertions, and inferencing can be defined over those assertions to conform to that defined over the abstract sentences and expansions. Specially defined causal and state links can be incorporated into the inferencing scheme through the expansions, which eventually expand into atomically normalized form that have no expansions under the rules of the system. Expansions seem to capture the structures and logical relationships that human beings appreciate when they reflect on the meaning of the associated concepts, and since SMS conducts inferencing over representations of those structures and relationships, there seems to be some sort of correspondence, at least at some level, between the way humans reason over these concepts and the way SMS reasons over representations of them. In English, for example, one might say, "John shortened the rope." In SL, one might say '<john shortened rope>'. Assuming default values for time references, so that the statement would become '<john

<shortened<t-over tr-k>> rope>', the meaning of this SL expression may be taken to be its expansion, which would be produced by instantiating the abstract expansion given above for the link *shorten*. The result would be:

<<rope <has-dimension <t-at tr-i>> <length$_i$ <c* 1>>>

and

<john causes <<rope <the>> <has-dimension <t-at tr-j>> <length$_j$ <c* 2>>>>

and

<<length$_j$ <c* 2>> is-less-than <length$_i$ <c* 1 >>>

and

<tr-i is-prior-to tr-j>

and

<<tr-i within tr-k> and <tr-j within tr-k>>>

This results from substituting 'john' for $\Phi_i$ and 'rope' for $\Delta_i$ in the formalism for *shorten*. Because of the presence of the special individuating terms 'c*' and 'the', this result can be individuated under the individuation methods described earlier in this chapter to produce something like:

<rope-77 <has-dimension <t-at tr-1>> length-24>

and

<john-12 causes <rope-77 <has-dimension <t-at tr-2>> length-25>

and

<length-25 is-less-than length-24>

and

<tr-1 is-prior-to tr-2>

and

<<tr-1 within tr-3> and <tr-2 within tr-3>>>

In addition, as part of the process the following relations would be created and recognized: <rope-100 isa rope>; <length-24 isa length>; and <length-25 isa length>. The entire representation would constitute the individuated notation. Each component of each sequence bears a recognized position in relation to other components in the representation. The components are related to one another both through links and through position. This representation would be processed further by SMS and cast onto related frame structures that capture the entailed relations. The frames bear *isa*, *member-of*, and *has-members* slots, as well as other special slots, that help define those relations. Results thus far suggest that efficient storage and retrieval strategies can be developed to take advantage of the specificity that is made available through individuated SL notation. Later chapters will describe some strategies being used in SMS to do so (see e.g. section 11.5). The point to be made here is that the individuated notation above is in itself a formal notation. The possibilities as to what might be done with it to preserve and bring out entailed relationships are open. Regardless of which system of processing, storing and retrieving one chooses to employ to draw inferences from this information, the logical theory behind the notation is specifiable independently of that system. By using parenthesis instead of wedges, SL notation becomes LISP code and is directly usable in a Lisp environment. One might compare these results with those that might be produced under FOL by writing out in first order notation the equivalents of these SL representations, and doing so in a form that would be suitable for direct use in a LISP or PROLOG environment. It seems that SL and SMS, working together, are able to capture natural language meaning in a more natural way than some other systems because of the special links that are made available through SL and because SMS allows the production of expansions that correspond almost directly with ordinary human analysis and understanding of the corresponding natural language concepts. This point will be strengthened in later chapters when examples on the use of quantifiers in SL and SMS are given. The strengths of FOL in this area are well known (see e.g. Hayes, 1977).

Before closing this chapter, it should be pointed out that when an *unquantified*, plural form of a label is used in expression, it is interpreted as a reference to a group or CE (for cluster-entity) and is assigned a CE marker of the form ce-$_{i}$. The marker is taken to name a set, each member of which conforms to the sign of the singular form of the label that introduced the CE marker. The statement '<teachers know students>' asserts that a group of 'teachers' knows a group of 'students'. By default, the CE is taken to be a subset of the extension of its associated label. Thus, the reference to 'teachers' in the statement above is a reference to a subset of the extension of the label 'teacher'. If a plural form of a label is *quantified*, it is individuated into a quantifier-marker rather than a CE marker. Section 10.2.4 describes how quantified plural forms of labels are handled in SMS.

When an *unquantified* singular form of a label is used in expression, it is interpreted as a reference to an individual or UE (for *u*nary *e*ntity) and is assigned a UE marker of the form ue-$_{i}$. Such a marker is taken to be an individual in the system. Most of the examples of SL notation given in the rest of this book contain singular forms of labels to avoid unnecessary complications. Chapter 10 will discuss how plural forms of labels affect the meaning of SL statements.

## CHAPTER 3

# ADDRESSING THE PROBLEM OF IMPRECISION

### 3.1 Preliminary Remarks

Chapters 1 and 2 introduced SMS as a system that employs a many-valued system of evaluation. Chapter 3 discusses the need for a many-valued approach and briefly describes the basis of the qualified response component of the system. The problem of imprecision in communicative discourse is discussed to reinforce the need for a many-valued approach and to set the context for a description of multiquerying, a strategy designed to address some aspects of imprecision. The problem of imprecision is described as a dual problem. One aspect of the problem is grounded in lack of denotative and temporal specificity. It is suggested that the best way to handle this problem under current automated technology is through interaction with the user. The other aspect of the problem is rooted in inadequate query construction. A query often does not precisely represent what the questioner actually wants to know. The many-valued approach is described as an effective means by which to address certain aspects of this problem. A multiquerying strategy is described that employs multiple values in generating responses to queries.

### 3.2 Need for a Many-Valued Approach

SMS employs a many-valued approach designed to accommodate a conversational mode in which the system responds to input in a way traceable to the way human beings respond to one another in ordinary discourse. It has long been recognized that ordinary conversation lacks the formal rigor of logic and mathematics. Human beings employ a multiplicity of highly complex cognitive processes as they communicate through loosely stated utterances (e.g. Winograd, 1983). If one wishes to build an AI system that either directly or indirectly will be used to simulate human conversation, the system should be designed to accommodate the leeway that is built into that kind of discourse. Some researchers believe that such a system should rest upon a theory of commonsense reasoning that incorporates both plausible inference and exact deduction (see e.g. Schank and Nash-Webber, 1975). The need for nonmonotonic logic to handle certain aspects of the leeway problem is now recognized by many logicists and other researchers who wish to maintain a logic-oriented approach to resolving representation issues (e.g. McCarthy, 1980). Indeed, the specification of a formal theory of nonmonotonic reasoning has been the subject of much recent literature (e.g. McCarthy, 1986; Reiter 1987).

The position taken in this book is that the employment of a many-valued approach is an effective way to deal with the problem of incorporating leeway into a system. The following example helps illustrate the point. Given that a person knows that a flock of birds descended on his fig tree and ate all the figs on the tree, how should that person respond in ordinary conversation when faced with the following question:

Did a bird eat all the figs on your fig tree?

Although there may be some individuals who believe that the appropriate response should be a mere "no" (since it is not true that just one bird ate all the figs), most people would have more to say based on the fact that they recognize that the person asking the question might not have stated the question in a way that precisely calls for the information sought. The words 'a bird' instead of, say, 'some birds' may have been used even though the questioner actually may have wanted to know whether one or more birds ate the figs. Recognizing this, some people would tailor their responses to cover that possibility, a technique typically employed in human conversation. Although a considerate and perhaps overly precise-thinking individual might respond, "No, a bird did not eat all the figs, but a flock of birds did eat all the figs," it would not be surprising for a person to respond simply by saying, "A flock of birds ate them." This last response seems to imply that the person giving it is aware that the questioner actually may wish to know whether one or more birds ate the figs, and the response provides the appropriate information, yet at the same time it disspells the notion that only one bird was involved. The disspelling of that notion, however, seems to be only a secondary point, the primary point being couched in the positive assertion that a flock of birds ate the figs. The reason for responding in this way might very well be that the person may be assuming that the original question does not precisely reflect what the questioner wants to know. This kind of assumption opens the door for the employment of a many-valued approach of the sort used in SMS. The approach rests in part on the assumption that a query does not *necessarily* specify with precision what information is being sought. This approach is quite different from that taken in FOL in which a conclusion to be proved is taken to be fixed.

AI researchers are keenly aware of the fact that without sufficient specificity of description available, there is little hope of enabling a system to handle free conversation with a user. This is evident since human beings have difficulty communicating with one another when specificity is lacking. It seems that a significantly large part of human discourse involving questions and responses is devoted to determining precisely what is is that the questioners wish to know. Indefinite reference inherent in ordinary human conversation often drives the conversation, with participants groping for specificity to increase their understanding of the communications taking place (see section 6.1 for example). Even if a system would have the ability to solicit precising information from the user, the problem alluded to previously pertaining to the sufficiency of questions would nonetheless persist. In other words, given that through interaction with the user, the denotative and temporal reference in a question can be set with sufficient precision to optimize scope of the question, the problem still remains whether the question accurately reflects what the questioner actually wishes to know. The many-valued approach is particularly useful in addressing this and the other problems mentioned in this section. It employs systems of qualified response and multiquerying to deal with these problems. These systems are described in sections 3.3 and 3.4.

### 3.3 Qualified Response

In FOL the truth function maps wffs into the set {T,F} (or {1,0}) so that every closed sentential formula, whether atomic or compound, has the value 'T' or 'F'. So-called many-valued logics in one way or another extend the range of the truth function to include values other than 'T' and 'F', such as 'U' for 'undetermined'. Some logics allow for an infinite set of values (see, for example, discussions in Rescher, 1969, at pages 36-45). SMS employs a system of qualified response that is built upon a mapping of *wfsss* into a set of symbols that are related to one another based on a ranking of strength. Given an SMS database, a valuation function can be defined to assign any *wfss* a value that is indicative of its 'strength of presence' in the database. The symbol 'IPR' marks the top of the ranking. It indicates that the given sequence 'is present' in the database in the strongest sense known to the system, whereas 'NPR-IC', the symbol at the bottom of the ranking, indicates that the sequence is 'not present' in the database in any sense recognized by the system and could not possibly be present. The concept of the impossibility of presence of an item is understood to mean that the presence of the item would cause an inconsistency in the database. Between these two extremes are other values that indicate some sort of 'presence' or 'nonpresence' in the database. The value 'NPR' signifies the absence of presence but leaves open the possibility that the presence of the associated *wfss* might be introduced at a later date. The system has been designed to allow flexibility in the selection of the number of symbols that are ranked in the scheme. In the version described in this book, the valuation function maps *wfss*s into the set of symbols {IPR,APR,SPR,WPR,FPR,NPR,NPR-IC}, where 'APR','SPR', 'WPR' and 'FPR' are ranked in the following decreasing order of strength and may be taken to have the connotations indicated below:

1) APR (almost present);
2) SPR (somewhat present);
3) WPR (weakly present);
4) FPR (faintly present).

This approach treats the concept of *presence* (or of being *present*) as a linguistic variable, that is, a variable whose values are words or sentences in a natural or artificial language, the values constituting a *term-set* of the variable (Zadeh, 1975). In this case the 'term-set' would be {IPR,APR,SPR,WPR,FPR,NPR,NPR-IC}. Sections 4.6 and 4.10 have more to say about the use of linguistic variables in SMS. For a treatment of truth and probability as linguistic variables, see [Zadeh, 1975]. The meaning of each symbol is defined with reference to the the type of match (e.g. partial or total) made, if any, during the evaluation process. The system has a set of matching rules that cover exact matches, near misses (e.g. singular form of word almost matches plural form of word) and matches based on shared properties or relations. If the database contains the expression '<birds sing>', for example, and the sequence to be evaluated is '<bird sings>', the sequence would be assigned the value 'APR' under the current version based on the fact that the sequence to be matched bears recognized relations to the database sequence. The relations indicate to the system that the evaluated sequence is 'present' in the database sequence in a recognized way. However, if the location of the two sequences is reversed so that '<birds sing>' becomes the sequence to be evaluated, the value 'SPR' would be returned under the current version of SMS since given that a formula holds for a singular form of a term, it does not follow necessarily that it holds for the plural form of the term. Measuring presence in this way corresponds in some respects to the approach used in fuzzy reasoning to handle partial matching (Zadeh, 1983a) and the detection of similarity through use of similarity functions (Zadeh, 1971; Chen, 1988).

The reader may not be accustomed to having so much emphasis placed on the notion of presence, but a little reflection should convince one that the notion is quite common and is frequently employed in logic-oriented systems. When talking about databases and the CWA (closed world assumption), for example, Reiter makes the following statement: "If a positive fact is not explicitly present in the database, its negation is assumed to hold" (Reiter, 1987, at page 150). He goes on to describe problems of formulating the CWA for deductive databases. One problem is that the lack of explicit presence of a fact cannot be the only test for concluding its negation because the fact may be derivable from the database. Reiter's remarks are mentioned not to introduce discussion on the CWA, but to point out the relevance of the idea of presence in that area. If any positive information (fact) not specified is to be assumed to be false under a particular formalization of the CWA, the assumption of falsehood rests upon a prior determination of nonpresence. In this respect, the notions of presence and nonpresence are more basic than the notions of truth and falsehood. The approach used in SMS is to define operations at the basic level of presence in an attempt to avoid making the semantic ascent to the truth predicate. This seems to be consistent with an austerely formal approach. An ascent is made in SMS, but it is the non-truth-functional, many-valued one described in section 3.5.

It is interesting to note that Reiter uses the expression 'explicitly present' in his remarks reported above, and does so to contrast the case in which a fact is explicitly present from one in which the fact is merely *derivable*. In SMS, a derivable fact is taken to be nonexplicitly present and is thus 'present' in a sense recognized by the system, so there appears to be a correspondence between the notions of presence in SMS and the senses of 'present' and 'derivable' used by Reiter. As will be described in section 3.3, SMS employs a many-valued system to describe presence. For any query term $\alpha_i$ and any database term $\alpha_j$, a valuation function can be defined to assign values indicative of the 'presence' or 'nonpresence' of $\alpha_i$ in $\alpha_j$ (see section 3.5). Since a two-valued system would be inadequate to cover all the desired results of possible evaluations, a many-valued system has been adopted for expanded coverage.

The philosophy behind the qualified response approach is that although a database formula might not exactly match a query formula, the two might nonetheless be related in a way that justifies a response of some sort. The 'measures of presence' used in the many-valued scheme are not technical descriptions of presence (understood in its normal sense) because sometimes it is not fair to say that a sequence is actually present in the database when a qualified response is given. The values produced are called 'qualified responses' because they represent qualifications of the strongest possible response the system is allowed to give. Whenever a qualified response is given to a query, the derivability of the query, taken as a conclusion to be proved, is considered to be *tainted* to some extent, which corresponds to treating the derivability relation as a fuzzy relation (see Zadeh, 1971, and Yager, 1986, on fuzzy relations), that is, one that may hold in varying degrees of strength.

For readers who might have reservations about treating the derivability relation as a fuzzy relation, it should be noted that the relation can also be handled in a more traditional, non-fuzzy way based on a total valuation of SL statements. One can easily envision the conversion of a flat SMS database (i.e. a database consisting solely of the original SL statements entered to create the database) into a partial valuation using a valuation function that would assign the value 'IPR' to each statement based on the fact that acceptance of a statement into the database in itself bestows full presence on the statement. SMS can be thought of as providing inflating operations (rules) by which statements bearing appropriately assigned values can be added to the database to produce what amounts to a total valuation. Section 4.2 on inferencing gives details on how this would be done. Assuming for the moment that the product of these operations would be a total inflation (i.e. an inflation containing every possible statement of SL, each statement bearing an appropriately assigned value), the inflated database would constitute a total valuation on SL. It would be but a simple step to convert this database into a database of *signed statements* simply by prefixing the values to the statements (see Smullyan, 1968, and Fitting, 1986, on creation of signed statements by prefixing *T* or *F* to the statements). The theoretical basis of derivability for *signed statements* can then be defined with reference to the totally inflated database of signed statements. The derivability of a signed statement $V_i\Phi_j$ (where $V_i$ represents the value that has been prefixed to the statement $\Phi_j$) would be defined in terms of whether the signed statement could be matched in the totally inflated database. Under this scheme, the derivability relation would not be fuzzy since any signed statement either would or would not be provable from the database of signed statements.

### 3.3.1 Qualification Based on Multiple Senses of a Term

As a way of acquainting the reader with how a many-valued system can be used to produce qualified responses, this section and section 3.3.2 will describe some techniques that are employed to address problems of indefinite reference. The examples given are quite simple and are intended to introduce the reader to the basic principles that ground the higher level methods employed in the system.

The qualified response scheme described in section 3.3 can be broadened to include a subcategorization of the value system itself. Each value in the scheme can be taken to be the the top node in a hierarchy of values. This can increase the power of the approach significantly, as the following example illustrates. Given that the term 'school' has two recognized meanings in a system, as in 'school of fish' and in 'school for students', one way to distinguish the meanings is to have each meaning represented by a different term. The term 'school-1' could be reserved for the first sense of 'school' and 'school-2' for the second sense. The assignment of markers to terms to individuate them is a technique commonly employed in AI systems (Charniak and McDermott, 1985). As long as one or the other of these terms is used in expression, the associated ambiguity is avoided. It is somewhat inconvenient to have to worry about representing different senses in this way during expression. In ordinary conversation, the context is usually consulted to disambiguate uses of terms, and often a term having multiple senses can be used on frequent occasion in conversation without causing problems of ambiguity.

The use of the many-valued scheme makes it possible to capture some of the convenience that attends ordinary English expression, which would allow the term 'school' to be used in the two senses mentioned above without the attachment of distinguishing marks to differentiate the senses. A hierarchy of values can be established to accommodate different senses of a term. If a term has only one sense and is sought in a search and is found to be present in the database, a value may be chosen from the set of symbols given previously to describe the nature of the presence of the term. If a term has multiple senses, as does the term 'school' in the example under consideration, a separate value can be assigned to each sense, and these values can be cast into subtype relationships with the parent value. For example, the values 'APR-1' and 'APR-2' may be classified as subtypes of the value 'APR' and may be respectively assigned to sense 1 and sense 2 of the term 'school'. Thus, if in a given case the value 'APR' is the appropriate value for a use of the term 'school', the subvalues can be activated and used to generate responses. If, for example, the term 'school' is present in the database at a unique location, say represented by the symbol 'loc-10', and one asks whether the term 'school' is present in the database, the following responses might be given in the case under consideration (the listing would be arbitrary in the sense that the order in which responses are listed is not indicative of a ranking of preference):

1) APR-1 $\rightarrow$ loc-10; and

2) APR-2 $\rightarrow$ loc-10;

where each arrow points to the location of the basis of the response. This blatantly ambiguous mode of response indicates that each sense of the term 'school' is somehow present at 'loc-10'. The reader should note the difference between a response like 'APR', a parent value response, and one like 'APR-1', a subvalue response. The former flags that the 'presence' is tainted in the way normally indicated by 'APR'. The response 'APR-1' indicates that the presence is tainted in the same way because, being a subtype of 'APR', the symbol 'APR-1' inherits the meaning of its parent 'APR'; in addition, 'APR-1' indicates that the presence is tainted by ambiguity rooted in multiple senses of a term. The symbol 'APR-1' thus carries important, additional meaning.

For any term of SL that has multiple senses, there corresponds a sequence of alternative meanings that can be used in the derivation process. The correspondence is diagrammed below:

$$\alpha \rightarrow \{\beta_1, \beta_2, \ldots, \beta_n\} \rightarrow <\beta_1 \text{ or } \beta_2 \text{ or} \ldots \text{or } \beta_n>$$

where $\alpha$ represents a term with multiple senses, and '$\beta_1, \beta_2, \ldots, \beta_n$' represent the multiple senses of $\alpha$. Given that the sequence '$<\beta_1$ or $\beta_2$ or . . . or $\beta_n>$' can be generated from the set of multiple senses of $\alpha$, each alternative (e.g. '$\beta_2$') in the sequence can be assigned the value '$V_{indefinite\text{-}ref.}$' to indicate tainted presence based on indefinite reference. Sections 11.3 and 11.4 describe how this correspondence can be used in the derivation process.

The power of the scheme can be augmented by establishing a ranking of preference for the subvalues. If one decides, for instance, that sense 1 of the term 'school' should be ranked higher than sense 2, perhaps under certain contextual conditions, the preference could be represented by attaching letters indicative of rank to the appropriate subvalues. It follows that if 'A' has a higher ranking than 'B', the exact order of response listed below would be dictated in this example:

1) APR-1-A → loc-10; and

2) APR-2-B → loc-10.

Thus, if one decides that sense 1 of the term 'school' is to be preferred over sense 2 in the context of the expression '<school <fish>>' (which corresponds to the English expressions 'fish school' and 'school of fish'), the system can be made to respond in the way indicated above, that is, with the ranked letters attached to the responses. Although still ambiguous, the response at least indicates that one of the response values is a stronger indicator of presence than the other. Figure 4 diagrams a simple comparison between this scheme and one in which there is no such ranking of preference.

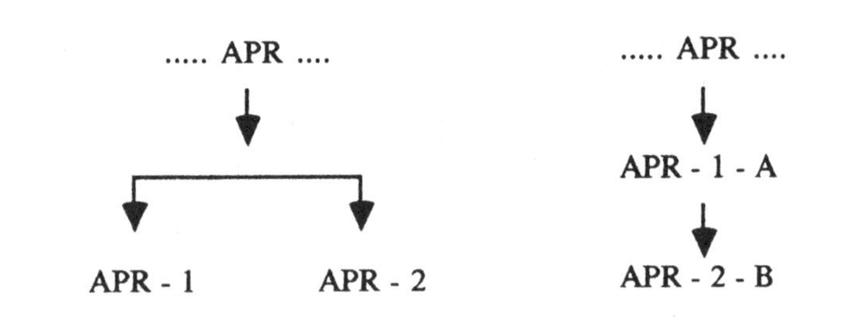


Figure 4. Comparison of Value Schemes

It should be noted that, consistent with the many-valued approach, a ranking of this sort does not necessarily render lower ranked responses useless. After all, it is possible that a person might place the expression '<school <fish>>' in the database having in mind a place where a professor (teacher) is teaching fish (students if the term 'students' covers animals as well as persons) how to react to some stimuli. That person would not be unreasonable, perhaps, to think of such a place as being a 'fish school', the term 'school' being used in sense 2. The many-valued approach produces lower ranked responses to cover this kind of contingency.

### 3.3.2 Qualification Based on Indefinite Reference

The approach described in section 3.3.1 that deals with multiple senses of a term can be conveniently extended to address the problem of indefinite reference. If, for example, two tokens (cf. 'instances') of a sign (cf. 'concept') are entered into an SL database, and subsequently, reference is made to one of them without precisely identifying which one, a different response value can be associated with each token just as was done for each sense of 'school' in the example above. This approach can produce benefits. Assuming, for instance, that the database has only two instances of 'john' seeing a 'person', one in which he saw 'mary' and another in which he saw 'jim', how should the system go about handling a query like:

<john saw <person <the>>>? (21)

In this query the term 'the' is supposed to point to a specific 'person', but it is not clear which 'person' is the referent of the expression '<person <the>>'. One possible way to proceed when faced with this kind of problem is to solicit precising information from the user. Accordingly, the response of the system might take the form:

> Please restate your query in a way that identifies the referent of '<person <the>>'.

Assuming the response from the user would be:

<john saw jim> ?

the system could go about giving a response by indicating that this sequence is present in the database. The form of the response might be something like:

<IPR → <john saw jim> → $\sigma_1$>

where 'IPR' indicates full presence of the query; where the first arrow points to the statement in the database that matches the query; and where $\sigma_1$ represents indexing information that would give the location of the database statement.

Another approach to handling query (21) would be to employ the scheme mentioned previously that entails the assignment of values to possible referents. Under this scheme the initial response to the query would be something like:

<$V_{indef}$-1 → <john saw mary> → $\sigma_2$>

<$V_{indef}$-2 → <john saw jim> → $\sigma_1$>

where $V_{indef}$-1 and $V_{indef}$-2 are values indicative of tainted presence due to indefinite reference, each number indicating the presence of a different referent. This turns out to be a more useful and efficient response than was given under the previous approach since everything achieved in multiple steps under the other approach is achieved in this one-step response. This places the user in a position to select relevant information from the response, assuming of course that the user is familiar with the entailed values. This way of doing things corresponds to the way that a human being who knows what the system knows in this example might respond to the original query. In such a case, instead of asking:

"Which person do you mean?"

a human being might respond:

"John saw two people, Mary and Jim."

The assignment of values to possible referents might not be feasible in some instances, as would be the case when the list of possible referents is too lengthy. The scheme, of course, should be designed to take this into account, but at the very least, the system could resort to the first approach mentioned above.

Theoretically, the many-valued approach can be defined to allow an unlimited number of factors and circumstances to govern the creation of response values. Depending on the depth and the degree of relevancy one wishes to admit into conversation with the system, lines can be drawn to limit appropriately the number of factors to be considered. The task of having to decide where to draw lines seems to be more of a luxury than a problem since systems that do not have such a depth of possibilities are short of information to that extent and seemingly have no way to compensate for the deficiency.

As will be discussed in Chapter 6, the SMS approach employs a non-truth-functional, many-valued semantical scheme that borrows features from fuzzy logic and many-valued logic. Later it will be shown that because of the local nature of fuzzy logic (see Bellman and Zadeh, 1977), it is possible to employ some of the underlying features of fuzzy logic to address particular problems in the SMS environment, and there appears to be no reason why mechanisms similar to probability and possibility distributions (e.g. Zadeh, 1975; Farreny and Prade, 1986) cannot be employed effectively in the system. If, for instance, the set $U = \{u_1, u_2, u_3, u_4\}$ is taken to be the universe of discourse, a fuzzy subset F of U is a subset in which the grade of membership of any element of F is drawn from the unit interval [0,1]. The following is an example of what would be referred to as a fuzzy subset of U:

$$\{ .5/u_1, .7/u_2, 1/u_3, 0/u_4 \}$$

where each element-pair of the form $a_i/u_i$ (e.g. '$.5/u_1$') is understood to signify that the element $u_i$ has the membership grade $a_i$ in the fuzzy subset F (cf. Yager, 1986). Thus, in the example given, the element $u_1$ has the membership grade .5 in the fuzzy set F. The larger the grade, the stronger the membership in the fuzzy set. Any member of F whose grade of membership is above 0 is said to be a member of the *support set* of F. In this example, all elements except $u_4$ would be members of the support set of F. Using a somewhat standard example, given that U is the set of positive integers and that *small integer* is the name of the fuzzy set { 1/0, .8/1, .6/2, .4/3, .2/4, 0/5, .... }, the value .8 would represent the compatibility of the integer 1 with the concept *small number*. Given that X is a variable that may take values in U, the propositional function 'X is a small integer' is said to induce a *possibility distribution* $\Pi_x$ that associates with each integer in U the *possibility* that the integer could be a value of X. The possibility distribution $\Pi_x$ equates the possibility of X taking a particular value in U to the grade of membership of that value in the fuzzy set, which in this case is the set *small integer*. Given that 'X is a small number' and given that the number 1 has the membership grade of .8 in the set *small number*, the possibility that X = 1 is equal to that membership grade. The fuzzy theorists claim that much of the imprecision intrinsic in natural language is possibilistic rather than probabilistic (Zadeh, 1979), but it should be noted that proponents of probability theory argue that there is a probabilistic (degree of belief) model for vague sets that provides quantitative and computable measures for vague classifications (e.g. Cheeseman, 1985).

A distinctive feature of fuzzy logic is that terms such as *tall, beautiful*, and *approximately* are assumed to have meanings that are not only subjective, but also local in the sense of having limited validity in a special domain of discourse. The definition of the term 'small number', for example, as a subset of the real line might be valid only for a designated set of propositions (Bellman and Zadeh, 1977). This section and section 4.8.1 give examples of how the many-valued approach can be used effectively in addressing certain problems of imprecision without resorting to possibility and probability distributions of the sort typically employed in fuzzy systems (see e.g. Gaines, 1977; Zadeh, 1978). Section 4.10 describes how those distributions can be used effectively when the task at hand requires extra precision.

The methods described in this section for handling imprecision do not employ the kind of finely graded concepts used used in fuzzy applications (e.g. Zadeh, 1978; Yager, 1980; Farreny and Prade, 1986; and Turksen, 1986). Instead, the scheme employs simple rankings that perhaps are best thought of in terms of *utility* rather than probability or possibility (understood in terms of feasibility; see e.g. Eoy and Kuss, 1986). The fuzzy theorists maintain that an ordinary set can be represented as a fuzzy set (Yager, 1986). Given U = { $u_1$, $u_2$, $u_3$ } as a universe of discourse, the ordinary (crisp) set { $u_1$, $u_2$ } can be expressed in fuzzy notation as:

$\{ 1/u_1, 1/u_2, 0/u_3 \}$

where 1 indicates membership and 0 indicates nonmembership. It could thus be said that in handling the indefinite reference problem in the way described previously, a possibility distribution is implicitly being employed since '<person <the>>' may be taken to name a fuzzy set in which each possible referent would be assigned the grade of 1 by the membership function, so that the determination of the referent of the expression '<person <the>>' amounts to determining what possibility each possible referent has of being in that fuzzy set. Something similar could be said about the examples involving the term 'school' in which response values were cast into a ranking of preference (as was done for the responses 'APR-1-A' and 'APR-2-B'). The ranking could be taken as being defined over an interval, say [0,100], in which the responses would be mapped to integers whose natural order in the interval would represent the ranking. Thus, sense 2 of school could be represented by a linguistic value that could be mapped into the interval to produce a result similar to the one described in the example. Admittedly, the problems of imprecision described in this section could be handled in this way. What is meant by the statement that certain problems of imprecision can be handled without resorting to probability and possibility distributions of the sort used by fuzzy logicists is that the problems can be handled without having to determine subjective gradations of the sort that would have to be made to treat a concept like *attractive appearance* as a fuzzy set. To handle such a concept, one might very well have to assign each member of the database a grade of attractiveness, say one member the grade of .87, another the grade of .83, and yet another the grade of .79 (cf. Zadeh's treatment of 'attractiveness'; see e.g. Zadeh, 1986). This is not to say that SMS can completely avoid such difficulties, but only that in some instances it can deal with this kind of concept without reference to fine gradations. Section 4.10 describes how this might be done by employing natural language hedges.

Since a grade of 'presence' indicates the extent to which one expression is present in another, the grade being taken as the measure of strength of the derivability relation between the expressions (see section 3.5), derivability in SMS is not to be understood in terms of *feasibility*. It would be difficult, for example, to determine the possibility of X taking the value '<birds sing>' in the expression 'X is derivable from <<animal<one>> sings>' when possibility is thought of in terms of feasibility. However, when one considers how the relation between the two expressions might be relevant for human conversation, it is somewhat easy to assign a *utility* value to the relation that describes its usefulness in a conversational mode. This perhaps compares to using the feasibility test in a figurative way (see Zadeh, 1978, and section 4.10 on the use of the 'degree of ease' test in a figurative way).

The sense of utility used to describe derivability in SMS differs from the sense sometimes used in the logic of assertions in which propositions are assigned values indicative of the strength of commitment to them by those who assert the propositions, the commitment being defined with reference to utility, at least in part (Giles, 1985). Following the notion that one should not try to be any more precise (understood in terms of linguistic precision) than necessary (see Popper, 1976, cited in [Gaines, 1977]), there seems to be no reason to employ devices such as probability distributions and commitment measures if the conversational task can be handled without them. Unfortunately, not all situations can be dealt with in a simplistic way, and it is sometimes necessary, though perhaps less often than one might expect, to consider possibility valuations and probability measures. Section 4.10 discusses how mechanisms similar to possibility and probability distributions can be used effectively within the SMS environment.

### 3.4 Multiquerying

In SMS it is assumed that each query implies a set of queries (referred to herein as the 'expansion' of the query) and that each member of the set is within the scope of the original query. The effect is that a query is taken to be a set containing the original query, generalizations and other deformations of it, plus other queries that are related to it in determinate ways. It can be specified (postulated), for example, that if the query employs a singular form of a word, its expansion should at least contain the given query plus one that employs a plural form of the word, the latter constituting a deformation of the given query based on the substitution of the plural form for the singular form. A well defined subset can be produced from the set based on specifications that define which deformations, generalizations and related queries are to be included in the subset. Each query in the subset is therefore related to the original query in determinate ways. The relations are traceable to the relations that exist between the components of the original query and the components of the queries in the subset. Subtype/supertype, part/whole and singular/plural relations are examples of relations that might hold between components. The system subcategorizes the elements of the subset based on how closely they resemble or are related to the original query. A particular response value is assigned to each subcategory so that if a member of that subcategory is matched in the database, a response is given that contains the value assigned to the category. This value serves as a qualification of the response. In other words, the following mapping is defined:

$$f : Q \to \mathrm{V}$$

where '$Q$' is a family of categorized subqueries produced from the original query, and 'V' is the range of values to be used to qualify responses to the query. The fact that V contains more than two values provides one basis for characterizing the response system as a many-valued one. Figure 5 diagrams this scheme. In

Figure 5, $Q_1$ is the original query to which there corresponds a set of multiple queries $\{Q_1, ..., Q_n\}$, where $n \geq 1$. Each member of the set is assigned a value by the function $f$, after which an attempt is made to satisfy that member in the data-base (DB).

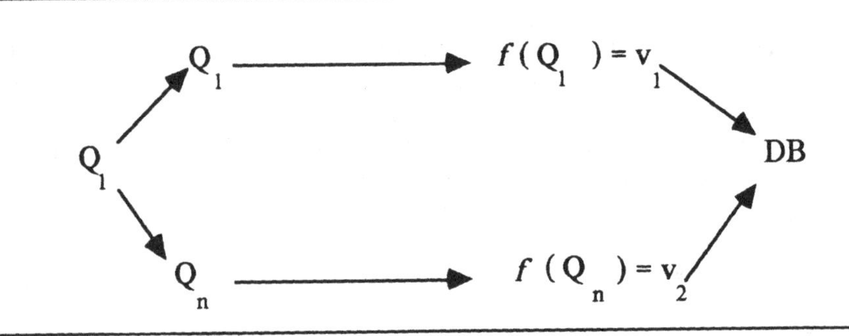


Figure 5. Multiquerying Scheme

It should be noted that by having defined specifications for membership in the subset, SMS distinguishes itself from any many-valued system that fails to reveal the basis for using multiple values. By avoiding the truth predicate, SMS avoids having to answer the troublesome question whether it makes sense to speak of different degrees of truth. The qualified responses described in this section are not based on belief in the existence of 'shades of truth' but on the special view that:

1) a query is possibly imprecise in its request for information;

2) there are well founded principles that can be used to determine what information reasonably might fall within the scope of a query; and

3) there are well founded principles by which to categorize and rank information that is within the scope of a query, the ranking being indicative of the reasonableness of particular information being included within that scope.

More details about the system of qualified response is given in section 4.6. It should be pointed out that the techniques employed in the examples dealing with individual terms such as 'bird' and 'birds' ground the methods that are employed at the sentential level. Section 11.5 describes some of those methods as part of a discussion of the querying process employed in SMS.

### 3.5 Justification for Use of a Many-Valued Approach

A somewhat coarse yet accurate justification for the many-valued approach can be explained with reference to the following scheme.

Given that A is the set of all possible ordered pairs of SL terms, that R is a set of selected binary relations that may hold between SL terms, and that B is the product set of A and R, it is possible to define a function $f$ so that $f\,(\langle\langle a_i, a_j\rangle, r_i\rangle)$ returns 1 if the relation $r_i$ (where $r_i \in R$) holds between $a_i$ and $a_j$ (where $a_i$ and $a_j$ are terms of SL) and 0 if the relation does not hold. Given that set C includes all ordered pairs $\langle\langle a_i, a_j\rangle, r_i\rangle$ such that $\langle a_i, a_j\rangle \in \{\, x \mid f\,(x, r_i) = 1 \,\}$, the function $g$ can be defined as follows:

$$g : C \rightarrow V$$

so that $g\,(\langle\langle a_i, a_j\rangle, r_i\rangle) = v_i \in V$, where V is a set of values used to describe the derivability of $a_i$ from $a_j$. Given that the range of $g$ consists of more than two elements, a many-valued system can be distinguished based upon the multiplicity of elements in V. In other words:

$$g : C \rightarrow \{v_1, v_2, v_3, \ldots, v_n\}$$

where $n \geq 3$. In SMS, the values in V are not truth functional nor are they probabilistically based. The values are based on criteria that define usefulness in a precisely determined conversational mode. These values are used to qualify responses in ways traceable to the ways human beings qualify their responses in ordinary discourse. A trivial example can illustrate the point. Given that ‘<<worker <a>> helped john>’ is the only database sequence that is relevant to the query ‘<<workers <several>> helped john>’, it should be obvious that the query cannot be satisfied because the query calls for more than one worker to be related to ‘john’ in the way of having helped him, yet the database has only one worker that is so related to him. The system would not respond in such a case merely by indicating that the query could not be satisfied (derived) but would indicate that a tainted derivability relation holds between the query and the database sequence. This response corresponds to the way a person might respond to the query if the person knew that ‘a worker’ had helped someone named John and was asked the whether several workers had helped John. Instead of responding something like, "No" or "No, it is not true that several workers helped John, but a worker did help him," the person might respond, "A worker helped John." This response gives more information than a mere "No" and is more efficient than the other possible response mentioned above. SMS captures this kind of efficiency by using the many-valued approach described above. This approach to handling leeway in human conversation has promising potential for use in AI. Figure 6 gives information that might be used in the response processes that are employed in the conversational mode of SMS. From a study of Figure 6 one can see that three values can be associated with the term 'bird' (the first element of each ordered pair), to wit:

1) '$v_1$' if 'bird' is associated with 'bird' based on the identity relation;

2) '$v_2$' if 'bird' is associated with 'birds' based on the singular/plural relation; and

3) '$v_3$' if 'bird' is associated with 'animal' based on the subtype/supertype relation.

| ORDERED PAIR | RELATION | RESPONSE VALUE |
|---|---|---|
| <bird, bird> | identity | $v_1$ |
| <bird, birds> | singular/plural | $v_2$ |
| <bird, animal> | subtype/supertype | $v_3$ |

Figure 6. Information That Might Be Used in Response Scheme

If one considers the first element of each ordered pair to correspond to a query that asks whether the element is present in a given database, and if one considers the second element of each ordered pair to correspond to a term in that database, one can see that a number of response values are possible for a term depending on what relations it holds to one or more terms in the database. For example, given the database {bird, birds, animal}, the query 'bird', and the information in Figure 6, the system could be made to produce the values '($v_1$, $v_2$, $v_3$)' based on the indicated associations. If the database had just one item x such that $x \in$ {bird, birds, animal}, one of three possible values would be returned. The possible responses in such a case would range over the set $\{v_1, v_2, v_3\}$. It is but a simple step to the position that the the set $\{v_1, v_2, v_3\}$ may be used as values that describe the derivability or provability of 'bird' from the database. Under such an interpretation, the term 'bird' would be derivable or provable from the original database in three ways, each of which would be based on the *presence* of a term that bears a *recognized* relation to the term 'bird'. Each instance of provability would be associated with a different value. The derivability of 'bird' based on the presence of 'bird', for instance, would be associated with the value '$v_1$', whereas the derivability based on the presence of 'animal' would be associated with the value '$v_3$'. The relations that are recognized for defining derivability between terms of SL have been carefully selected based on their relevance for simulating the way human beings respond to one another in ordinary conversation.

By limiting the number of recognized relations, the number of terms that have to be considered when setting the derivability specifications for a given term is minimized. Given any term of SL, a function called a relevance function (see section 4.10) can produce all the terms that are related to the given term through any of the recognized relations. When the given term is used in a communication, the set of terms produced by the relevance function are employed to simulate the way a human being might think about and respond to that communication. Each term in the communication is treated in isolation as part of the simulation process. The terms produced by the relevance function are employed while the given term is being viewed in isolation. If the communication is a query, for example, the terms can be used to help construct deformations of the query in preparation for giving a response (see section 3.4 on multiquerying). Sections 11.6 gives details about how the terms are used in the query satisfaction process. Basically, the terms are treated as parts of the original query, and if any of the terms are matched in the database, a predetermined value is assigned to the match and is used to determine the response that is to be given to the original query.

What this amounts to is that response values can be postulated for the ordered pairs and relations. As will be explained in section 11.5 on querying, each instance of provability can be considered to be a line of reasoning about the derivability of 'bird' from the database. This permits one to speak of a degree of strength of a line of reasoning based on the response value that is associated with that line of reasoning. Response values can be ranked to indicate the strength of 'presence' of the derived term in the database (see section 3.3). This approach can be extended to include not only individual terms, but also sentential expressions so that it becomes meaningful to speak of lines of reasoning that yield sentential expressions. Section 4.6 describes the basis for the extension. It should be noted that the lines of reasoning are not rooted in probabilities but are based on predetermined relevancies. It thus seems that these results can be produced without employing a probabilistically-based or truth-functional approach.

From what has been described thus far, one can see that given any two terms $\alpha_i$ and $\alpha_j$ and a set of selected relations R, the derivability of $\alpha_i$ from $\alpha_j$ can be assigned values by postulation based on the correspondence defined by the function $g$. As is described in section 4.6, it is possible to assign derivability values to all ordered pairs of SL terms using these correspondences. Since $g(\langle\langle\alpha_i, \alpha_j\rangle, r_i\rangle) = v_k \in \{v_1, v_2, v_3, \ldots, v_n\}$, where $n \geq 3$, and since $\{v_1, v_2, v_3, \ldots, v_n\}$ contains more than two values, the conclusion that derivability so defined is a many-valued relation seems inescapable. The only thing left open to question is whether the mapping into a multiple-valued set instead of into a 2-valued set, say {T,F}, is proper. An affirmative answer seems in order. It is true that the many-valued approach can be explained in terms of a 2-valued approach, but this has little consequence in an environment like SMS. One could say, for example, that the approach described thus far can be explained as follows. For any SL term $a_1$, a set $\{a_1, \ldots, a_n\}$ (where $n \geq 1$) can be specified for it so that to ask whether $a_1$ can be derived from $a_2$ is to ask whether any member of $\{a_1, ..., a_n\}$ matches $a_2$. A function *h* can be defined to map any ordered pair into {T,F} so that $h(\langle a_i, a_j \rangle) = F$ (where $a_i \neq a_j$) and $h(\langle a_i, a_i \rangle) = T$ (since $a_i = a_i$). The response to be given to the question whether $a_1$ can be derived from $a_2$ would amount to determining whether one could find a term to satisfy $a_i$ in:

$$h(\langle a_2, a_i \rangle) = T.$$

where $a_i \in \{a_1, ..., a_n\}$.

The process viewed in this light is based on a 2-valued system. However, with equal force it can be said that it is not necessary to define the approach in this way since for any two terms $a_i$ and $a_j$, a set of relevant relations R can be specified so that the derivability of $a_i$ from $a_j$ can be described by postulation to be: $g(\langle\langle a_i, a_j \rangle, r_i \rangle) = v_k$, where $r_i \in R$. The potency of the argument in favor of the two valued approach seems to evaporate when one considers the pressure that would be imposed by a conversational environment. In a conversational mode, one need not employ the 2-valued approach at all but can depend on the function *g* from the outset. Thus, given the database {birds} and the query term 'bird', the value '$v_2$' would be produced based on postulation and would be used to qualify the response. The need to know the basis of the postulation simply would not arise in conversation. The point is that the response qualified by the value '$v_2$' might be a more appropriate and efficient response in a conversation mode than would be a 2-valued-based response such as:

> F, but if you also wish to present the query term 'birds', the response would be 'T'.

Within the formal limits of SMS, the response qualified by the value '$v_2$' at the very least stands on equal footing with this last type of response.

Given a provability function P that takes two propositional arguments and returns a value indicative of whether the first argument is derivable from its second argument, and given two formulas x and y, the issue at hand seems to reduce to:

Which of the following approaches to the provability relation is more appropriate?

1) $P(x,y) = z \in \{$ valid, invalid $\}$; or

2) $P(x,y) = z$, where z is qualified by a member of $\{v_1, v_2, v_3, \ldots, v_n\}$ (where $n \geq 3$).

Within the plain, symbolic environment of SMS, a 2-valued approach is no more legitimate than a many-valued approach. It does not appear that any advantage can be gained for a 2-valued system by defining validity with reference to the truth predicate, which would be amount to defining the provability relation as follows:

$$P(x,y) = z \in \{T,F\}.$$

This definition would be based on the correspondence between 'y/ therefore x' and 'y ⊃ x', where '⊃' represents material implication.

At the level at which SMS is defined, it does not seem reasonable to argue that the characterization of the argument:

Given: A flock of birds ate all the figs.

---

therefore: A bird ate all the figs.

as being 'invalid' is somehow better than assigning it a value such as 'SPR' (as defined in section 3.3). An important point can be made here. Given that the premise of this argument is contained in a database and that a user wants to know whether the conclusion follows from that database, the reader might consider how the response 'invalid' would compare to the response 'SPR' in terms of usefulness to the user. The response 'SPR' lets the user know that the derivability relation is tainted and at the same time indicates that the database contains information that is somehow related to the conclusion, perhaps in a way that would be of interest to the user. The response 'invalid', on the other hand, does not make it known that related information is available. All the user obtains from the response is that the conclusion *as stated* is not derivable from the database. How many people are consistently capable of stating with exact precision what they wish to know in ordinary conversation? Upon receiving the response 'invalid', the user indeed might wonder whether the conclusion was stated with sufficient accuracy to cover his actual rather than stated derivational interests.

The essence of the argument in favor of the 2-valued approach seems to be that as long as the reducibility relation holds between a given KR system and 2-valued FOL, the KR system is not really needed because the generally recognized and well understood notation of FOL can be used in its place. It does not appear that this argument can give the 2-valued approach much of a boost in the current context even if the the notion of truth is adopted as part of the scheme. The reason for this is that it can just as well be argued that the 2-valued approach can be explained in terms of the many-valued approach. The two values can simply be mapped into the many values. The circularity of the argument in favor of the two-valued approach has been observed by others. Rescher, for example, states:

> "If we insist upon setting out from a two-valued point of view, we will, of course, be able to regard the variant logical systems from its perspective. But . . . there is no fundamental reason why we could not have set out from a multivalued point of view and then developed other pluri-valued systems -- two-valued logic specifically included -- from this vantage point."
>
> (Rescher, N., *Many-Valued Logic*, McGraw-Hill, Inc., 1969, at page 229)

If one is interested in only two values, the rest of the values can be ignored. On balance, although two-valued logic is generally recognized and perhaps even well understood, this is not sufficient to outweigh the benefits produced by the many-valued approach when employed in a conversational environment. In the last analysis, the two approaches should be evaluated based on criteria of usefulness and efficiency in their domain of application, which is something that has long been recognized by logicians. As C. I. Lewis put it:

> "Sufficiency for the guidance and testing of our usual deductions, systematic simplicity and convenience, accord with our psychological limitations and our mental habits, and so on, operate as criteria in our conscious or unconscious choice of "good logic"."
>
> (Lewis, C. I., "Alternative systems of logic," *The Monist*, vol. 41, 1931, at page 484).

For complementing discussions of arguments favoring many-valued logic over two-valued logic, see Chapter 3 of (Rescher, 1969).

CHAPTER 4

# INFERENCING IN SMS

## 4.1 Preliminary Remarks

Chapter 3 described how a many-valued approach can be combined with multiquerying to address problems of imprecision. The discussions now turn to the subject of inferencing. SMS generates two kinds of inferences that correspond to deductive inferences and nondeductive inferences. Derivation processes use these inferences, along with the relation of identity and relations between sentential expressions and their corresponding expansions and normal forms, to produce both unqualified and qualified proofs. In SMS, proof of a conclusion amounts to demonstrating its 'presence' in the premises (database). The notion of presence is specially defined to suit the needs of a conversational mode of expression in which queries are taken as conclusions to be proved. A 'conclusion' is merely a well formed sentential sequence. It is proved by demonstrating that its components are *present* in the database and that they hold the same or equivalent relationships with one another in the database as they do in the conclusion to be proved.

Section 4.5 describes how ontological distinctions affect the derivation process. Ontological inconsistency is described as a somewhat independent basis for tainting the derivability relation. The ontological scheme employed in SMS is described as a set of realms or spaces that are reserved for specific types of objects. Improper use of an object in a space in inferencing results in the production of tainted inferences. Section 4.6 briefly describes the derivation process and gives a few examples of how these factors can affect the process. Section 4.7 briefly describes how SMS operates in the modal realm, and section 4.8

introduces the approach used to handle nonmonotonic reasoning. Section 4.9 covers the use of expansions and formalisms in the inferencing scheme to set the stage for a description of how fuzzy set theory can be gainfully employed in SMS. Section 4.10 discusses how fuzzy reasoning can be incorporated into the overall inferencing scheme if one wishes to do so.

It should be pointed out here that most of the schemes in SMS are adjustable to suit particular needs. For the most part, the schemes described in this book are merely illustrative of the general approach that is being recommended. The methodology described for producing penumbral (nondeductive) inferences, for example, may be changed as one sees fit as long as consistency specifications are met. Thus, within somewhat well defined limits, the SMS approach allows one to specify which nonstandard inferences are to follow from a given formula. Likewise, one may make ontological distinctions as one chooses as long as consequences produced by the distinctions are consistently defined throughout the system. An important requirement in this regard is that for whatever change is made in one of the schemes, a corresponding change must be made in the many-valued aspect of the system that is to deal with that scheme. There is a plus side to this requirement. One of the strong points of the many-valued approach is that it serves as a buffer for changes within the system. An attempt has been made to design SMS so that all one need do to add new types of inference or ontological distinctions is to specify the affects they will have on the many-valued system. One may even specify that absurdities are to follow from formulas of SMS as long as the many-valued component is apprised of their status as absurdities so that it can assign appropriate values to them. This indeed gives developers an opportunity to incorporate a significant amount of flexibility into their systems.

## 4.2 Inferencing

Inferencing in SMS depends on defined relations between a variety of types of linguistic objects ranging from individual terms to highly complex sequences of considerable length. This section describes the basis for classifying different types of inference and defines some crucial relations that may hold between sentential expressions that are of particular importance for the derivation process. The relations between sentential expressions and their expansions and normal forms and the relation of identity are distinguished in this regard. For expository convenience, two types of inferencing will be distinguished: *intrasentential* inferencing and *intersentential* inferencing. The former covers the processes that determine what inferences follow from individual sentential formulas. The latter covers processes that specify how derivations are drawn from combinations of independent sentential formulas, that is, from formulas that are connected by conjunctive links (which correspond to conjunctive connectives in FOL). Admittedly, this distinction is somewhat tenuous since, technically speaking, a series of *wfss* connected by conjunctive links may be taken to be a single, independent formula. In this sense, the database of SL statements could be considered to be a single sentential sequence if implicit conjunctive links are read into the database. The same is true of a first-order database, at least when implicit conjunctive connectives are read into it. Nonetheless, there are benefits to be realized by maintaining the distinction between intrasentential and intersentential inferencing. By distinguishing the rules for each type of inferencing, it becomes easier to describe the overall scheme. For the most part, the inferencing described in this chapter is intrasentential inferencing because it deals with individual formulas. The subject of intersentential inferencing will be taken up later in section 11.4.

An understanding of the derivation process in SMS requires that one be acquainted with the types of inference that the system generates. Two basic types of inference are recognized in the system: *direct* inferences and *penumbral* inferences. Direct inferences correspond to deductive inferences. Penumbral inferences correspond to what is known in AI circles as 'plausible inferences', yet there are differences between the two (see section 4.2.2 for an explanation of these differences). The following subsections will define and distinguish these types, but first, the theoretical basis of the derivability relation will be specified.

Section 3.3 mentions that an original SMS database can be inflated and converted into a partial valuation on SL, which, in turn, can be used to make a total valuation on SL. In the partial valuation, each original statement would be assigned the value 'IPR' since each statement would have full presence in the database. The following example, taken schematically, shows how one might go about making a total valuation on SL from a perspective that differs slightly from that described in section 1.3. Starting with an originally entered database (DB) containing $\Phi_1$ and $\Phi_2$ (where $\Phi$ ranges over sentence-sequences), a partial valuation can be made on SL by assigning the value IPR to each of these statements to produce the following:

$$<< \Phi_1 \;\; IPR >$$

$$< \Phi_2 \;\; IPR >>.$$

This database can be inflated by employing a syntactic operation $\Omega$ that would generate a penumbra for each statement using axiomatic formalisms (see section 11.3) and would then inflate the resulting database by adding statements using the basic inference mechanisms of the system (see section 11.4). The presence of the components in each statement added by $\Omega$ would be maximized to full presence, but the statement would be assigned a degree of presence that would reflect the degree of presence of the original components (see description of the function $v$ in section 1.3). It is being assumed here that the recursive application of $\Omega$ could be made to yield, eventually, a fixed point (FP). In other words, the following would hold:

$$FP = \Omega( \ldots \Omega (\Omega(DB)))$$

such that $\Omega(FP) = FP$. For the fixed point to be reached, $\Omega$ and the database would have to be restricted appropriately. For example, the operation of the rule of addition (i.e. p *therefore* <p or q>) would have to be ignored by $\Omega$ to avoid infinite recursion, and the database could not be allowed to contain functions that would not terminate automatically. The resulting database might take the form:

$< < \Phi_1 \;\; IPR >$

$< \Phi_{1\text{-}1} \; Vi >$

$\ldots$

$< \Phi_{1\text{-}a} \; Vj >$

$< \Phi_2 \;\; IPR >$

$< \Phi_{2\text{-}1} \; Vk >$

$\ldots$

$< \Phi_{2\text{-}b} \; Vl >$

$< \Phi_x \;\; IPR >$

$< \Phi_{x\text{-}1} \; Vm >$

$\ldots$

$< \Phi_{x\text{-}c} \; Vn > >$

Here concatenations to the numbers flag penumbral inferences (e.g. $\Phi_{1\text{-}1} \ldots \Phi_{1\text{-}a}$ represent the penumbral inferences of $\Phi_1$), and $\Phi_x$ represents a statement produced from $\Phi_1$ and $\Phi_2$ by the inference rules of SMS. V ranges over a set of multiple values that indicate varying degrees of presence, a, b and c $\geq 1$, and x $\geq 2$. It should be noted that this inflated database would not yet constitute a total valuation. The total valuation would be produced by first adding statements to the database that are *inconsistent* with the statements already present. Methods by which that could be done are described in section 11.7. Each statement so added would be assigned the value 'NPR-IC'. After that, all statements not already present in some way would be added and would be assigned the value 'NPR'. Thus, one can envision the employment of an n-valued (n > 2) syntactic projection system that would produce a total valuation from an initial partial valuation. One can conceive of the total valuation being converted into a totally inflated database of signed statements by simply prefixing assigned values to statements. As is explained in section 3.3, the *untainted* derivability of a signed statement of the form $V_i\Phi_j$ (where $V_i$ is the value and $\Phi_j$ is the SL statement) from the database of signed statements can be understood theoretically to depend on whether the signed statement can be made to match a signed statement in that database.

Chapter 11 describes some inferencing and proof methods that implement the alternative version of this theory that was described in section 1.3. The alternative version of the theory is specified with reference to a database that has been inflated as described above, but only to the extent that would result from the application of the inference rules of the system. In other words, inconsistent statements and statements not otherwise present in the database would not constitute part of the inflated database under this alternative version of the theory. The relation of entailment, represented by the symbol $\models$, can be defined with reference to such an inflated database. To say that $\Gamma_i \models V_i\Phi_i$, where $\Gamma_i$ represents one or more signed objects of SL, is to say that if $\Gamma_i$ constitutes an SMS database, the inflation of $\Gamma_i$, includes $V_i\Phi_i$. Such an inflated database consists of what is *entailed* in $\Gamma_i$. SMS theory is thus specified with reference to a database of signed statements, each of which, as a signed statement, is understood to have the maximum degree of presence in the database. A signed statement that is not derivable from one or more other signed statements serves as an axiom in that database. Taking $\Gamma_i$ as a set of one or more premises, a *derivation* in SMS can understood to be a sequence of signed statements $V_i\Phi_i$, ..., $V_k\Phi_k$ such that each member of the sequence is a member of $\Gamma_i$, an axiom, or a result of the application of an inference rule to one or more of the previous elements in the sequence. The symbol $\vdash$ will be used to represent the derivability relation so that to say that '$\Gamma_i \vdash V_i\Phi_i$' is to say that $V_i\Phi_i$ is derivable from $\Gamma_i$.

As will be explained in section 4.6, any atom, phrase or sentential object can be assigned a degree of presence, and it will be legitimate to speak of a relation of the form '$V_i\Phi_i \vdash V_j\Phi_j$' even if $\Phi$ is allowed to range over atoms and phrases. As will be discussed in sections 11.3 and 11.4, the SMS environment can be taken to consist of a multitude of inference patterns, there being one such pattern for each sentential formalism or expression from which inferences can be drawn. Thus, under this conception, to prove $V_i\Phi_i \vdash V_j\Phi_j$, where $\Phi$ ranges over atoms, at least one of those inference patterns would have to be invoked. An alternative conception is possible in terms of the 'if ... then ....' operator, which is treated as a special construction in SL. A sentence of the form <if $V_i\Phi_i$ then $V_j\Phi_j$> means that if $V_i\Phi_i$ is present, then $V_j\Phi_j$ is also present. The sequence does not assert the presence of $V_i\Phi_i$ or $V_j\Phi_j$. Using this conception, the SMS environment can be taken to consist of a set of axioms written in 'if ... then ....' form, and instead of having a separate inference rule for each expression as described under the previous conception, only one inference rule (here represented as an argument pattern) would be needed, that is:

<if $V_i\Phi_i$ then $V_j\Phi_j$>

$V_i\Phi_i$

---

$V_j\Phi_j$

This rule would be extended to cover situations in which the second premise in the argument pattern would consist of an expression that would unify with the antecedent of the first premise, thereby yielding as a conclusion the resulting substitution applied to the consequent of the first premise. Sections 11.3 and 11.4 discuss how the 'if ... then ....' construction is used in inferencing.

It was mentioned in section 3.3 that the derivability relation can be treated as a fuzzy relation that may hold in varying degrees of strength. This conception of derivability can be usefully employed in the scheme of automated reasoning so that weaknesses in the relation can be reflected in associated responses, which, in turn, can enable the system to simulate ordinary human conversation more effectively. The move from a crisp to a fuzzy conception of the derivability relation can be made quite easily, as the following schematic example illustrates. The derivability of $< \Phi_{1\text{-}1}\ Vi >$ from $< \Phi_1\ IPR >$ can be represented as follows:

$$< \Phi_1\ IPR > \vdash < \Phi_{1\text{-}1}\ Vi >$$

(where $Vi$ is a value signifying tainted presence). Under this conception, the relation is maximally strong. In other words, it holds. However, it is possible to conceive of the relation in another way that allows it to hold in varying degrees of strength. This can be accomplished simply by shifting the taintedness of the conclusion to the relation itself. Thus, in this example, the value $Vi$ would be made to qualify the relation $\vdash$ instead of the statement $\Phi_{1\text{-}1}$, so that the representation of the result would be:

$$< \Phi_1\ IPR > \vdash^{Vi} < \Phi_{1\text{-}1}\ IPR >.$$

The value IPR can be defined to be a default value so that it is not necessary to represent it explicitly in expression. The conversion of the crisp derivability relation into a more flexible relation of degree is easier to appreciate using this convention. The relation $\Phi_1 \vdash <\Phi_2\ APR>$, for example, can be expressed as $\Phi_1 \vdash^{APR} \Phi_2$. These examples are presented simply to show how easy it is to conceive of the one conception of derivability in terms of the other. In SMS, the relation is allowed to hold in varying degrees so that the system can sometimes deal with statements, say in matching processes, without having to deal with values attached to the statements. This eases computational tasks.

### 4.2.1 Direct Inferences

Direct inferences correspond to deductive inferences. A sentence-sequence $ss_i$ follows as a direct inference from another sentence-sequence $ss_j$ if:

1) $ss_i$ is equal to $ss_j$ (see section 4.3 for precise meaning of equality); or

2) $ss_i$ is explicitly entailed in $ss_j$ as a *wfss*.

3) $ss_i$ is derivable from $ss_j$ by an explicit direct inference rule of SMS.

For example, given the sentential sequence:

<john cause <mary has happiness>> (22)

the inference:

<mary has happiness>

follows as a direct inference because it is present as a well formed sentential sequence within the given sequence. On the other hand, the sequence:

<john cause happiness>

is not present in sequence (22) as a well formed sequence and thus does not follow as a direct inference. It, however, does follow as a penumbral inference, a special type of inference defined in the next subsection. The following schemata illustrate each type of direct inference:

Given: $< < \beta_1 \text{ or } \beta_2 > \upsilon_1 \; < \beta_3 \, \upsilon_2 \, \beta_4 > >$ (23)

where $\beta$ ranges over noun phrase-sequences or noun atoms and $\upsilon$ ranges over 2-place links, the following is a direct inference of type 1) above:

$< < \beta_2 \text{ or } \beta_1 > \upsilon_1 < \beta_3 \, \upsilon_2 \, \beta_4 > >$

This is a direct inference because it is equal to sequence (23). The following is a direct inference of type 2):

$< \beta_3 \, \upsilon_2 \, \beta_4 >$

This is a direct inference because it is explicitly entailed in sequence (23). The third type of direct inference is produced through application of the inference rules of the system. The rules recognize the transitivity of certain relations. One of the rules, for example, is based on transitivity of causal relations and takes the following form:

$< < \beta_1 \text{ causes } \beta_2 > \text{ and } < \beta_2 \text{ causes } \beta_3 > > \; \vdash^{P} \; < \beta_1 <\text{causes}<\theta>> \beta_3 >$.

where $\theta$ represents a causal qualifier that slightly taints the link 'causes' (see section 11.4). Despite the presence of $\theta$, the sequence '$< \beta_1 <\text{causes}<\theta>> \beta_3 >$' is classified as a direct inference. The inference rules also provide for the generation of inferences through instantiation and generalization (see Chapter 10). Given, for example, that '<<logician <any>> loves <logic <some>>>' and that '<john isa <logician <cl*>>>', the inference '<john loves <logic<the>>>' follows as a direct inference under the rules applied by the system.

Direct inferences are used in the derivation process as one might expect. A sentential sequence that matches a direct inference present in a database is derivable from that database. It should be noted that any well formed sentence-sequence will have at least one direct inference derivable from it since an exact syntactical match can be generated for the sequence, and that generated sequence would qualify as a direct inference under the criteria given in this section.

### 4.2.2 Penumbral Inferences

To say that an inference is penumbral is to say that its validity is tainted. A simple example can illustrate the difference between a penumbral inference and a deductive inference. Given that the statement:

John saw Mary in the park

is true, the inference "John saw Mary" would follow from it as a deductive inference, whereas the inference "John was in the park" would not follow as a deductive inference because it is not necessarily true that John would have had to have been in the park to have seen Mary, at least under one plausible interpretation of the given sentence. John may have been outside the park when he saw Mary walking in the park, for example (cf. discussions of predicate modifiers in Keenan and Faltz, 1985, at pages 158-160). In AI circles, this kind of inference is often referred to as a 'plausible' inference. In SMS the inference would be classified as a penumbral inference (see also deBessonet and Cross, 1985). As is explained below, the penumbral inference classification is broader than the the plausible inference classification, and hence the term 'penumbral' has been reserved to describe inferences of that type.

The term 'penumbral' is derived from the idea of Hart (1958) that an ordinary concept has a core of settled meaning that is surrounded by a penumbra, that is, an area of unsettled meaning. If it is not clear whether particular meaning is to be associated with a concept, the meaning is relegated to the penumbra of that concept and can be said to be associated with that concept in a penumbral way. In SMS, this scheme is extended to include inferencing, the core being taken to consist of direct inferences, and the penumbra being taken to consist of penumbral inferences. Some inferences lie closer to the core than do others based on the fact that they are related to core inferences in special ways. Figure 7 illustrates this scheme by diagramming relations between areas (CORE and PENUMBRA) and by indicating the basis (abstraction or concretion) for distinguishing penumbral regions. The areas in the penumbra are subdivided according to a ranking based on strength, the ranking being represented by the 'measures of presence' that are used to qualify responses (see section 3.3). The CORE contains direct inferences. The penumbral areas are subdivided into categories of inferences. Each category is demarcated by enclosure in the pair [ ] and is related by a bi-directional arrow to a measure of strength. Later, in section 11.2, it will be convenient to define the penumbra of a statement to include both the core inferences and the penumbral inferences, but for now the penumbra will be taken to include only those inferences that qualify as penumbral inferences under the description given in this section.

By avoiding a two-valued semantic ascent to the truth predicate, SMS is able to scale the strength of inferences without having to distinguish degrees of truth. The scaling is based on the relations between the components of the given sequence and the components of the inferences. The position of an inference in the penumbra depends on its strength. The weaker the inference, the farther its position from the core.

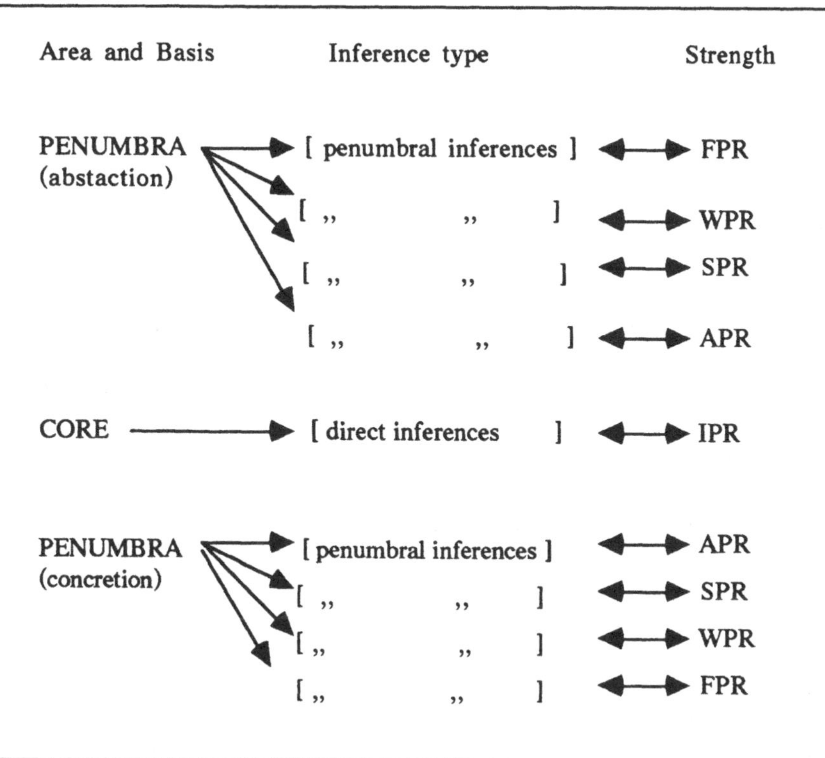


Figure 7. Diagram of Core and Penumbra

It should be noted that for the most part penumbral inferences are *defeasible* in the sense that they may be overridden by a statement that bears a stronger degree of presence. This means that the reasoning in SMS is nonmonotonic (see section 4.8.1 for an example) since the inference, as well as other inferences based on it, may be cast aside as new information is added to the database of SMS. Penumbras are postulated in advance for each sentential formalism. Semantic depth is achieved by creating a separate formalism to accommodate semantic nuances (see discussions below).

Penumbral inferences are generated based on a combination of syntactical and semantic factors, but the semantical aspects are defined wholly within the system through marker bindings and lexicographical code assignments. What this means is that penumbral inferences are constructed for a given sentential expression based on the syntactical structure of the expression and on the nature of the terms and relations it comprises. Terms that are noun forms of links, adjectives or adverbs, for example, produce different effects than do ordinary noun terms that correspond to persons and things. Type codes of terms are contained in LEX, the lexicon of SMS, and the system uses that information to build inferences. Each noun type is associated with one or more special links that are used to generate inferences when that noun type appears in a designated position within a sequence. As result, the inferences produced differ from one another, and it is in this respect that part of the inference generation process is semantically based. A simple example illustrates the point. Given the sequence '<john caused <mary has flowers>>', it does not follow from this sequence that '<john caused mary>' or that '<john caused flowers>'; however, given the sequence '<john caused <mary has happiness>', which is a sequence that bears the same structure and much of the same semantic content as the one above, it does seem to follow that '<john caused happiness>'. The difference between the results produced in these examples is rooted in the fact that 'happiness', being a noun form of a term that 'describes' an 'emotional state', is assigned a different semantical classification than the term 'flowers'. This kind of semantical difference is reflected in the inferences produced in the system.

In general, semantic nuances are handled by classifying them according to type and then creating special formalisms to deal with each type. The following examples demonstrate the need for this approach. The formalism/pattern:

<< ?A is ?B > caused < ?C is ?D >>

might be instantiated to produce the sentential sequence:

<<picture is created> caused <fred is pleased>>

which corresponds to the idea that the creation of a picture pleased someone named Fred. In such a case, the inferences (penumbra) specified for the formalism/pattern could be instantiated by the appropriate components of the sentential sequence, and the resulting instantiations would constitute the penumbral inferences of that sequence. It might be specified, for example, that '< ?A caused < ?C is ?D>>' follows as a penumbral inference, say of strength 'APR' (see section 3.3), from the formalism/pattern. In this example, the proper instantiation of this penumbral inference would be '<picture caused <fred is pleased>>', which, in turn, would follow as a penumbral inference from the sentence-sequence. The reader should note, however, that the same formalism/pattern should not be used to represent the idea that the improvement of a picture pleased Fred, as in:

<<picture is improved> caused <fred is pleased>>

nor should the same pattern be used to represent the idea that the destruction of a picture pleased Fred, as in:

<<picture is destroyed> caused <fred is pleased>>.

The ideas represented above share some of the same 'semantic' information, yet each idea has its own individuating semantic features. The idea of a person being pleased by the improvement of a picture presents a number of possibilities. In the first place the idea, as expressed, is imprecise in that it is not clear whether the process of improvement had been completed or was in progress when Fred was pleased. Even if it were given that the process had been completed, it is still not clear whether it was the process of improvement or the end product, or both, that pleased Fred. Each of these ideas carries its own imprecision. It should be noted that the SL representations given above do not remove those imprecisions and themselves carry imprecision of the same sort. SMS generates penumbral inferences in an attempt to deal with imprecision of this kind. The point to be stressed here is that the semantic differences that distinguish one idea from another can be reflected in the SL representations of those ideas.

In the examples discussed above, differences in the concepts of creation, improvement and destruction of an object provide semantic bases for distinguishing the ideas expressed. Corresponding semantical differences can be appreciated in the SL representations, and separate formalism/patterns can be created to accommodate each type of semantic difference. Thus, semantic depth can be achieved by tailoring the penumbra of each formalism/pattern to fit particular semantic situations, which consist of the constraints and requirements dictated by the nature of the components and relations that may be used to instantiate the formalism/pattern. To a significant extent, these constraints and requirements can be recognized in advance, and the appropriate penumbra can be postulated. One might, for instance, include the inference that the 'picture' pleased 'fred' in the penumbra of the example involving the creation of the picture. This inference would be assigned a particular value that is reflective of its strength. The same inference might follow from the example about the improvement of the picture, but the inference might very well be assigned a different value based on the fact that the second idea seems to imply that the picture was already in existence when the improvement began. This opens up the possibility that Fred may have been displeased by the original picture but was pleased either because it was being improved or because of the results of the improvement process. At any rate, because of these semantical differences in the ideas, the inference that the picture pleased Fred might be more plausible in the one situation than in the other. The inference is much less plausible, it appears, in the third situation since Fred was pleased by the destruction of the picture, and thus the inference would be assigned a value indicative of its implausibility.

The penumbral inferences specified for each formalism function in a default capacity. They are defeasible and are subject to being overridden by other information in the system. Semantic precision can be achieved in some instances by overriding one or more penumbral inferences. The two primary ways to override a penumbral inference are:

1) to introduce a 'fact' into the database that is inconsistent with the inference; and

2) to introduce a rule or general statement that is incompatible with the inference.

If, for example, a general statement to the effect that no picture pleases Fred were to be introduced into the system, the inferences described earlier that imply the contrary would be overridden. On the other hand, if the system were to be told that Fred for some reason is always pleased when something he likes is destroyed, the inference that the picture pleased Fred might be upgraded in strength in the example involving the destruction of the picture. Whether or not the adjustment would be made in this last instance would depend on whether the system had a 'semantic rule' to the effect that if it is given that someone is pleased by the destruction of what they like, specified adjustments in penumbras are to be made.

Although discussions about the foregoing examples focus on plausible inferences, it should be pointed out that not all penumbral inferences are 'plausible' in the ordinary sense of that term. One might wonder why the system would be made to generate 'implausible' inferences. The answer to this lies in the fact that the inferences are generated for multiple and independent purposes. One purpose is to distinguish normal forms from one another. The normal form of a given sentential expression consists of a minimal set of sententially expressed binary relations that are necessary and sufficient to capture the essence of the given expression (see section 4.4). An expression that has penumbral inferences will have some of those inferences expressed in this way, that is, as sentential binary relations, and those inferences plus the direct inferences expressed in like fashion constitute the normal form of that expression. The syntactical features of these relations help distinguish one normal form from another, and to this extent the inferences function in a syntactic mode. They also have semantic roles. In the querying process, it is sometimes convenient to reduce a query to its normal form and then attempt to satisfy the normal form rather than the original query. This process is sometimes employed when the query is a *conjunctive* sequence (i.e. one that contains the term 'and'), an *alternative* or *disjunctive* sequence (i.e. one that contains the term 'or') or a *combinative* sequence (i.e. one that contains both 'and' and 'or'). When this occurs, the penumbral inferences comprised by the normal form are considered to be part of the meaning of the original sequence. Penumbral inferences also stand in their own right and may be matched as part of the qualified response process. This point can be illustrated by example. If one is given the English sentence:

John gave Mary some flowers, which pleased her (24)

it should be noted that it is not entirely clear from a reading of this sentence how one should answer the following questions:

Did John please Mary? (25)

Did the flowers please Mary? (26)

It is possible that Mary was most pleased by the fact that it was John who gave her something, the primary pleasing factor being John. On the other hand, it may have been the flowers alone that pleased her, or perhaps it was a combination of these factors. Ordinary discourse quite often does not precisely reflect intended meaning. SMS is being designed to handle some of the imprecision that is built into this kind of English sentence, and penumbral inferences play a crucial role in the processes that attempt to deal with the problems involved. The basic approach employed is to segment representations into levels by transforming the representations of higher levels into sets of more primitive representations called expansions. The expansions are equivalent to the higher level representations, the whole scheme amounting to an abstraction/expansion hierarchy (see section 4.9 for an example). Intermediate representations are chosen as targets for mappings from both higher and lower level representations, and penumbral inferences can be generated from them. The following sentential sequence is an example of a sequence that might be used at an intermediate level to represent English sentence (24):

<<john <cause <bmo give>> <mary <has <at t-1>> flowers>> (27)

caused

<mary <is <at t-2>> pleased>>

where the term 'bmo' acts as a pointer to the term that describes the type of act at the root of the causal relation (in this case an act of giving), and the terms 't-1' and 't-2' are sequentially related temporal descriptors. Basically, this sequence indicates that 'john' caused (by means of an act of giving) 'mary' to have some 'flowers', and this pleased her. It is this kind of sentential sequence that is used to generate penumbral inferences that could be used to respond to questions (25) and (26). It should be noted that sequence (27) does little in and of itself to resolve the question whether it was John, the flowers, the act of giving, or a combination of these factors that pleased Mary. The representation seems to accurately trace English description (24) in that the entire description of the act of giving the flowers is placed in a causal position in relation to the description of Mary's state of being pleased. This interpretation seems to conform to the use of the word 'which' in sentence (24). There the word is used somewhat loosely to refer to the whole act of giving. The system would construct penumbral inferences for this sequence by using special links that correspond to links in the given sequence. The special links are weaker than the links to which they correspond. The expression:

<flowers mcaused <mary <is <at t-2>> pleased>> (28)

is such an inference. The 'mcaused' link used in this inference is a penumbral link that, by postulation, is taken to be a weaker link that its corresponding link (i.e. 'caused') in the sequence from which it is derived. This correspondence is based on the structural position of the components that are to be related in the sequence and on a designation of which link in the given sequence is to serve as the source link from which to derive the penumbral link, which in turn, is to be used to relate those components. Although weaker than the source link 'caused', the link 'mcaused' used in inference (28) indicates that the system recognizes some type of causal connection between the 'flowers' and the state of 'mary' being 'pleased'. The inference could be used as a basis for responding to question (26) above. Although a definitive response perhaps would not be appropriate in this case, the system would be in a position to inform the user that there is some sort of causal connection between the 'flowers' and the state of 'mary' being pleased at 't-2'. The connection is of course the penumbral one represented in this penumbral inference.

It should be noted that the temporal indicators given in the example (27) above would have to be related properly to capture the meaning of the surface level expression. Lower level expressions such as (27) above can be generalized to serve as formalisms for representing surface level expressions. Combinations of these formalisms can be used to represent what corresponds to descriptions of ordinary world phenomena.

The inferencing processes used in SMS depend on abilities to recognize identical expressions and to handle partial matches. The notion of identity is thus very important for the inferencing process. Section 4.3 defines this notion for SMS, and section 4.4 describes how normal forms are being employed in an attempt to enable the system to determine when two expressions are identical.

### 4.3 The Relation of Identity

In SMS, identity is treated as a binary relation that has the same meaning as equality. The terms 'identity' and 'equality' are thus used synonymously in this book. The system recognizes two types of identity:

1) syntactic identity; and

2) semantic identity.

Syntactic identity between linguistic objects exists when the objects match one another geometrically. The symbol 'is≡' will be used to represent syntactic identity. Two expressions are semantically identical if they are bound to markers that are syntactically identical. The strongest relation of identity known to the system is one between objects that are both syntactically and semantically identical. This relation can exist only between two syntactically identical markers. A weaker form of semantic identity, referred to herein as *derived* identity, is also recognized by the system. The symbol 'is=' will be used to represent derived identity. Expressions are identical in the derived sense if they are not syntactically identical but can be made so by a process of transformation. The process is governed by a set of rules that allows expressions to be changed into new expressions that are equal to the original expression. These rules correspond to the definitional substitution rules of FOL. The following are examples of the relation of syntactic identity:

a) <a and b> is≡ <a and b>; and

b) person is≡ person.

whereas the following are examples of semantic identity:

c) john is= johnny;

d) john is= <brother <of james>>

where 'john', 'johnny' and the expression '<brother <of james>>' are bound to the same marker. If two markers are cast into the relation of semantic identity, as in '<ue-1 is= ue-2>', one of the markers may be dropped and replaced by the other marker. This, of course, should be done uniformly throughout the system.

It should be noted that SMS allows sentence-sequences to be individuated, that is, assigned markers (see section 10.5 on event individuation). It follows that both types of identity exist among the sentences-sequences of SL. Syntactic identity exists between sentence-sequences when they match one another geometrically, whereas semantic identity exists between them when they are bound to the same sentential marker. The sequences:

<<john and mary> are happy>

<<john and mary> are happy>

are identical in the syntactical sense, whereas:

<<john and mary> are happy>

<<mary and john> are happy>

are identical only in the derived sense (assuming they are bound to the same sentential marker) because the positions of 'john' and 'mary' are reversed in them, and hence the two do not match one another geometrically. Given that a particular sentence-sequence is present in the DB and that it is bound to a sentential marker, one might wonder how the system would go about determining whether another sentence-sequence bears the identity relation to that sequence? The question is easily answered if syntactical identity is at issue. The system simply employs its geometric matching capabilities to determine whether an exact match exists. Given that the sequences are not syntactically identical, the question of semantic identity arises. This question is again easily answered if the second sequence is bound to a sentential marker since the markers of the two sequences can be compared. The case in which the second sequence is not bound to a marker raises more difficult problems. This situation frequently arises as sentence-sequences are added to the DB . The system operates by first attempting to assign a marker to the entering sequence. As part of this process it must determine whether the sequence should receive a marker that has already been assigned to another sequence. Two sequences receive the same sentential marker when the two can be made syntactically identical by individuating the noun and link labels and by manipulating the resulting denotata by application of special transformation rules of the system (see section 10.5 on event individuation). Alternatively, each sequence may be reduced to its normal form, and the resulting normal forms may be compared to determine whether the sequences should be assigned the same marker (see section 4.4 for a description and explanation of this process), but as is the case for the previous alternative, all components must be individuated to make the proper comparison.

### 4.4 Normal Forms

This section describes the normalization process used in SMS. Each sentential expression, whether sentence or formalism, has a *normal form.* The correspondence between sentential expressions and their corresponding normal forms is important for a number of reasons. As stated previously, the relation of semantic identity (see section 4.3) between two sentential expressions can be determined in some cases by comparing the normal forms of the expressions. Through a normalization process, each sentential expression is transformed into a set of more basic expressions. The process corresponds to the process by which Boolean normal forms are produced in logic. Two ordinary sentential expressions are semantically identical if a one-one and onto mapping exists between the components of their normal forms. The way in which normal forms can be used to determine semantic identity between sentential expressions can be described schematically by example. Given that $f$ is a function that assigns a sentential formalism its normal form, consisting of a set of formalisms that meet specified constraints, and that $g$ is a function of two arguments (normal forms) that maps its first argument into its second argument, returning 1 if the mapping is one-one and onto and 0 if not, the following holds:

$$\forall(x,y)\ [\ g\ (f(x), f(y)\ ) = 1 \rightarrow x \text{ is= } y\ ]$$

where 'x' and 'y' range over *wfsfs*. Each sentential component of a normal form must meet the following specifications:

1) the sentential component must be a simple sentential sequence, that is, one that contains only atoms as elements; and

2) the component may contain no more than three elements.

Since the second position in a sentential sequence is the link position, it can be seen that each sentential component consists of a 'subject' followed by a link followed by an 'object'. Thus, the normal form can be understood to be a set of binary relations, expressed sententially, that are derivable from a given sentential expression. The following example is illustrative of these principles. An expression of the form:

$$< \alpha_1 \ \upsilon_1 < \alpha_2 \ \upsilon_2 \ \alpha_3 >>$$

(where $\alpha$, here taken to be a typed variable, ranges over noun atoms classified as persons or things and where $\upsilon$ ranges over 2-place links) might have the following normal form:

$$< < \alpha_1 \ \ \tau_1\upsilon_2 \ \ \alpha_2 >$$

$$< \alpha_1 \ \ \tau_2\upsilon_2 \ \ \alpha_3 >$$

$$< \alpha_2 \ \ \upsilon_2 \ \ \alpha_3 > >$$

where the $\tau$ attached to the links ranges over qualifiers, in this case penumbral qualifiers that produce penumbral links. The normal form of a given sequence is a subset of the union of the direct inferences and the penumbra of that sequence. Only those sequences that meet the specifications mentioned previously (i.e. that they be simple and binary) are included in the subset.

Normal forms can be effectively employed in the querying process. Whenever a query is conjunctive, alternative, or combinative, it can be transformed into its normal form, and an attempt can be made to satisfy the normal form instead of the original query. This enables the system to avoid some troublesome problems that might otherwise result from attempting to satisfy a query that has, say, multiple conjuncts and disjuncts. This situation presents well known combinatorial problems since the query can be expressed in a multiplicity of forms by simply manipulating the positions of the various conjuncts and disjuncts. Section 4.6 describes an alternative method by which to address this problem.

### 4.5 Ontological Distinctions

In SMS, objects are bound to particular realms. This affects the derivation process since if one wishes to derive an untainted conclusion about a particular realm, the linguistic objects comprised by the conclusion, itself a linguistic object, must be consistent with that realm. If they are not consistent, the derivability relation is tainted and the response to be given by the system must be qualified appropriately, that is, assigned a value indicative of the tainted derivability. On this count, the system bears strong resemblance to a many-valued logic system. These topics will be discussed in more detail in later sections. Figure 8 diagrams the scheme in which objects are bound to realms. Each column in Figure 8 represents a realm and indicates that the realms are reserved for special kinds of objects, which are represented in the figure by the object-type symbols. An English description is given of the kinds of objects that correspond to the object-types. Chapter 5 discusses the scheme in more detail.

| Realm-1 .... | Realm-2 .... | Realm-3 |
|---|---|---|
| Object-type-1 | Object-type-2 | Object-type-n |
| World objects | Fictional objects | Relations |

Figure 8. Use of Realms in SMS

In SMS, linguistic objects that correspond to nouns of ordinary English are classified ontologically. The ontological classification of a *wfss* is defined with reference to the ontological classifications of its noun components. The derivation process is defined to take into account the ontological status of any object, sentential or nonsentential, with which it deals, and derivability can be affected in a number of ways by the ontological classifications of the objects involved. The process is somewhat complex and is best described metalinguistically in terms of realms of objects. Because of the importance of ontological classification in SMS, a chapter in this book is devoted to that subject. Further discussion on the subject will thus be postponed until Chapter 5 entitled "Ontological Considerations."

### 4.6 Derivations

It is in the area of derivability that a major difference between SMS and FOL is appreciable. In FOL, derivability is defined over sentences, not individual terms like constants. In SMS the derivability relation is defined so that it may hold between any linguistic objects of SL, including:

a) atoms (individual terms);

b) phrase expressions (corresponding to phrases in English); and

c) sentential expressions.

Derivability at higher levels (e.g. sentential level) is defined in terms of derivability at lower levels (e.g. atomic level). At the atomic level, a defined correspondence between individual terms (atoms) can be fixed. As described in section 3.5, given any two SL terms $a_i$ and $a_j$, a set of mappings can be employed to produce a value that describes the derivability relation between $a_i$ and $a_j$. Figure 9 diagrams the scheme in abbreviated array fashion. The variables 'a1, ..., an' in the figure range over atoms of SL, and the variables 's1, ..., sn' range over phrase expressions and sentential expressions.

Derivability Values for Atoms

| | a1 | a2 | a3 | .......... | an |
|---|---|---|---|---|---|
| a1 | v1 | v2 | v3 | | |
| a2 | v4 | v1 | v5 | | |
| a3 | v6 | v7 | v1 | | |
| . | | | | | |
| . | | | | | |
| . | | | | | |
| . | | | | | |
| an | | | | | |

Derivability Values for Phrases and Sentential Expressions

| | s1 | s2 | s3 | .......... | sn |
|---|---|---|---|---|---|
| s1 | v1 | v2 | v3 | | |
| s2 | v4 | v1 | v5 | | |
| s3 | v6 | v7 | v1 | | |
| . | | | | | |
| . | | | | | |
| . | | | | | |
| . | | | | | |
| sn | | | | | |

Figure 9. Derivability Defined Using Array Structures

The scope of the derivability relation can be broadened to include any combination of atoms or phrase expressions, such as one consisting of a term and a quantifier. The derivability relation between the atom 'bird' and the phrase '<bird <any>>', for example, can be assigned a value in a way similar to that prescribed for atoms, the only difference being that the function *f* would receive ordered pairs consisting of any combination of atoms or phrases.

A phrase may consist not only of an atom and a quantifier, but also of an atom and other types of modifiers such as adjectives and prepositional phrases, as in the expression:

<bird <any><large><with feathers>>

which corresponds to the English expression 'any large bird with feathers'. The point is that defined correspondences can be set at any level of expression all the way up to the sentential level.

This scheme allows one to segment levels of response to ease communicative tasks. The derivability of a given sentential expression from a given SL database depends on whether all the components of the the expression are present in the database and, if so, on whether they bear the relations to one another that are called for by the query. An independent attempt is made to derive each component of the query, which means that an attempt is made to match each component in the database. If the match of a component is successful, an attempt is made to determine whether the matched component holds a position (relation) that directly corresponds to the position held by the query component. What this amounts to is that individual terms and their positions are brought within the scope of the inferencing scheme. This works out nicely from a syntactical perspective since position codes can be treated as modifiers and can thus be dealt with like other terms. The inference pattern:

$$\frac{\langle a_i \text{ IPR}\rangle}{\langle a_j \text{ IPR}\rangle}$$

(where $a_i$ and $a_j$ are individual terms) can be extended to include the pattern:

$$\frac{\langle\langle a_i \langle p_i\rangle\rangle \text{ IPR}\rangle}{\langle\langle a_j \langle p_j\rangle\rangle \text{ IPR}\rangle}$$

where $p_i$ and $p_j$ are position codes.

The process is not quite so simple as is being described since, as indicated in Figure 9, an atom might have a number of expressions in the database that could be 'matched' to produce a derivability value of some sort. The concept of matching is being loosely employed here to include penumbral matches, that is, matches that are not based on syntactic or semantic identity. In SMS, the term 'bird', for example, would match the term 'birds' in a penumbral way by postulation, although it hardly makes sense to say that these terms 'match' one another in the traditional sense of 'match'. The result of adopting this approach is that as attempts are made to derive a given component from a database, a branching effect occurs in the derivability quest. For example, when attempting to derive the component 'bird' from an SL database, the system not only seeks to find that term, but also related terms and expressions, such as: 'birds', '<bird <any>>', '<birds <all>>', 'animal', 'animals', '<animal <any>>', and '<animals <all>>'. The set of related terms and expressions correspond to 'term-sets' of 'linguistic variables' (in this case the sign of the token 'bird' would be taken as the linguistic variable). The scheme is diagrammed in Figure 10.

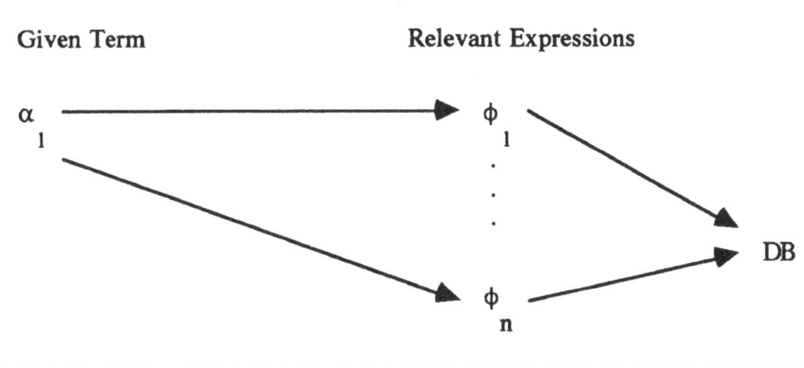


Figure 10. Derivability Scheme for Individual Component

The related expressions given here in example bear somewhat obvious relations to the given term, at least when those terms are assigned their English meanings. Other terms, such as 'tweety', '<pet <my>>', 'nest', 'egg' and 'feather' may likewise bear recognized relations to the given term and thus could be included among the relevant terms for 'bird'. What is included on the list of relevant terms is a matter of choice. As with other schemes in SMS, this feature is adjustable to suit particular needs. One might, for example, wish to include on the list not only terms such as 'beak' and 'claw', but also terms such as 'nose' and 'toe'. In fact, the list could be be made to include all SL terms and could be categorized based on shared values assigned to the derivability relation. On the other hand, the list may be kept small by selecting a compact subset of relations to define relevancy of terms. One might, for instance, restrict relations to subtype/supertype, part/whole, and singular/plural relations. The selection of the subtype/supertype relation would of course produce hierarchical branching, which would mean that if each term or expression is taken as a node, multiple branching is likely to occur at the nodes. Obviously, in a serial implementation, the list of relevant terms should be kept small enough to meet requirements of speed and efficiency .

The use of a many-valued approach is one way to address the age old problem of connectivity between objects, all objects being connected or related to one another in one or more ways. The problem is that unless one has some way of ruling out certain relations, all objects are relevant for a given object. Human beings are aware of many of the connections between objects in the world and employ knowledge of an amazing number of those connections in ordinary reasoning. For those who might have wondered why a term like 'nose' might appear on the list of relevant terms for 'bird', the following example is offered to illustrate the ability of human beings to employ knowledge of connections between objects. If a person has a bird named 'tweety' as a pet, and the bird on one or more occasions has perched on the person's shoulder and nibbled at the person's ear, how might that person respond to the question:

"Have you ever felt a cold nose in your ear?"

Assuming that to the person's recollection, no nose-like object other than tweety's beak has ever touched the person's ear, the response might very well be something like:

"My bird's beak has felt very cold to my ear on occasion."

It seems that part of the processes by which human beings make whatever sense they do out of this kind of dialogue bears important correspondence to the many-valued derivation process being described in this book.

As the scheme has been described thus far, the derivation process entails straightforward searches at the atomic level. By extending the derivability relation to hold between atoms (individual terms), phrases, sentential expressions, or combinations of these objects, it becomes permissible to speak of lines of reasoning defined over individual terms or phrases in addition to lines of reasoning defined over sentential expressions. In a search that proceeds from atom to atom, for example, multiple paths might be encountered at some of the nodes (atoms), and each path can be taken to represent a separate line of reasoning. Since each line of reasoning bears its own measure of strength, separate streams of reasoning become appreciable based on shared measures of strength. As the process proceeds, three possibilities exist for each line of reasoning:

1) it will retain its strength throughout the process;

2) it will become weaker; or

3) it will terminate prematurely.

A line of reasoning cannot become stronger under this scheme, and any penumbral match taints the line of reasoning. Once tainted in any way, it continues to be tainted throughout the process.

The segmented reasoning scheme of SMS can be explained by example. Given a sentential expression of the form:

$$< <<\beta_1 \text{ or } \beta_2> \text{ and } <\beta_3 \text{ or } \beta_4>> \upsilon_1\ \beta_5 >$$

(where $\beta$ ranges over noun atoms, and $\upsilon$ ranges over links other than conjunctive and alternative links), a grouping technique can be used to handle the boolean combinatorial problems presented by the presence of the special links 'and' and 'or'. A marker can be assigned to each conjunct or alternative, and the marker can be taken to designate a set consisting of the conjuncts or alternatives. Each set can be qualified by an appropriate modal qualifier to restrict the use of the set in reasoning operations. In this example, the following marker assignments could be made for the conjunctive and alternative sequences involved:

$$<\beta_1 \text{ or } \beta_2> \rightarrow \quad \text{AS-1}$$

$$<\beta_3 \text{ or } \beta_4> \rightarrow \quad \text{AS-2}$$

$$<<\beta_1 \text{ or } \beta_2> \text{ and } <\beta_3 \text{ or } \beta_4>> \rightarrow \quad \text{CS-3}$$

Markers 'AS-1' and 'AS-2', being bound to alternative sequences, could be bound to modal qualifiers indicative of their alternative nature. 'AS-1', for example, could be bound to the data-set $\{\beta_1, \beta_2\}$, which are the members of the corresponding alternative sequence, and the use of that set in reasoning could be restricted by the modal qualifiers assigned to 'AS-1'. Under this scheme the following sequences would be identical in the derived sense of identity described in section 4.3:

$$<<<\beta_1 \text{ or } \beta_2> \text{ and } <\beta_3 \text{ or } \beta_4>> \upsilon_1\ \beta_5 > \qquad (29)$$

$$< <\text{AS-1 and AS-2}> \upsilon_1\ \beta_5 > \qquad (30)$$

$$< \text{CS-3}\ \upsilon_1\ \beta_5 >. \qquad (31)$$

The reasoning process may be illustrated by a description of some of the key aspects of the processes that SMS would employ in attempting to derive the sequence:

$$< \beta_1\ \upsilon_1\ \beta_5 >$$

from the sequences given above. This sequence would not follow under ordinary reasoning since it is clear that what would be true of '$<<\beta_1 \text{ or } \beta_2> \text{ and } <\beta_3 \text{ or } \beta_4>>$' would not necessarily be true of one of its components such as $\beta_1$. The approach used in SMS attempts to satisfy the sequence by finding it present in the database either at the top or penumbral level (see section 11.3) or by deducing it as an intersentential inference (see section 11.4). The process proceeds by attempting to satisfy each component of the query. Thus, it would seek to satisfy '$\beta_1$', '$\upsilon_1$', and '$\beta_5$' independently of one another. Taking sequences (29), (30) and (31) above as the database, one can see that components '$\upsilon_1$' and '$\beta_5$' map nicely into sequence (31) and hence could be satisfied without difficulty. However, '$\beta_1$'

could not be satisfied directly in this way. The relation between $\beta_1$ and CE-3 is such that a tainted satisfaction of $\beta_1$ could be accomplished using the information given in Figure 11.

| Component | Property | Value |
|---|---|---|
| $\beta_1$ | $\varepsilon$ | AS-1 |
| $\beta_2$ | $\varepsilon$ | AS-1 |
| $\beta_3$ | $\varepsilon$ | AS-2 |
| $\beta_4$ | $\varepsilon$ | AS-2 |
| AS-1 | $\varepsilon$<br>type members | CS-3 alternative<br>$\{\beta_1, \beta_2\}$ |
| AS-1 | $\varepsilon$<br>type members | CS-3 alternative<br>$\{\beta_3, \beta_4\}$ |
| AS-1 | $\varepsilon$<br>type members | conjunctive<br>(AS-1, AS-2) |

Figure 11. Membership and Type Properties of Components

The information given in this figure indicates that $\beta_1$ is a member of AS-1 and that AS-1 is a member of CE-1. Under normal set-theoretic principles one could conclude that $\beta_1$ is a member of CE-3, and thus it might be tempting to entertain the possibility that what is asserted about CE-3 could also be asserted about its member $\beta_1$. Unfortunately, this cannot be allowed because of the modal qualifiers that are associated with the sets. SMS would trace $\beta_1$ into AS-1 using the membership path given in Figure 11 but would encounter the 'alternative' modal qualifier in the process. This encounter would be interpreted as a qualification on derivability. The process is designed so that as paths are traversed, a description is constructed that reflects what weakening effects, if any, have been occurred along the path. In the example given, the first weakening effect would occur when membership in an alternative set is recognized. An additional weakening effect would be produced when membership in the conjunctive set CE-3 is recognized. Anything less than an exact match produces some kind of weakening effect on the strength of the derivability relation. Predesignated type codes for these effects are added to the description as the process continues. Thus, there are two types of description available at any point in the process:

1) the strength value of the line of reasoning at that point; and

2) the detailed description of what weakening effects have been encountered.

The strength value gives a general description of the derivability relation. The detailed description enables the system to engage in a fine point discussion about the derivability relation.

As mentioned previously, defined correspondences can be set at any one or more levels in the abstraction/expansion hierarchy. The multiquerying process described earlier in section 3.4 can be extended to include multilevel querying so that multiquerying can occur at multiple levels. An implementation of this scheme seemingly would greatly benefit from having concurrent processing techniques available. Consequently, SMS is being developed with parallel processing in mind (cf. Fahlman, 1979).

Thus far, discussions have focused upon derivability at the atomic level. Derivability at the sentential level has been said to be grounded, at least in part, on derivability at the atomic level. Unfortunately, discussions about sentential derivability will have to be postponed until some additional concepts have been defined and the ontological scheme of SMS has been introduced. Sections 11.3 and 11.4 will describe sentential derivability, and section 11.5 on querying and the proof process will describe how derivability at the atomic level grounds derivability at the sentential level. Chapter 5 will describe the ontological structure of the SMS universe and will cover some aspects of modal and nonmonotonic inferencing. Before presenting those discussions, some comments about modal inferencing and default reasoning will be made to introduce the reader to the general approach used in SMS in these areas.

## 4.7 Modal and Epistemic Inferencing

In SMS, modal inferencing is defined to include epistemic inferencing (i. e. reasoning about knowledge and belief) because for the most part the same methods are used to handle each type. Unless otherwise specified, what is said to be true of modal inferencing in this book is to be taken to be true of epistemic inferencing. This is not to say that epistemic reasoning lacks features that can be used to distinguish it from other forms of modal reasoning (e. g. reasoning about possibility and necessity). Indeed, epistemic reasoning has unique features (see discussions on *belief* below), but much of the discussion that follows does not require that a distinction be drawn between the two. Reference will be made to modal inferencing only unless there is need for distinction.

Techniques by which to handle modal inferencing problems in SMS are still under development; however, the general methodology has been specified in a few areas in sufficient detail to warrant description. The basic approach is to recognize qualifications on objects that are within the scope of whatever modal term happens to be at hand. The link 'believe' (or any derivative thereof), for example, has a specified modal scope when it is used in an SL statement. The scope is taken to be the *belief*, that is, the sentential expression that appears in the statement as the object of the link. Every linguistic object within that expression (belief) is tainted by a modal qualifier, the purpose of which is to represent the difference between fact and belief. Once a modal qualifier is assigned to an object, it continues to taint the presence of that object until the qualifier is removed. Any attempt to derive an unqualified object from a qualified one taints the derivability relation. The hope is that this approach and the many-valued scheme described in Chapter 3 can be combined to solve some of the problems associated with inferencing over modal concepts. Section 4.8.1 on nonmonotonic reasoning discusses how this combination of approaches can be used to treat the concept of typicality.

The general approach used in modal inferencing in SMS is to treat modal terms as qualifiers that either detract or add emphasis to the assertions of which they are a part. SMS recognizes three types of modal objects:

1) atomic modal qualifiers;

2) sentential modal qualifiers; and

3) modal links.

Because SMS allows events to be individuated (see section 10.5), the the techniques for handling items 1) and 2) above can be described together since sentential markers assigned to events can be treated as atoms. Modal qualifiers are divided into:

1) those that do not detract form the 'presence' of the atom; and

2) those that detract from the 'presence' of the atom.

An example of a use of a nondetracting modal qualifier is contained in the following sequence:

<john <loves <unquestionably>> mary>.

Here the modal qualifier 'unquestionably' does not detract from the presence of 'loves', the term modified by the expression '<unquestionably>'. This being so, it does not detract form the presence of the embedded sequence '<john loves mary>' since for a modifier to affect the status of a sequence in SMS, it must first affect the atom to which it is attached. In contrast, a modal qualifier like 'perhaps' has a detracting effect on the presence of the term it modifies and, consequently, detracts from the presence of the sequence of which it is a part, as in:

<john <loves <perhaps>> mary> (32)

Here the qualifier has a detracting effect on the presence of the embedded sequence:

<john loves mary> (33)

and hence sequence (33) does not follow as an untainted derivation from sequence (32).

The basic scheme for handling modal qualifiers is to process and individuate the root atoms in sequences as usual and then place modal qualifications on the results. This process is used in conjunction with the querying process that operates at the atomic level as described in section 11.5. Whenever two atoms or sentential sequences are identical, the association of a modal qualifier with one of them can taint the derivability relation. In other words, the following holds:

$$\Phi_1 \vdash^{IPR} \Phi_1$$

but when a detracting modal qualifier is added, as in:

$$< \Phi_1 <\sigma_1>>$$

(where $\sigma_1$ represents a detracting modal qualifier), the same result does not obtain. Instead, the following holds:

$$< \Phi_1 <\sigma_1>> \vdash^{IPR} <\Phi_1 \; V_{tainted}>$$

(where $V_{tainted}$ indicates that the presence of $\Phi_1$ is tainted by the presence of the modal qualifier). In other words, although the derivability relation does not hold in the strong sense, the many-valued approach recognizes a tainted or penumbral relation of derivability. This aspect of the approach is described in more detail below as part of the discussions on inferencing over modal links.

As indicated in the foregoing discussions, the handling of modalities of atoms is a somewhat straightforward process in which detracting modal qualifiers are allowed to taint the derivability relation. Modal links are more difficult to handle as can be gleaned from the following schematic examples. The belief link, being one of the most difficult links to handle, has been chosen to illustrate the scheme. Given a belief-sequence, the basic technique consists of tainting both the belief and the components of the belief with detracting modal qualifiers to indicate mere belief status. The effect is to qualify inferencing in determinate ways. Responses generated during the inferencing process are qualified as indicated above because of the presence of detracting modal qualifiers. In addition, the process for generating derivative beliefs from the original belief is qualified as described below.

Given that $\Phi$ ranges over sentential sequences, and given a sentential sequence of the form:

$<\alpha \text{ believes } \Phi_1>$ (34)

where $\alpha$ ranges over atoms that may qualify as believers and $\Phi_1$ is a belief expressed as a sentence-sequence, the following sets can be specified for $\Phi_1$:

1) $I_{DI\Phi_1}$ (consisting of the direct inferences of $\Phi_1$, excepting those based on transitivity or substitution);

2) $I_{PI\Phi_1}$ (consisting of the penumbral inferences of $\Phi_1$, including those based on relations with objects other than those within $\Phi_1$); and

3) $I_{TI\Phi_1}$ (consisting of inferences based on transitivity of relations or on substitution principles).

Given these specifications, the following holds for any $\Phi_i$:

a) If $\Phi_i \in I_{DI\Phi_1}$ (35)

then $<\alpha \text{ believes } \Phi_i>$

b) If $\Phi_i \in (I_{PI\Phi_1} \cup I_{TI\Phi_1})$ (36)

then $<\alpha <\text{believes } <\phi_i>> \Phi_i>$

(where $\cup$ represents union, and $\phi_i$ is an appropriate detracting modifier that acts as a penumbral qualifier on the link believes).

Thus if $\Phi_i$ is not a member of $I_{DI\Phi_1}$ of $\Phi_1$, the derived belief '$<\alpha \text{ believes } \Phi_i>$' would be mapped into V, where V is a set of qualified response values used to described tainted derivability.

These principles operate as constraints on the inference generation process as it pertains to belief. Given, for example,

$<\text{john believes } <<p \supset q> \text{ and } <q \supset r>>>$

(where 'p', 'q' and 'r' are FOL variables, here assumed to be recognizable within SMS, and '$\supset$' represents material implication, also assumed to be recognizable within SMS) and given that the belief part of this sequence (i.e. '$<<p \supset q> \text{ and } <q \supset r>>$') is $\Phi_1$ of sequence (34), it should be noted that the derived belief:

$<\text{john believes } <p \supset r>>$

would not follow as an untainted inference from the original sequence because under principle (36) above, '$<p \supset r>$' would be a member of $I_{TI\Phi_1}$ and hence would be mapped into V for that reason. The same set of principles, however, would allow the generation of the following derived belief as an untainted inference under principle (35):

$<\text{john believes } <p \supset q>>$

The reason for this is that '$<p \supset q>$', being a direct inference, would be a member of the set $I_{DI\Phi_1}$.

In addition to the constraints on belief-inferencing mentioned above, the consistency specifications pertaining to belief (see section 9.4) are also applicable.

The many-valued approach seems particularly well suited for use in this area. The reader should note that the difficulties associated with having to determine which beliefs should be allowed as derivations from a given belief are somewhat lessened when one is allowed to choose from a range of values in describing the derivability relation. Given that a person believes that a doughnut is in a particular box and that the box is in a particular refrigerator, the problem of having to decide whether it follows that the person believes that the doughnut is in the refrigerator can be a difficult one when one considers that a young child might very well answer 'yes' to each of the questions:

Is the doughnut in the box?

Is the box in the refrigerator?

yet failing to give the same response when asked:

Is the doughnut in the refrigerator?

This example is intended to convey the idea that in the belief realm some hard choices have to be made about the kind of inferences that are to be allowed. A many-valued scheme can be employed effectively in this area. The result of employing such a scheme for the example above might be that the derivability relation should be tainted to some extent, but perhaps only slightly. Having that kind of choice available enables one to specify with more confidence which rules are to govern the derivation process. A decision not to allow the ranking 'IPR' (i.e. the strongest indicator of derivability) to be assigned to derivations based on transitivity principles applied in the belief realm, for example, is easier to make knowing that a weaker form of derivability may be recognized for those inferences.

### 4.8 Nonmonotonic Reasoning

The province of nonmonotonic reasoning has been asserted to be the derivation of "plausible (but not infallible) conclusions from a knowledge base viewed abstractly as a set of formulas in a suitable logic" (Reiter, 1987). The conclusions drawn are taken to be tentative and may be withdrawn after new information is added to the knowledge base. Monotonic reasoning, on the other hand, does not allow conclusions to be retracted. Once a valid conclusion is drawn in a monotonic system, it stands regardless of what new information is added to the knowledge base. The reasoning in SMS is clearly nonmonotonic since any penumbral inference can be overridden by new information. Discussions in this section will focus on a couple of aspects of the default reasoning problem to illustrate the general approach to nonmonotonic reasoning used in SMS . The areas chosen for discussion are reasoning based on the concept of typicality and reasoning that involves adverbial, adjectival, and other descriptive expressions.

### 4.8.1 Default Reasoning Involving the Concept of Typicality

It has been observed that examples of nonmonotonic reasoning discussed in AI seem to fit the following pattern (or one similar to it; see Reiter, 1987):

Typically, Φ is the case. (37)

This pattern can be used to produce plausible inferences by employing the following rule pattern:

In the absence of information to the contrary, assume Φ.

The rule pattern thus provides for the assumption of Φ by default.

A number of formalizations of nonmonotonic inferencing have already been developed (e.g. McCarthy, 1980, 1986; McDermott and Doyle, 1980; Reiter, 1980; and Pearl, 1988; see also Yager, 1987a, and Dubois and Prade, 1988, on default reasoning within the framework of possibility theory). A good overview of the subject can be found in (Reiter, 1987). A full treatment of the subject is beyond the intended scope of this book. Methods by which to handle default reasoning problems are still under development in SMS. Nonetheless, the general methodology is sufficiently developed to warrant a description of it in illustration of how the many-valued approach might be used effectively in this area.

Few people would doubt that the following argument schema is invalid:

Given: Typically, Φ is the case.

-------------------------------

Therefore: Φ is the case.

Although the schema is invalid, the plausible reasoning approach can render the conclusion useful by assuming it to be true until contrary information is made available. The plausibility of this assumption is, of course, based on the typicality indicated in the premise. In SMS, the conclusion 'Φ is the case' would follow as a penumbral inference. In this respect, penumbral inferencing and nonmonotonic inferencing produce very similar results. The corresponding argument in SMS would be represented as follows:

IPR: Typically, Φ is the case.

--------------------------------

$V_i$: Φ is the case.

where $V_i$ indicates tainted, but nonetheless 'plausible', derivability.

Considering the standard example that deals with flying birds, the sentence "Birds fly" can be taken to be an instance of pattern (37), thus yielding:

Typically, birds fly. (38)

If given that Tweety is a bird, by further invoking the plausible reasoning approach, one might be inclined to assume that Tweety flies based on the assumption that Tweety is a typical bird. It should be noted that even if it is known that Tweety is a typical bird, the conclusion that Tweety flies is still a mere plausible inference. For the inference to be a deductive one, pattern (38) would have had to have been something like:

All typical birds fly

but this pattern is not synonymous with pattern (38). This becomes clear when one considers that the sentence:

Typically, typical birds fly

makes sense under some interpretations. The problem being alluded to is that internal qualifiers (in this case 'typical') are not necessarily defined by the same criteria that define the corresponding sentential qualifiers (in this case 'Typically'). The ability to fly may not have been included in the criteria that defines the qualifier 'typical.' This point can be illustrated by example. Given the objects:

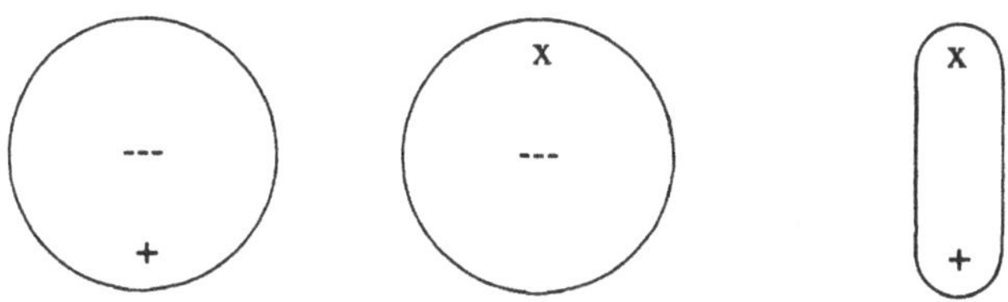


and given that each object is something called a 'ramble' and that the objects constitute the total population of rambles, the features listed below (miniaturized for convenience), along with their indicated frequency of occurrence in the population, could be used to define the features of a typical ramble.

1) ○ → 2 instances

2) ⬯ → 1 instance

3) --- → 2 instances

4) x → 2 instances

5) + → 2 instances

Seemingly, it would not be unreasonable to define typicality in terms of features 1) and 3), especially if features 1) and 2) were to be placed in the category of basic features, as might be the case, for example, if they were to be taken as body shapes and the rest of the features were to be taken as attributes of the body shapes. In such a case, the typical ramble might be taken to conform to the pattern: (---)

Under such an interpretation, the other features could be considered to be anomalies. Given that any ramble that conforms to this last pattern is a typical ramble, the reader should note that the statement:

Typically, a ramble has a '+'

would be true if 'Typically' is construed in this context to mean that *most* rambles have a '+'. Yet the truth of the assertion:

The typical ramble has a '+'

is at least questionable since it is not true that most 'typical' rambles have a '+'. Difficulties of this kind will be ignored for the moment to facilitate discussion about how the many-valued approach might be employed in default reasoning. Later in this section, a scheme for recognizing multiple types of typicality will be described that can be used to overcome some of the mentioned difficulties.

Unfortunately, the SMS approach does not provide any short-cut solutions to default reasoning problems. It does, however, present an environment in which problems can be addressed straightforwardly, and the many-valued approach can be used advantageously in dealing with problems of typicality. At the outset there seem to be two alternatives from which to choose:

1) explicit representations of typicality can be required; or

2) typicality can be assumed by default.

Each approach has well known advantages and weaknesses. The first alternative causes notational inconvenience since each time one wishes to speak of an object in a typical sense, an explicit term must be employed to represent that sense. Thus, to represent the English sentence 'Birds fly', where the intended meaning is that 'All typical birds fly' or something to that effect, an expression like:

<<birds <all><typical*>> fly>

would have to be used, where 'typical*' is an operator of SL that is used to invoke special procedures to bring about effects of the sort described below. Alternative 1 above was chosen for the prototype of SMS because the many-valued scheme can be defined to take up slack whenever a modifier like 'typical*' is omitted, which incidently might be done unintentionally. In such a case, the system can be made to assume that the object represented is not a 'typical*' one but can compensate for the absence of the modifier by using the many-valued approach to recognize a penumbral presence of the modifier. The following example illustrates the point. Given that an SMS database contains the following sequences (where the term 'can' functions as an auxiliary):

<<birds <all><typical*>> <fly<can>>>

<tweety isa bird>

the system could generate the following values in preparation for responding to the query '<tweety <fly<can>>>':

1) $V_1$ (a value indicative of tainted derivability) → <<birds <all><typical*>> <fly<can>>>

2) $V_2$ (a value indicative of untainted derivability) → <<birds <all>> <fly<can>>>

(where the arrows point to the source statements from which the query has been derived). The first value indicates that the query follows from the source statement as a tainted derivation. The reason the derivation is tainted is because it is not given in the database that 'tweety' is a '<bird <typical*>>'. The second value indicates that the derivability is not tainted. The source statement of the second value is a mere penumbral inference. As the system is being implemented to deal with the default reasoning problem, by postulation the sequence '<<birds<all>> <fly<can>>>' follows as a penumbral inference from the sequence '<<birds<all><typical*>> <fly<can>>>'. Penumbral inferences of this sort are recognized when a statement contains the special modifier 'typical*'. Given the presence of '<<birds<all>> <fly<can>>>' as a penumbral inference, the conclusion '<tweety <fly<can>>>' follows from it as an untainted derivation because it is given in the database that '<tweety isa bird>.' However, any response based on this valuation would have to be qualified (tainted) because the valuation is based on a penumbral inference. A response that is qualified in this way might prompt the user to recognize that one or more statements in the database should be amended to include indicators of typicality. This especially might be the case if the user did not expect to receive a tainted response, as would be the case in this example if the user knew that 'tweety' was supposed to be able to 'fly'. In such a case the statement '<tweety isa bird>' would be a likely candidate for amendment to incorporate an appropriate indicator of typicality. The nonmonotonic nature of SMS can be shown in this example. If later the statement '<tweety <fly<cannot>>>' were to be added to the database, the penumbral inference '<<birds <all>> <fly<can>>>' would be cast aside because of its inconsistency with the new statement that carries a stronger degree of presence.

For a system to be able to reason by default when dealing with typicality, it must first know the meaning(s) of typicality in its domain. Different senses of typicality are appropriate for different types of objects. Given a listing of numbers, for example, one might wish to define the typical number as something like the mode or mean of the list. For physical objects, on the other hand, one might choose to define typicality in terms of features cast into a model. Considering again the example involving the population of rambles, the typical ramble could be defined by a model or prototype consisting of any of the following combinations of features:

1) the most frequently occurring body shape plus the most frequently occurring attribute of that shape;

2) the most frequently occurring body shape plus any one attribute of the set: {x, +, ---}; or

3) the most frequently occurring body shape plus any two attributes of the set: {x, +, ---}.

Given the database statement:

<ramby isa <ramble <typical*>> >

(where 'ramby' is a proper name) and given that these three senses of typicality are defined within the system and that the system is able to recognize features, how should the system respond to a query such as:

< <appearance <of ramby>> is= < (---) <at least>> > ?

The following response values could be generated in preparation to giving a response to this query:

(a) IPR → '○' plus '---'

(b) $V_1$ → '○' plus any one of the set: {x , + , ---}

(c) $V_2$ → '○' plus any two of the set: {x, +, ---}

where each value (e.g. 'IPR') is associated with a sense of typicality; where each arrow points to the features that define the associated sense of typicality; and where the values '$V_1$' and '$V_2$' indicate tainted presence based on the fact that although 'typical*' in the sense associated with the value, ramby may not have the exact features called for by the query. Since the modifier 'typical*' in the database sequence is indefinite because it fails to identify which sense of typicality is being employed, each of the above responses must be further qualified to reflect this indefiniteness. Under the SMS approach, the penumbra of the database sequence can be defined to entail the presence of each sense of typicality, and the query would be satisfiable in three ways, all penumbral, based on the database sequence. Using the technique described in section 3.3.1 to handle terms with multiple senses, the following response values could be generated in preparation for responding to the query:

<IPR <$V_{typicality\text{-}sense\text{-}1}$>> → $\Phi_{DB}$

<$V_1$ <$V_{typicality\text{-}sense\text{-}2}$>> → $\Phi_{DB}$

<$V_2$ <$V_{typicality\text{-}sense\text{-}3}$>> → $\Phi_{DB}$

where $\Phi_{DB}$ represents the original database sequence and where the values '$V_{typicality\text{-}sense\text{-}1}$, ..., $V_{typicality\text{-}sense\text{-}3}$' indicate tainted presence based on multiple senses of the term 'typical*'. These values have been added as qualifiers on the values previously generated (i.e. 'IPR', '$V_1$' and '$V_2$'). Each nesting of response values represents an independent penumbral satisfaction of the query, and each nesting reflects the penumbral nature of that satisfaction.

Generalizing these ideas, given that $\alpha$ stands for a general sense of typicality and that $\alpha_1, ..., \alpha_n$ stand for particular subsenses of typicality for a class of objects, say class A, it follows that for every $a_i \in A$, the following associations and mappings can be defined:

$$a_i \rightarrow \{ \alpha_1, \ldots, \alpha_n \}$$

$$\downarrow \qquad \downarrow$$

$$V_{\alpha 1}, \ldots, V_{\alpha n}$$

This indicates that $a_i$ can be associated with one or more senses of typicality (represented here by the set $\{ \alpha_1, \ldots, \alpha_n \}$). The values $V_{\alpha 1}, \ldots, V_{\alpha n}$ indicate presence (perhaps tainted presence) or nonpresence of $a_i$ as an object that is 'typical*' in the corresponding sense of typicality. Given a statement of the form:

$$< a_i \text{ is } \alpha >$$

the following associations and mappings would hold:

$$< a_i \text{ is } \alpha > \rightarrow \{ <a_i \text{ is } \alpha_1>, \ldots, <a_i \text{ is } \alpha_n> \}$$

$$\swarrow \qquad \downarrow$$

$$<V_1 <V_{\alpha 1}>>, \ldots, <V_n <V_{\alpha n}>>$$

where $V_1, \ldots, V_n$ are values that indicate presence tainted by multiple senses of $\alpha$.

Typicality is a difficult concept to deal with in an automated reasoning system because the concept may be localized or defined with reference to select criteria. Clyde, a white elephant, might be typical in the sense of being large and having four legs, a tail and a trunk, but he is not typical with respect to color. Man-made objects such as houses and boats may be defined with reference to a multiplicity of purposes and features, each of which may bear on a particular sense of typicality. A boat typically floats, and one designed for people typically is used for transportation over water. Each purpose, type or feature may become a criterion for a particular sense of typicality. The expression 'typical boat' has at least as many interpretations as there are kinds of boats. Under the many-valued approach, all senses of typicality associated with an object are drawn into relevance unless otherwise eliminated from consideration. Using the techniques described in sections 3.3.1 and 3.3.2, the senses can be assigned a ranking of preference with the result that the presence of an object in one sense of typicality may be stronger than another. This allows one to employ a more traditional default scheme by simply postulating that only the highest ranking senses are to be drawn into relevance in a given case.

Another aspect of the default reasoning problem involves the use of adverbial, adjectival and other descriptive expressions. A statement of the form:

<$\beta$ is $\phi$>

(where $\phi$ ranges over descriptive expressions) is handled in SMS in the following way. Every such expression is expanded into the following form:

<$\beta$ is <$\phi$ <iaw $\alpha$>>>

(where 'iaw' means 'in accordance with' and '$\alpha$' represents some standard that determines or measures $\phi$). The meaning of $\phi$ is defined with reference to the standard $\alpha$. If, for example, $\phi$ = 'small', $\alpha$ might consist of a set of rules that define smallness, e. g.:

If < $\beta$ has size-measure >

and

< <size-measure <the>> $\leq$ $\sigma$ >

then < $\beta$ is small >

(where $\sigma$ is a numerical measurement). Where $\alpha$ is totally unspecified in the sense that no set of standards has been associated with $\phi$, $\alpha$ would be marked as an unspecified standard. This amounts to giving $\phi$ an indefinite measurement or value. Thus given the statement:

<jupiter is small>

and given that no standard is associated with the term 'small', the expansion would be:

<jupiter is <small <iaw <standard <some>>>>>.

In SMS, it is easy to give a standard a name, as in:

<jupiter is <small <iaw <standard <n=i rule-1>>>>>

where 'n=i' is a special preposition that introduces the name of an object (see section 2.3.4). If the standard to be used to determine smallness has not been specified, whether in expression or otherwise, and there are multiple standards for smallness defined within the system, a problem of indefinite reference is created and processes similar to those described in sections 3.3.1 and 3.3.2 would be used to address the problem. A default value can be used to represent some unspecified standard when no standard whatsoever exists for 'smallness' within the system. In any case, the many-valued approach would interpret the statement in a penumbral way, that is, it would give each possibility some penumbral status within the system.

A discussion of inferencing in SMS would not be complete without describing how causal formalisms and expansions are used in the process. Section 4.9 discusses this topic.

## 4.9 Expansions and Causal Formalisms

It now seems to be recognized that a representation language should have sufficient expressive power to represent a wide range of world phenomena and that its semantics should correspond to our intuitive notions about the meanings of the objects and constructs of the language (Patel-Schneider, 1985). The language SL is being developed to possess sufficient expressive power to handle a variety of descriptions of world phenomena. At present, given an English description of an event, one would represent the description in SL in a way that corresponds to the way one would represent it in FOL. Hopefully, at some point SL will be developed into an even more English-like notation to ease the representation task. Causality is one of the most difficult notions to handle. The current version is being designed to accommodate causal relations as well as factors and modalities that serve to distinguish one causal event from another. In particular, the scheme is being built to allow temporal, modal, and other qualifying information to accompany causal event descriptions. This information can be used to increase causal reasoning power. A simple example illustrates the point. If one is informed that John amused Mary by playing the piano and is given a set of descriptions of world events and is asked to find the event that caused Mary to be amused, assuming it is among the descriptions given, a system might encounter problems if it finds several instances of piano playing by John and none of them are explicitly linked to the Mary's state of amusement. The point is that unless one has available some means by which to distinguish and order events, the ability to draw causal inferences is limited. Methods are being developed to enable SMS to mark events based on temporal information and the denotata of the components and relations entailed in those events (see section 10.5).

It seems desirable to preserve uniformity of expression at all levels in an automated reasoning system so that components of different levels can communicate with and be transformed into one another. This produces certain advantages as the examples in this section illustrate. Interaction between levels can be accomplished by mapping lower level expressions into higher level expressions through intermediary expressions or formalisms. Representations of causal relations are particularly useful in serving as intermediary expressions into which to map expressions of higher and lower levels, thereby relating those expressions to one another. The scheme is diagrammed below.

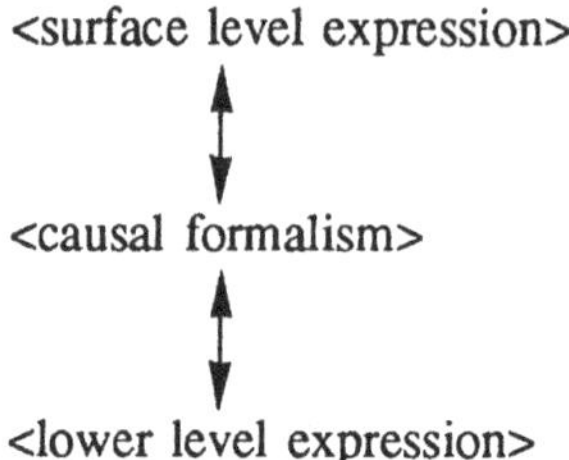


Given the English sentence:

John pleased Mary by giving her some presents

and given that the 'giving' was of the type that would cause the recipient to have possession of the thing given, the hierarchical scheme can be illustrated by example. Figure 12 presents such an example. Sequence 1 of that figure represents what might be called the surface level of the current version of SMS. The surface level is the level at which SL is employed to represent an English description. Where the mappings are not obvious, arrows in the figure indicate how the components of expressions 1 and 3 map into expression 2, which functions as an intermediary causal formalism. The term "bmo" flags the term that describes the type of act at the root of the causal relation. The terms "tr-0", "tr-1", and "tr-2" are sequential temporal indicators. The term 'the' is used to indicate that all the references are to the same emotional state. The link 'has-possess' corresponds to the English expression 'has possession of'. The negation of this link is 'has-possess-not. The link 'has-emot' corresponds to the English expression 'has emotion'.

The information in Figure 12 represents an abstraction/expansion hierarchy. The surface level expression has been expanded into an intermediary representation, and that representation, in turn, has been expanded into a lower level expansion. The lower level expansion is approaching the atomic level, that is, the level at which the sequences involved cannot be expanded further under the expansion rules of the system. A sentence-sequence that is not reducible to more primitive sentential expressions is called an atomic sentential expression. The top level of the hierarchy consists of SL versions of English sentences. The bottom level consists of an atomically normalized versions of top level representations.

A similar scheme is employed in CCLIPS (*C*ivil *C*ode *L*egal *I*nformation *P*rocessing *S*ystem), a system being developed to process legal information (deBessonet and Cross, 1986). CCLIPS employs a language called ANF (*A*tomically *N*ormalized *F*orm) that employs a set of formalisms cast into an abstraction/expansion hierarchy. The idea is to reduce each sentence to a set of atomic sentences that is to serve as a normal form for the original sentence. The goal is for the atomically normalized form to capture the essential meaning of the original sentence. If that goal is achieved, equivalence between dissimilar surface level expressions can be determined by matching their corresponding normal forms. A similar process is being developed for SMS (see section 4.4).

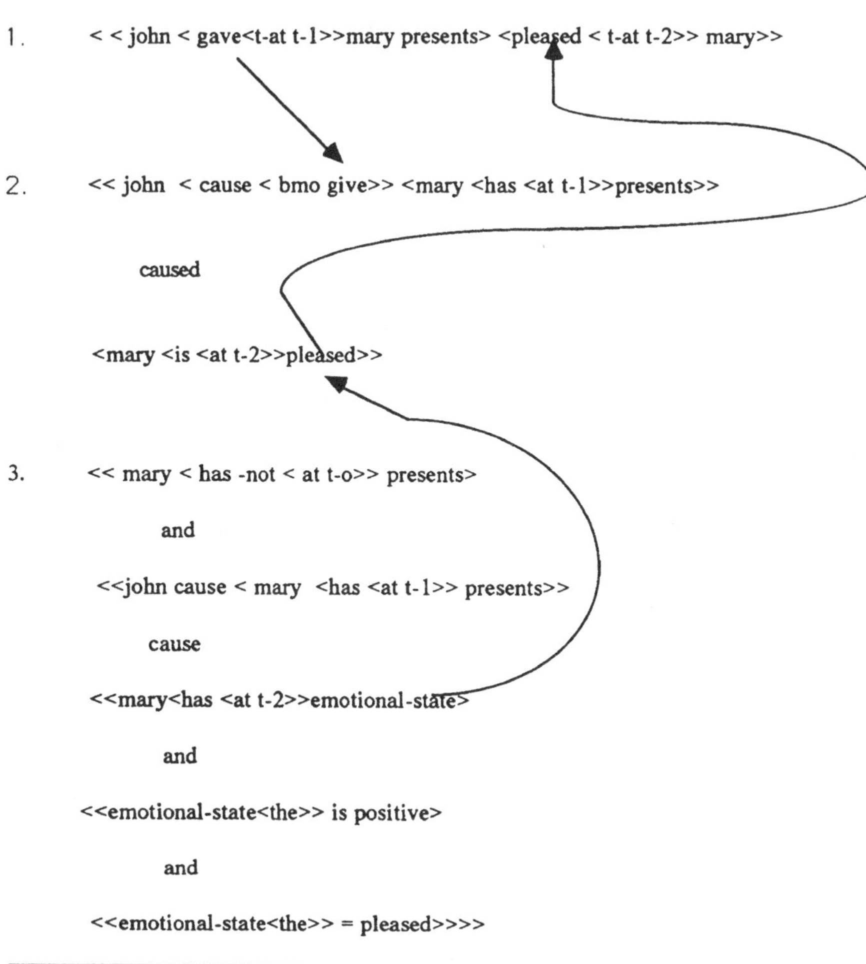
1. < < john < gave<t-at t-1>>mary presents> <pleased < t-at t-2>> mary>>
2. << john < cause < bmo give>> <mary <has <at t-1>>presents>>
caused
<mary <is <at t-2>>pleased>>
3. << mary < has -not < at t-o>> presents>
and
<<john cause < mary <has <at t-1>> presents>>
cause
<<mary<has <at t-2>>emotional-state>
and
<<emotional-state<the>> is positive>
and
<<emotional-state<the>> = pleased>>>>

Figure 12. Mapping Between Expansions

The primary reason for producing the atomically normalized lower levels is to have things expressed in a standardized way so that the system can determine whether syntactical differences at higher levels represent semantical differences. The sequence pairs:

1) <john saw <school <fish>>> <--> <john saw <school <of fish>>>

2) <john caused <mary is happy>> <--> <john caused <happiness <of mary>>>

each contain equivalent yet syntactically different sentential sequences. The idea is to produce expansions that are syntactically identical. Each sequence of pair 2), for example, can be expanded into:

<<john caused <mary has-emot emotional-state>>

and

<<emotional-state<the>> is positive>

and

<<emotional-state<the>> is= happiness>>

Each sentence in the pair would thus map to the same expansion at the lower level. The importance of all this can best be understood by considering the fact that matching problems caused by deviations in query formulation can be addressed by expanding queries into expressions that can be matched at the atomically normalized levels.

The employment of an abstraction/expansion hierarchy, along with thesauri-oriented processes, allows query satisfaction to be conducted at multiple levels. This gives the system the flexibility it needs to handle deviations in query formulation, as the following example illustrates. Given that the sentential sequences in Figure 12 constitute an SL database, and given the query:

<mary is pleased>

one can see that the query matches the root terms of one of the sequences embedded in sequence 2 of Figure 12. The match would be made in the core of sequence 2 as part of the process described in section 4.2.2 when talking about a similar example. The process would generate the sequence '<mary is pleased>' as a direct inference from sequence 2. Suppose, however, that the query was:

<mary is amused>.

This query does not match any sequence within the scope of the sequences in Figure 12. SMS is being designed so that when this kind of matching difficulty occurs, the system employs auxiliary procedures that operate at the basic level of the abstraction/expansion hierarchy. The reason for producing the atomically normalized level is to have it serve as the target of mappings from higher levels. Sentential expressions that are equivalent in the derived sense have normalized expansions (normal forms) that are equivalent. Once an atomically normalized form is produced, thesauri-oriented processes can be used to enhance the matching capabilities of the system. The example under consideration can be used to illustrate this point. The query '<mary is amused>' could be expanded to read:

<<mary has-emot emotional-state>

and

<<emotional-state<the>> is positive>

and

<<emotional-state<the>> is= amused>>.

This expansion almost matches the sequence below that would be present as a direct inference in the penumbra of sequence 3 of Figure 12:

<<mary has-emot emotional-state>

and

<<emotional-state<the>> is positive>

and

<<emotional-state<the>> is= pleased>>.

Except for the term 'pleased', everything in this sequence matches the query expansion through unification (see section 10.2 for comments on unification). That in itself serves as a basis for giving a response to the query, although the response would have to be qualified to reflect the difference between a state of being 'pleased' as opposed to being 'amused'. In other words, a qualified response could be given based on a substantial, partial match. The query asks, among other things, whether 'mary' has a positive emotional state, and that much of the query can be matched in the database. The query, of course, identifies a particular kind of emotional state, and no match would be found for it. It is at this point that thesauri-oriented processes can be employed to give a more descriptive and relevant response.

The sequences given in example above consist of a set of atomic sequences connected by 'and' links. Using a little imagination, one can see that the sequences can be converted into syntactically identical formalisms simply by replacing the terms 'mary', 'amused' and 'pleased' by blank spaces or variables. The sequences, as given, can thus be considered to be instantiations of the formalisms. The advantage of treating them as such is that the formalisms can be treated as indexing mechanisms [cf. material and citations on 'indexing the formulas' in (Charniak and McDermott, 1985, at page 396)], and the matching procedures can focus attention on instantiated terms, in this case 'mary', 'amused' and 'pleased'. By narrowing matching tasks to those described in Figure 13, the system can make more effective use of thesauri lists, associative lists and other matching aids. In this example, the system would attempt to match the term 'amused' with the term 'pleased' and could resort to whatever associations have been specified for these terms, if any.

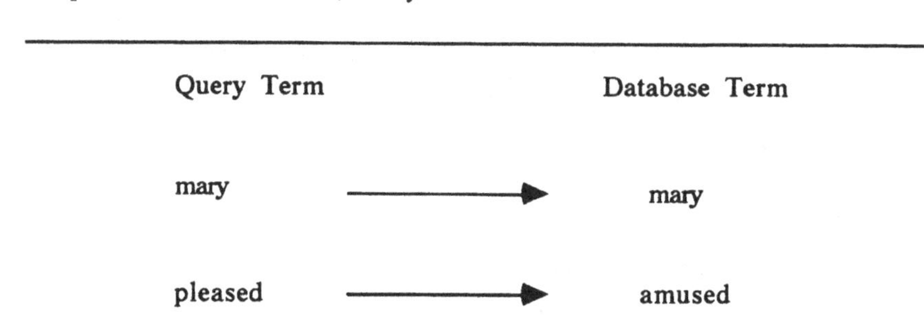

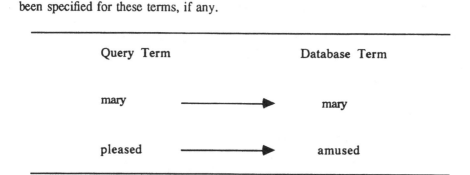

Figure 13 Terms to be Matched

The advantage of having representations related to one another in an abstraction/expansion hierarchy should be obvious when one considers that sequences 1, 2 and 3 of Figure 12 are equivalent to one another. Regardless of whether the query would be sequence 1, 2 or 3, or any well formed sentential part thereof, the system would be in a position to go about the task of satisfying it by first identifying the level at which the query is expressed and then searching that level and more basic ones for information upon which to base unqualified or qualified responses. It is at this point that an important connection is made with fuzzy set theory that allows SMS to deal more effectively with vague or imprecise concepts than otherwise would be the case. Section 4.10 deals with this subject.

## 4.10 Using Fuzzy Set Theory and Probabilistic Methods in SMS

One of the most important reasons for employing the abstraction/expansion hierarchy and the atomically normalized forms described in sections 2.5 and 4.9 is to enable inferencing processes to capture some of the flexibility enjoyed by fuzzy reasoning systems. By employing fuzzy sets and linguistic variables, fuzzy systems are able to handle imprecise concepts such as *small*, *young*, and *approximately* through use of possibility and probability distributions. Somewhat elaborate methods have been developed for incorporating the values provided by these distributions into the inferencing scheme (see Zadeh's *test-score semantics* in [Zadeh, 1986]).

Perhaps the best way to show the connection between SMS and fuzzy set theory is to trace the connection through possibility theory (e.g. Zadeh, 1978). Given that U represents the universe of discourse and that F is a fuzzy set in U determined by the membership function $f_F$, which associates a real number in the interval [0,1] with any $u \in U$ so that $f_F$ represents the grade of membership of u in F, one can speak of F as being a fuzzy restriction on X, where X is a variable that takes values in U. In such a case, $f_F$ (u) would be interpreted as the degree to which the constraint F is satisfied when u is assigned to X. A fuzzy restriction on X can be written as:

$$R(X) = F$$

and an attribute (e.g. 'A' for Age) of X that takes values in U may be added, so that the expression:

$$R(A(X)) = F$$

signifies that 'X is F' has the effect of assigning F to the fuzzy restriction associated with the values of A(X). For purposes of simplicity, the 'A' will be dropped so that R(X) will be used instead of R(A(X)). Using Zadeh's example:

John is young → R(Age (John)) = young

where 'young' is the name of the fuzzy set, and given that u = 28 and that $f_F$ (28) = 0.7, the value would be interpreted as the degree of compatibility of 28 with the concept labeled 'young'. Under this approach, the proposition 'John is young' converts the degree of compatibility into the degree of possibility that 'John is 28'. In other words, the compatibility of the value assigned by $f_F$ (28) is converted into the possibility of that value of u given that 'John is young' (Zadeh, 1978). A *possibility distribution*, $\Pi_x$, can be associated with X so that $\Pi_x = R(X)$. The possibility function $\pi_x$ is postulated to be equal to $f_F$ so that $\pi_x$ (u), that is, the possibility that X = u, is equal to $f_F$ (u). Possibility is distinguished from probability under this approach. Zadeh (1978) uses the example:

Hans ate X eggs for breakfast

with X taking values {1,2,3,4 ....}. A possibility distribution can be associated with X so that $\pi_x$ (u) would be interpreted as the 'degree of ease' with which Hans can eat u eggs. A probability distribution can be associated with X so that $P_X$ (u) would be interpreted as the probability that Hans ate u eggs for breakfast. Given the possibility distribution:

$$\Pi_x = 1/1 + 1/2 + 1/3 + 0.8/4 \ldots.$$

(where + stands for union), one can easily conceive of a probability distribution in which the values for 'u =1', 'u=2' and 'u=3' would be 0.1, 0.8 and 0.1 respectively, which would indicate that there exists a high probability that Hans ate two eggs for breakfast and low probabilities that he ate one or three eggs. In contrast, the possibility measures for 'u=1', 'u=2' and 'u=3' are 1, 1 and 1 respectively, meaning that the degree of ease with which Hans can eat one, two or three eggs is the same in each case. Thus, possibility differs from probability under this approach, although if an event is impossible, it is also improbable under this way of looking at things.

The 'degree of ease' test can be understood in a figurative sense, so that 'Age(John) = 28' may take the value 0.7, with 0.7 representing the degree of ease with which 28 may be assigned to 'Age(John)' given the elasticity of the fuzzy restriction labeled 'young'. The statement that the compatibility of 28 with 'young' is 0.7 has no relation to the probability of the age value 28. The compatibility-value 0.7 is "merely a subjective indication of the extent to which the age-value 28 fits one's conception of the label *young*" (Zadeh, 1978, at pages 223-224). In this respect, the SMS approach is similar to possibility theory since the rankings of presence in SMS are based on subjective indications of the measure to which derivability relations between expressions of SL fit one's conception of their *usefulness* in a conversational mode. It has been asserted that Zadeh's possibility theory seems to fall under a general theory of valuation, whereas probability is perhaps best thought of as part of a general theory of measure and thus has the property of additivity (Kaufmann, 1977).

Proponents of probability theory have criticized some of the conceptions of probability theory that have been expounded by the fuzzy theorists. Cheeseman (1985), for example, has asserted that the view that probabilities are necessarily frequencies is a fallacy. He maintains that there is a probabilistic model for vague sets that provides quantitative measures for vague classifications. A set can be defined by a *prototype* and expectations of divergence from the prototypical features of the members of the set. Each object is given a numeric 'degree of membership' based on the likelihood of the occurrence of observed features, given that the object is a member of the set. Classification of an object is optimized based on the maximization of the probabilistic 'similarity' measure. An object may be so dissimilar from the prototype that it forms a new set. An object can also be probabilistically similar to more than one set simultaneously (see Wallace and Boulton, 1968, for the underlying theory of probabilistic set membership).

Under the fuzzy approach, the concept of truth can be treated as a linguistic variable and assigned a term-set containing terms such as *true*, *very true*, and *somewhat true*. The scheme employs what is termed a 'base variable'. The linguistic values (e.g 'true') of the linguistic variable (e.g. 'Truth') serve as labels for the fuzzy restrictions on the values of the base variable. The base variable for 'Age' would be 'age', whose values might be taken to be the numbers 0, 1, 2, 3, 4, ..., 100. Where *Truth* is treated as a linguistic variable, the values of the base variable can be taken to be included in the interval [0,1]. A compatibility function can assign each linguistic variable in the term-set a number in the interval [0,1] to represent the compatibility of the linguistic values with the numerical values of the base variable. Figure 14 diagrams the scheme in abbreviated form.

In SMS, each linguistic object x can be assigned an associated set T consisting of terms that correspond to members of a term-set of a linguistic variable (as defined by Zadeh; see section 4.6). The elements of T can be taken to be postulated gradations of the object x. A derivability function (cf. compatibility function; Zadeh, 1978) can be defined to assign a derivability value to any pair, one element from T and the other element from another set R generated by a relevance function that generates all expressions that are relevant for x in the derivation process.

---

Truth

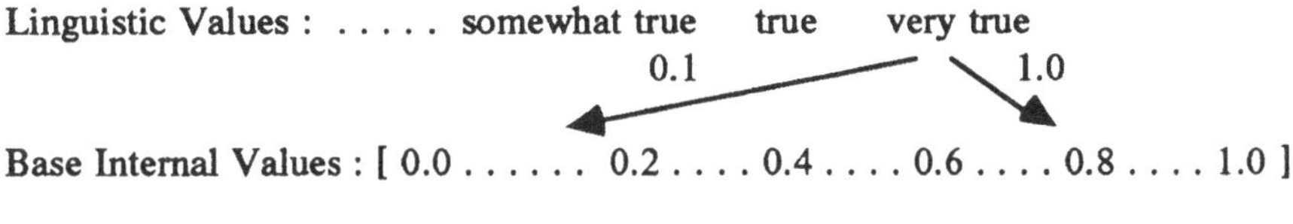


---

Figure 14. Truth as a Linguistic Variable

The set to be returned by the relevance function can also be postulated in advance. As is mentioned in section 4.6, it is theoretically possible for the derivability function to assign a value to any pair of SL expressions, but since most of those valuations would be irrelevant for the derivation tasks to be performed by the system, it would not be not necessary to produce the irrelevant valuations. The expressions in set R determine the scope of the search that must be made to determine the derivability of x from an SMS database. The object x will be deemed to be derivable from that database if any $r_i \in R$ matches a term in the database. The strength of the derivability relation is measured by the value postulated for the ordered pair $\langle x, r_i \rangle$ (see section 11.6). For any pair $\langle t_i, r_i \rangle$, where $t_i \in T$ and $r_i \in R$, the derivability function can assign a value $v_i$ that indicates the extent to which $t_i$ is 'present' in $r_i$ (see section 3.5). It thus becomes possible to determine the derivability of $t_i$ (which represents a gradation of x) from the database based on the relation that $t_i$ holds to any member of R that matches a database term.

As the scheme has been described thus far, all the values are linguistic. By using linguistic values, one avoids the problem having to make difficult, subjective grade assignments on a large scale, a problem alluded to in section 3.3.2. The scheme is diagrammed in Figure 15 in abbreviated form. The reader should note that the mappings are into a set of linguistic values instead of into the interval [0,1] and that the values associated with the mappings are all linguistic. In conformity with Popper's idea (Popper, 1976) that one should not employ any more linguistic precision than necessary, matters should be handled without employing fine numeric gradations whenever possible. The determination of membership in each set (i.e. T and R) is a matter of choice. Obvious candidates for inclusion in these sets would be the supertypes of the existing members of the sets. The power of this scheme can be augmented by allowing *wfsss* to be included in the sets T and R. Thus, for example, sentential sequences of the form '<age is= x>', where x is a variable ranging over positive integers, might be included. It follows that the derivability function could assign a value to '<young, <age is= 25>>' if the sentential sequence '<age is= 25>' were to be included in the relevance-set R.

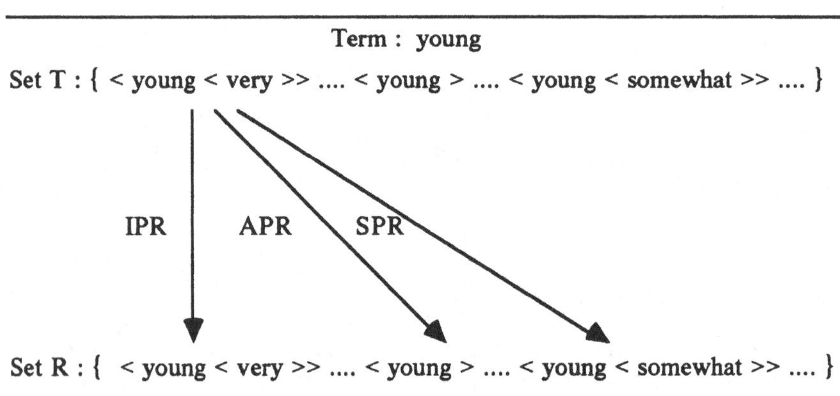


Figure 15. Relation Between Term-Set and Relevance-Set of SL Term

A viable alternative to the inclusion of sentential sequences in the sets T and R is to employ linguistic variables that range over components of sentential expressions. The term '?age-years', for example, could be included in R instead of an expression like '<age is= 25>'. The term could be used as a variable to range over numeric values for age and could be associated with linguistic sub-values, possibility distributions, probability distributions or any combination of these devices. This is where the contact between SMS and the fuzzy approach is made. Section 4.9 describes how basic level expansions can be treated as formalisms in which key terms are highlighted for matching. The following sequence, for example, could serve as a formalism for age (given in years):

<< x has ?age-years>

and

<?age-years is= y>>

(where 'x' ranges over noun labels, 'y' ranges over positive integers, and '?age-years' is a label that may be instantiated by a marker). If the database of SMS were to contain an instantiation of this formalism, in which say 'john' would instantiate 'x', 25 would instantiate 'y', and 'age-years-2' would be the marker that would instantiate '?age-years', and the query:

<john is young>?

were to be asked, the system could take advantage of having linguistic variables included in the relevance-set R for the term 'young'. Using the information given in Figure 16, one can see that the term 'young' would yield a term-set that would contain '?age-years' as a member. Associated with '?age-years' would be a possibility distribution and a set of linguistic values, one of which would be the marker in the instantiated formalism. That marker (i.e. 'age-years-2') would be bound to the age-years-value 25. When 25 would be found on the possibility distribution for ?age-years, the value 0.7 would be yielded, and this value could be taken to measure the compatibility of the query with the information in the instantiated formalism.

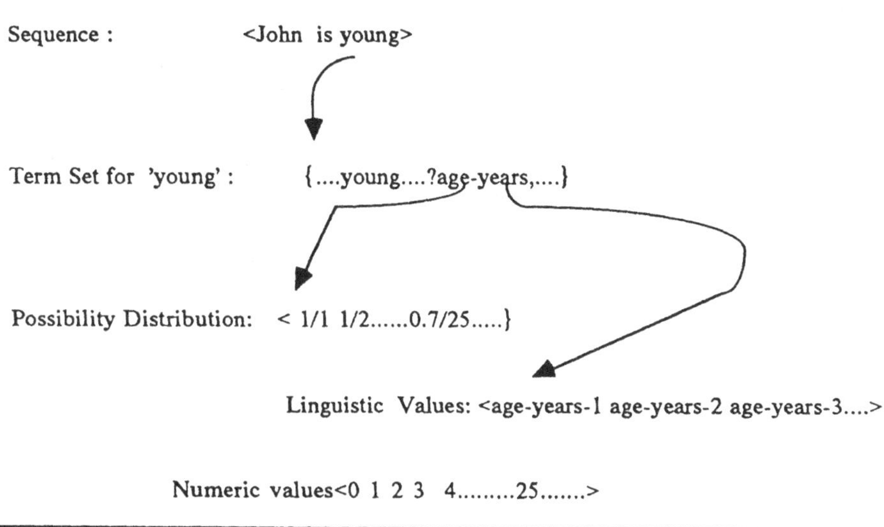


Figure 16. Relation between Term, Term-Set, Distribution and Values

Just as the SMS approach is compatible with the possibilistic approach, it is compatible with the probabilistic approach. The assertions made in Chapter 6 to the effect that some of the inferencing patterns recognized in the system are based more on utility than on probability does not mean that inferencing rooted in the latter cannot be usefully employed in an SMS setting. Probabilistic methods can be introduced into the system through probability distributions, for example. Inferencing based on probabilities fits well into the many-valued scheme because qualified responses to queries can be made to reflect probabilities. Given, for instance, that the system knows that there are only two possibilities, say $\Phi_1$ and $\Phi_2$, in a given situation and knows that at least one of those possibilities holds but does not know which one, under the principles described in Chapter 3 (e.g. sections 3.3.1 and 3.3.2), the system could give a qualified response to a query of the form '<$\Phi_1$ IPR>'. The response would be assigned a value to indicate that $\Phi_1$ is present as a mere alternative possibility. If the system also knows, say through some probability distribution, that $\Phi_1$ is just as likely as $\Phi_2$, that information could easily be incorporated into the response to reflect the 50/50 chance that $\Phi_1$ holds.

Default probabilities can be gainfully employed to make the responses of the system more meaningful. If the system knows, for example, that some set A has ten elements and that some relation holds for some element of that set but does not know which element, the default probability that the relation holds for some $a_i \in A$ could be set to a chance of 1 in 10.

Probabilistic reasoning capabilities were not implemented in the initial version of SMS but are currently under development for the enhanced version of the system. The point to be stressed here is that probabilities can be incorporated into the many-valued setting by allowing the presence of items to be tainted by probabilities and by allowing response values to reflect those probabilities.

Now that that some of the key features of SMS have been outlined, the discussions will turn to a description of the ontological scheme used in the system in preparation for a detailed comparison of SMS to FOL and further discussions on modal inferencing and the derivation process.

# CHAPTER 5

## ONTOLOGICAL CONSIDERATIONS

### 5.1 Ontological Realms

This section describes some ontological distinctions drawn in SMS. Human beings employ a multiplicity of classifications of the objects they refer to or describe in ordinary discourse. One finds, for example, reference to spiritual reality as opposed to physical reality, and reality itself is said to be distinct from the realm of imagination. Objects bear the ontological status of the realms to which they belong (e.g objects from the physical realm are referred to as 'physical objects'). Mental objects (e.g. beliefs) and emotional objects (e.g. desires) are thought to somehow partake of the nature of the objects that have or produce them, yet they obviously deserve special classification in their own right.

In designing SMS an attempt was made to capture the bare, uninterpreted structure of an ordinary ontological scheme, but before describing this aspect of SMS, a more general description of the system seems in order. The three primary components of SMS are:

1) LEX (for lexicon);

2) DB (for database);and

3) ID (for input domain).

SMS employs a set of functions to govern the flow of symbols from one component to another. The relations in DB and LEX are constrained by a set of ontological categories and associated specifications. For the most part the constraints are imposed upon the vocabulary of SL, that is, upon the signs in LEX. The basic idea is to relegate signs to categories. Relations between tokens of the signs are classified based on the categories to which the signs belong. This allows categorical distinctions to be drawn in the assertive component of the DB. The effect is that discourse within categorical limits becomes possible. Assertions containing the linguistic objects 'Superman' and 'Mighty Mouse', for example, can be kept distinct from assertions about 'Bush' and 'Gorbachev', assuming of course that the latter two objects are relegated to a different category than the former ones (no disrespect intended). Ontological distinctions are important for the derivation process. Of particular importance are distinctions drawn between assertions that contain objects categorized as mental objects (e.g. beliefs) and assertions that do not contain such objects. FOL systems have had difficulty in incorporating this distinction into the derivation process. Sections 5.8 and 4.7 describe how mental objects are handled in SMS. The ID component is used to enter SL statements to be processed either as queries or as candidates for admission into the DB.

The scheme of ontological classification employed in SMS establishes an environment in which it is convenient to specify and impose constraints on special objects, such as those classified as mental objects. The overall effect of the scheme is to establish different worlds or realms within the system, and it thus becomes possible to describe the system in terms of partitioned realms. When reference can be made to realms, such as the realm of mental objects and the realm of fiction, it becomes easier to appreciate how the ontological status of an object can affect the derivation process. The listing in Figure 17 gives the abbreviation for each realm and a brief description of it to facilitate an understanding of the following discussions.

---

1) OW -- everyday world;

2) FW -- fictitious world;

3) AW -- abstract world of defined concepts;

4) SW-- spiritual world;

5)NW -- nether world, a world of contradiction and inconsistency;

6)UW -- undetermined world, a world of objects of undetermined status;

7) MW -- mental world, a realm of beliefs, desires and the like;

---

Figure 17. Listing of Ontological Realms

The version of SMS described in this book is intended to reflect ontological diversity and flexibility. Accordingly, seven distinct realms have been specified for the system. These realms are intended to correspond to the classifications of objects that people generally recognize when they engage in ordinary conversation. The realms are assigned familiar descriptions for the convenience of the reader. Admittedly, the scheme of classification described in Figure 17 is somewhat arbitrary, yet for reasons stated below, the approach seems harmless enough. The goal here is simply to establish a scheme that can be used to demonstrate the general approach. As will be seen, SL statements are assigned values based on the ontological status of their components. Derivations in SMS are also assigned values that are descriptive of their ontological status, and these values are used as part of a qualified response program to assist the system in describing the strength of the derivations (see section 3.3). The following sections briefly describe the realms listed in Figure 17.

## 5.2 The Realm of OW

The realm of OW contains all linguistic objects that are explicitly assigned to OW and all objects that are not restricted to other realms. Hence, to some extent, it functions as a default realm. For expository convenience, 'OW' will be used autonymously, that is, as a symbol in both the metalanguage and in the object language. In the metalinguistic sense, 'OW' can be taken to correspond to the ordinary world, but in SMS, it is merely a symbol that is to be associated with particular constraints or specifications. All the abbreviations for ontological realms given in this section are used autonymously, and as far as SMS is concerned, they are merely symbols to be associated with constraints and specifications.

As mentioned previously, restrictions can be imposed on objects either in LEX or in DB statements. A linguistic object (token) that appears in an SL statement belongs to OW if:

1) it is not accompanied by an explicit modifier that relegates it to another realm;

2) its *sign* in LEX does not explicitly restrict it to another realm; and

3) it is not relegated to another realm because of the presence of a special link such as a MO(mental object) link.

## 5.3 The Realm of FW

FW contains linguistic objects that are excluded from OW because of some explicit constraint given either in LEX or in a wff of the DB. FW can be taken to correspond to the world of fiction. In the examples presented in this book, the terms 'Superman', 'Mighty Mouse' and 'yeti' will be used consistently as terms restricted to FW.

## 5.4 The Realm of AW

The realm of AW is confined to LEX. It consists of the *entries* of LEX and of associated lexical information.

## 5.5 The Realm of SW

This realm contains objects that correspond to spiritual objects (e.g. 'angels', 'heaven', and 'paradise'). The objects of this realm are treated specially in that they are allowed to partake of the character of another realm. An object classified as an 'angel' may act in the realm of OW, and the relation will be valid for OW. In other words, a statement such as '<mary saw <angel<some>>>', where 'mary' is an object of OW, may be assigned the ontological value 'OW' even though an 'angel' is involved.

## 5.6 The Realm of NW

This realm was made part of SMS to handle contradictions and inconsistencies. Any statement that fails to be admitted into one of the other realms because of inconsistency of any sort is placed in NW. As might be expected, special constraints are placed on operations in this realm, especially those that attempt to employ the derivation process. For all practical purposes, this realm is ignored in reasoning operations. It will also be ignored in most of the discussion in this book. Hence, when reference is made to the 'world' or 'universe' of SMS in discussions about inferencing, the reference should be understood to exclude the realm of NW.

## 5.7 The Realm of UW

Any object whose status is in some way undetermined is placed in the realm of UW. The realm is subpartitioned into:

a) undetermined world of links (UWL); and

b) undetermined world of relations (UWR).

The realm of links contains expressions that function like *open* sentences in FOL. In UWL, links are assigned the number of arguments or places they are to have. An individual link has no particular ontological assignment, but once the link is used in a wfss, it takes on the ontological value assigned to that wfss. A function can be defined to map the set $\{x \mid x \text{ is a wfss} \bullet x \in DB\}$ into the set of symbols {OW,FW,AW,MW,UW,NW,SW}. The mapping depends on the ontological status of what is referred to herein as the 'key nouns' of the sequences. Key nouns are the terms that occupy positions such as subject, object or indirect object of a sentence-sequence. If all such components of an $ss_i$ are of the same realm, the sequence is assigned a value that corresponds to that realm, and for all practical purposes, the sequence belongs to that realm. When two or more components belong to different realms, the assigned value is 'UWR', and the sequence is considered to be a member of the undetermined world of relations. These ontological values or assignments are used in the derivation process. A $ss_k$ with the ontological value 'OW', for example, cannot be derived from $\{ss_1,...,ss_n\}$ as an untainted derivation when each element of that set has, say, the ontological value 'FW'.

### 5.8 The Realm of MW

MW contains linguistic objects that are qualified in some way because of the presence of special links that are definitionally associated with MW. These links constitute a subcategorization of the *labels* category (see section 2.3.1). A linguistic object is relegated to MW based on its having a particular syntactic relation with one of these special links. The links will be referred to metalinguistically as 'MO links' ( mental object links). The term 'believe' is such a link. Any linguistic object that appears in a sequence immediately after the term 'believe', or any of its 'tenses', is classified as an object of MW. A sequence that contains such an object will be referred to as a 'belief-sequence', and every position in a belief-sequence has associated constraints and specifications in SMS. The sequence:

<john believes <mary is happy>> (39)

is a belief sequence that would place '<mary is happy>' in the realm of MW.

Schematically speaking, MW stands in the midst of OW, FW and SW. Each object of MW is a MO (mental object) of some kind, such as a thought or belief. For convenience, a host of other objects are treated as mental objects in this version of SMS although they technically deserve special classification. Objects of desire and emotion, for example, are treated as MOs in the current version.

The objects of MW are unique in that each is bound to some object of another realm. As used in these discussions, the term 'bound' implies correspondence between objects based on some scheme of individuation or marking. Every belief, for example, is marked in MW and thereby corresponds to some member of another realm, that is, to the object that occupies the first position in the belief-sequence involved, which is considered to be the position of *believer*. In addition, every constituent of the belief is deemed to have a corresponding object in another realm. In sequence (39) above, 'john' is the believer, and '<mary is happy>' is the belief. The terms 'mary' and 'happy' are constituents of the belief and thus have corresponding objects in other realms. The constituents are bound in MW within the scope of that particular belief. Part of the scheme for handling belief-sequence (39) is diagrammed in Figure 18.

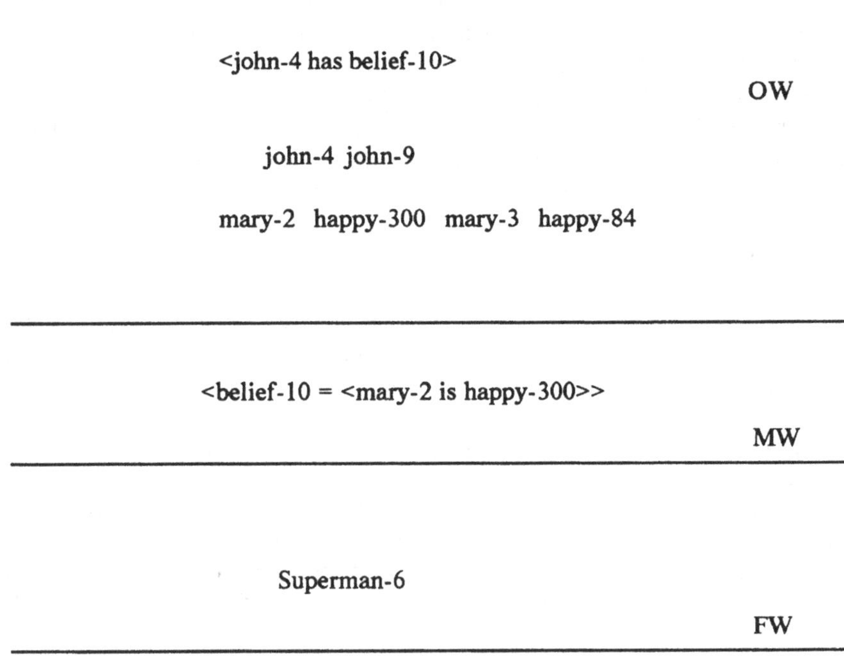


Figure 18. Belief Mappings

Markers have been assigned to the objects in Figure 18 to illustrate the mappings. The example in Figure 18 presupposes that the original belief-sequence identified both 'mary' and a known state of happiness of 'mary' as being objects of OW. The marked belief (i.e. belief-10) is mapped into the realm that contains the object that qualifies as the believer in the belief-sequence, in this case 'john-4'. The link 'is' would be mapped to the realm UWL.

One of the most important constraints placed on MW is that the substitution principle and the relation of derived equality, that is, equality that is not based on syntactic identity (see section 4.3), are not allowed to operate as usual when mental objects are involved. Ordinarily, if given the sequences:

< lear is happy > and < mimi is= lear >

(where 'is=' is a link that indicates that its subject and object are bound to the same marker and hence are identical), the sequence '< mimi is happy >' would be derivable from them simply through substitution of 'mimi' for 'lear' in the first sequence based on the given relation of identity. FOL recognizes a similar process. If, however, the given sequences are:

<patty believes <lear is happy>> and <mimi is= lear>

the sequence '<patty believes <mimi is happy>>' does not follow as an untainted derivation because of the aforementioned constraint on the objects of MW. Since '<lear is happy>' is a mental object, the substitution process is not allowed to operate as usual. The only substitution allowed in such cases must be based on the relation of syntactic identity or must consist of the substitution of the marker of a name or label for that particular name or label. The reasons for these constraints have been noted in AI and logic circles (e.g Quine, 1986). It simply does not follow logically that if Patty believes that Lear is happy that she also believes Mimi is happy because she may not know, for example, that Lear is Mimi. On the other hand, if Patty knows exactly which human object it is in the world that she believes is happy, it follows that she believes that object is happy regardless of what name it might have. In the plain, symbolic environment of SMS, however, a marker, say 'ue-10', would take the place of the object in the world, and just as it follows in logic that Patty believes that the human object is happy, it would follow in SMS that '<patty believes <ue-10 is happy>>'.

Although the sequence '<patty believes <mimi is happy>>' does not follow as an *untainted* derivation in SMS, it is nonetheless a derivation, albeit a weak one. The soundness of the derivation is tainted because of the constraints on mental objects discussed above. The result is that the sequence follows as a *qualified* derivation under the qualified response mechanism employed in SMS. That mechanism and other constraints on beliefs and other MOs are discussed in section 4.7.

Another somewhat obvious restriction on beliefs that perhaps should be mentioned is that a concrete marker cannot be introduced into the realm of OW through a mere belief since the belief may be about an object of another realm.

## 5.9 Interaction Between Realms

There is no prohibition in SL that prevents one from making statements that relate components of different realms. It is permissible, for example, to speak of a yeti living on the moon even when 'yeti' is restricted to FW and 'moon' is an object of OW. Likewise, one can describe a yeti having a thought about a unicorn and an apple even when 'yeti' and 'unicorn' are restricted to FW and 'apple' is not so restricted. Such a statement would assert that a yeti (individuated in FW) is related to a thought (individuated in MW) and that the thought has one constituent (i.e. 'unicorn') individuated in FW and another (i.e. 'apple') individuated in OW, assuming of course that the thought is about an apple in OW. The nesting of beliefs that contain objects of different realms is also permitted. The following *belief-sequence* is a *wfss* in SL:

<john believes <superman believes <mary saw yeti>>> (40)

where 'superman' and 'yeti' are restricted to FW and 'john' and 'mary' are known objects of OW. The scheme is diagrammed in Figure 19.

---

<john-2 has belief-20>

OW

john-2 john-5 john-8.....

mary-3 mary-4 mary-9...

---

<belief-20 = <superman-6 believes belief-21>>

MW

<belief-21 = <<mary-9 saw yeti-10>>

---

FW

yeti-10 yeti-11...

superman-6 superman-19...

---

Figure 19. Nested Belief Mappings

Numbers have been attached to terms in this figure to reflect individuation so that mappings can be traced. This diagram by no means captures all the complexities involved. Sequence (40) (the original *belief-sequence*), for example, has a set of direct and penumbral inferences (see sections 4.2.1 and 4.2.2), but those inferences are not represented in this figure. Inferencing over statements that contain objects of different realms falls well within the scope of modal inferencing, a subject covered in section 4.7.

CHAPTER 6

# PHILOSOPHICAL CONSIDERATIONS

## 6.1 The Many-valued Approach

The formal system described in this book is being developed for use in artificial intelligence and related disciplines. AI researchers are keenly aware of the fact that without sufficient specificity of description available, there is little hope of enabling a system to handle free conversation with a user. This is evident since human beings have difficulty communicating with one another when specificity is lacking. It seems that a significantly large part of human discourse involving questions and responses is devoted to determining precisely what it is that the questioners wish to know. Lack of specificity can actually drive such a conversation, as the following example illustrates. Assume that the following dialogue took place between two persons, John and Mary.

Mary: "John, did you see the movie?"

John: "Which movie?"

Mary: "The one you said you were going to see."

John: "When did I say that?"

Mary: "Last Sunday."

John: "Oh! Yes, I saw it the other day."

Mary: "Which day was that?"

John: "I believe it was Tuesday."

Mary: "Are you sure of that?"

John: "Come to think of it, I believe it was Monday instead of Tuesday."

From what is given, it appears that the course of this dialogue is determined in part by lack of specificity in questions and responses. Apparently it was not until Mary replied, "Last Sunday" that John was able to determine which movie was being referred to by the original question. Mary's first question failed to set the denotation of the expression "the movie" precisely, and her response to John's request that she identify the movie likewise failed to set the denotation due to a failure to specify time. Once John knew which movie was being referred to, he responded somewhat imprecisely by stating that he saw the movie "the other day." Why did John respond so imprecisely? Perhaps he was not aware of exactly what it was that Mary wanted to know. Her original question seems to indicate that she was only interested in finding out whether he saw the movie, but the whole conversation implies that she may have also been interested in other details about his activity and whereabouts. John answered the question about whether he saw the movie and volunteered additional, yet imprecise, information pertaining to time. One can speculate based on experience why he volunteered that information. He might have added it somewhat gratuitously as part of a habitual mode of expressing himself, or he may have done so intentionally to see whether Mary was interested in pursuing a line of discourse about the temporal reference. He may have been imprecise about the time simply because he might not have been immediately conscious of when he saw the movie and thus chose a convenient type of response, that is, one that would not require him to compute the exact time. The possibilities are numerous. The conversation continued with Mary seeking a more precise determination of time and with John exhibiting what appears to be lack of adequate recall, which forced him to qualify his responses as mere beliefs or approximations. At the end of the reported conversation, Mary still had not received definitive information about when John saw the movie.

The conversation between John and Mary is loaded with imprecision, and it should not take much effort for the reader to realize that the same is true of typical conversation. This example points out that lack of specificity as to time and objects can significantly thwart communication between human beings. Even if a system could understand the language used to communicate, it would have difficulty handling conversation unless it could cope with this kind of imprecision. For example, without having information available that could be used to narrow the scope of reference of the words 'the movie' in Mary's original question, any movie would qualify as a possible referent. A reasonable approach for an AI system to use to solve this kind of problem is the one used by John in this example. He simply solicited the information from Mary. This kind of interactive approach is quite popular in AI perhaps because of a lack of a reasonable alternative under the current state of technology. As discussed in Chapter 3, the many-valued approach holds promise for handling a wide range of problems of imprecision, including problems of the sort given in this example and problems of inadequate query formulation (see section 3.2). This chapter will shed light on the philosophical considerations that led to the adoption of the approach described in this book.

As is diagrammed in Figure 20, the SMS approach draws upon a number of disciplines, including FOL, many-valued logic, modal logic, fuzzy logic and free logic. The reader may wonder whether these logics, classified by some logicians as rivals or extensions of one another, can be employed successfully within a single system. Many-valued logic, for example, is thought by some to rival FOL, whereas modal logic is believed by some to be an extension of FOL (see Haack, 1978; Turner, 1984). Fuzzy logic (e.g. Gaines, 1977; Zadeh, 1979, 1983a) reportedly extends many-valued logic by employing fuzzy quantifiers (e.g. Zadeh, 1983b) and by allowing *truth* itself to become fuzzy (Zadeh, 1975). This book describes how some of the underlying features of these logics have been transformed and incorporated into a single approach. The approach has been used to implement a system called SMS (for 'Symbolic Manipulation System') and is being referred to in this book as the SMS approach. From FOL, the approach borrows certain aspects of quantification, a many-sorted scheme (see e.g. Kleene, 1967, for meaning of 'many-sorted logic') and certain principles of logic, although the principles are stripped of their truth-functionality. From many-valued logic, the approach adopts a many-valued system of evaluation, yet avoids commitment to the truth predicate. From modal logic, the approach adopts some modal concepts but employs them in a many-valued context set in a unique environment. From fuzzy logic, the approach borrows the concept of a linguistic variable, that is, a variable whose values are words or sentences (Zadeh, 1975). From free logic (see e.g. Bencivenga, 1986; LeBlanc and Thomason, 1968; and Cocchiarella, 1966), the approach borrows the idea of using multiple sets of quantifiers to range over the realms of SMS.

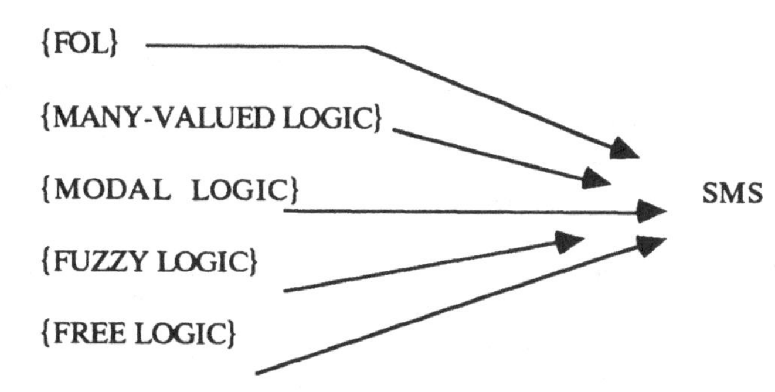


Figure 20. Sources Drawn Upon by SMS

The views expressed herein rest on the belief that a multiple-valued approach that ranges over modal and nonmodal concepts is sorely needed in AI to handle reasoning about the ordinary world. The system SMS employs such an approach. Although some progress along more traditional lines is being reported, the need for this kind of approach has been especially appreciable in the area of knowledge and belief. A case is being made in this book for the position that the SMS approach is appropriate for use in this area, especially in systems that implement some form of conversational mode in which reasoning and responses to queries about the world are to be based on a database of world 'knowledge'. The term 'database' is being used in this book instead of 'knowledge base' because the use of the term 'knowledge' in describing a collection of statements may be taken to require some sort of commitment to a theory of truth. Most people define 'knowledge' in terms of truth. The writer will not quibble with that but does wish to avoid an unnecessary commitment to a theory of 'truth'.

Although the SMS approach employs features of modal logic, many-valued logic, first-order logic, fuzzy logic and free logic, it should be pointed out that the distinction and the legitimacy of these logics are not universally recognized. Some appear to believe that modal logic is not truth-functional, whereas others appear to recognize truth-functionality in the modal realm. Some logicians speak of modal logic and many-valued logic as if the two belong to different realms (e.g. Haack, 1978; Turner, 1984), yet others describe what appear to be many-valued modal logics (Rescher, 1969). Some doubt the very basis of some of these 'deviant' or extended logics, while others doubt the correctness of FOL (e.g. Heyting, 1966). Despite these controversies, these standard and nonstandard logics continue to be usefully employed in AI. Examples of applications of logic in AI can be found in (Dubois and Prade, 1980; Turner, 1984; Genesereth and Nilsson, 1987; Yager *et al*, 1987b; and Smets *et al*, 1988), to name just a few sources.

It is very difficult to sort out and evaluate the views held by logicians on the aforementioned logics. Topics such as whether there is a need for anything more than a two-valued logic seem prone to endless debate. It seems, however, that it not necessary to take sides on some of these issues to develop a formal system suitable for use in AI. The SMS approach is described as being a many-valued *approach* rather than a *logic* because of its avoidance of the truth predicate. It seems appropriate to describe it as being many-valued because it assigns values to statements (cf. propositions) that indicate the extent of their 'presence' (cf. truth) in the system, and those values are drawn from a set containing more than two values. It appears to be well recognized that many-valued logic is concerned with the assignments of values to propositions without necessary regard to whether those values are appropriately called 'truth-values' (McCawley, 1981). Under this view, SMS would qualify as a many-valued logic, yet one most often finds that many-valued systems are described with reference to a theory of truth. Thus, to avoid needless objection and confusion, the term 'approach' rather than 'logic' is being used to describe the system. Sections 6.2 and 6.3 have more to say about whether SMS qualifies as a logistic system. For descriptions of some systems that employ values that, strictly speaking, are not truth-values, see [Belnap, 1977] and the discussions in [McCawley, 1981, at pages 360-361].

The terminology 'many-valued approach' is being used to describe SMS for the purpose of distinguishing it from traditional many-valued logistic systems and from fuzzy systems grounded in fuzzy set theory. Zadeh (1975) has asserted that fuzzy logic differs from many-valued *logic* because fuzzy logic employs fuzzy quantifiers, whereas many-valued logic employs only 'all' and 'some' as quantifiers, and because fuzzy logic allows *truth* itself to become fuzzy. The term 'many-valued approach' can be construed in a broad sense to include any approach that employs a many-valued system. Under this construction the many-valued approach would include the fuzzy approach since a fuzzy subset of a given domain of objects can be seen as a predicate whose truth-values are drawn from the unit interval [0,1] rather than from the set {0,1}, as would be the case for an ordinary set (Yager, 1986). Since the interval [0,1] contains an infinite number of values, it can be seen that the notion of a fuzzy subset rests upon a system of multiple values (Yager, 1986). It has been noted in [Gaines and Kohout, 1977, at page 415], for example, that a close relation exists between Zadeh's fuzzy logic and the infinite-valued logic $L_1$ first studied by Lukasiewicz (1920). Thus, in the sense that fuzzy logic may be viewed as a generalization of multiple-valued logic (e.g. Zadeh, 1985), the fuzzy approach seems to fall within the scope of the many-valued *approach*.

## 6.2 Is a Theory of Truth Really Necessary?

The fact that validity in SMS is defined with reference to a many-valued set might cause those who are accustomed to thinking in terms of standard truth theory to shy away from the approach as an initial reaction. In commenting on the importance of explicitly representing in the data structures of a program as much as possible of what a system needs to know, Levesque (1986) describes some properties he believes that structures forming a knowledge base must possess. One of the properties he mentions is that for the structures to represent knowledge, it must be possible to interpret them as propositional expressions in a language with a *truth theory*. In other words, one should be able to say what the world would have to be like for one of those propositional expressions to be true. Having described this property in terms of propositions and a truth theory, he goes on to assert that:

> " Wanting to deal with truth-preserving operations over symbolic structures puts us in the domain of *logic*." (Levesque, 1986, at page 258)

Later, he asserts that it is generally recognized that representation languages need an accompanying theory of truth and maintains, citing Hayes (1974), that without "some concrete specification of the meaning of a notational convention, what is implied by an expression in that language is unclear . . . ." (Levesque, 1986, at page 260). It appears, however, that not everyone would agree with this view. It has been asserted for example that "the truth-conditional conception of meaning is far from being commonly accepted" (Wojcicki, 1988, at page 180). Considering the fact that a truth theory has not been specified for SMS, how does the system stand in view of these remarks? SMS has been defined as a set of formal operations over SL representations without making any commitment to a theory of truth. This is not to say that such theory cannot be specified, but only that it has not been done. SMS has been sufficiently developed from a syntactical perspective to qualify as a formal system, and at first glance it would seem that a theory of truth could be specified for it without much difficulty. Seemingly, all one would have to do to establish such a theory would be to map the values of the many-valued system of SMS into the set {T,F} where appropriate. The value 'IPR', for example, could be mapped to the value 'T'.

Although it appears that a theory of truth can be specified for SMS, one might question whether it is needed. SMS is a system into which one enters SL statements to build a database. All SMS is designed to do when presented with a query (also an SL statement) is to determine whether the query is 'present' in the database in one of the specially defined senses of 'presence' recognized by the system. SMS assigns values to statements that indicate the extent to which, if any, they are present in the database. The values are drawn from the set {IPR, ..., NPR-IC}, where 'IPR' signifies presence ('*i*s *pr*esent') and 'NPR-IC' signifies nonpresence due to inconsistency ('*n*ot *pr*esent because of *in*consistency'). Section 3.3 gives a complete enumeration of the elements of the set. Given any SL statement, a determination of whether that statement is present in the database of SMS amounts to determining whether it matches a statement present in the database in a sense recognized by the system. It might be said that if a query matches a database statement, it is *true* that the query is present in the database, but in this context, what does being *true* contribute beyond that which is given by being *present*?

It is sometimes asserted that the meaning of a sentence of classical logic is given by the conditions under which it is true (Giles, 1985). This principle can be broadened to accommodate many-valued logic (MVL). The meaning of a sentence $\Phi$ in MVL might be given by stating for each $v_i \in V$, where V is a set of values containing more than two elements, the conditions under which the value of $\Phi$ is $v_i$ (Giles, 1985). In SMS, since V = {IPR, ..., NPR-IC} (see section 3.3), the *meaning* of $\Phi$ would be defined by stating the conditions under which the following value assignments would be made: $\Phi$ = IPR, ..., $\Phi$ =NPR-IC. Any SL statement either is or is not in the database of SMS. Any statement in the database receives a value of 'IPR', which signifies the strongest sense of presence known to the system. Any other SL statement receives a value indicative of the extent to which it matches a statement present in the database. Thus the meaning of Φ would be defined by the procedures (cf. Woods, 1968) that determine the presence or nonpresence of an identical statement (see section 4.3 on the relation of identity) in the database, which means that meaning in this sense is determined by the derivational and matching procedures of SMS. This corresponds to the way meaning is defined in expert systems in terms of matching and proof procedures. Within the fuzzy realm, it corresponds to the approach used in *test-score semantics* in which the meaning of a semantic entity (e.g. a proposition or quantifier) is taken to to be a *test*, which when applied to the database yields a collection of partial test scores. The scores are then aggregated into an overall vector test score whose components are numbers in the unit interval. The overall score measures the compatibility of the semantic entity with the database (Zadeh, 1983b, 1986). In SMS, there are six possibilities for a statement Φ, where Φ ranges over *wfsss*:

1) Φ precisely matches a database statement;

2) Φ matches a database statement in a penumbral (cf. fuzzy) way (see sections 4.2.2 and 4.6);

3) Φ is directly derivable from the database;

4) Φ is derivable from the database in a penumbral sense (see sections 4.2.2 and 11.3);

5) the negation of Φ matches a database statement in a way that excludes the possibility of the presence of Φ; or

6) Φ does not match a database statement and is not derivable from the database.

All statements present in the database in a physical sense as well as all statements derivable from those statements are deemed to be *present* in the database. Any external SL statement either matches a database statement or receives the value 'NPR' or 'NPR-IC', either of which signifies nonpresence of some sort. The *presence* of a statement Φ in the database of SMS indicates that:

a) Φ is *consistent* with all other statements in the database (see section 11.7); and

b) any statement that matches Φ will be assigned the same value as Φ.

No statement is allowed to enter the database if it is internally inconsistent or if one or more of its derivations are inconsistent with any statement already present. Section 11.7 on consistency describes consistency maintenance (cf. truth maintenance) in more detail.

The power of SMS has been augmented by the adoption of a flexible concept of value. A 'value' is defined to be any expression, whether atom, phrase or sentential expression, that is assigned to another expression or to itself by any valuation function within the system. Thus, a statement $\Phi_i$ may have either itself or another statement, phrase or atom as its value. This feature allows for a database statement such as '<john isa person>' to be assigned a value in the form of a related expression such as '<<person<male>> or <person <female>>>' in certain contexts.

One could argue that the statements 'present' in the database can be taken to be true statements, and thus it could be asserted that the notion of 'presence' as used in SMS is nothing more than the notion of truth in disguise. In defense of the SMS approach, one may question whether the notion of truth is really appropriate for use in the system. As is discussed in section 4.2.2, derivations in SMS serve multiple purposes, some of which have nothing to do with truth-based semantics. Thus, to impose truth-functional semantic interpretations on notational conventions could have adverse effects, as the following example illustrates. The sequence:

<john cause <mary is happy>> (41)

is a sentential expression in SL that relates the linguistic object 'john' to the linguistic object '<mary is happy>'. The sequence corresponds to an English statement that would assert that 'John made Mary happy'. When one views the matter from a truth-functional perspective and is given the truth of sequence (41), one might be inclined to conclude that the sequence '<mary is happy>' is true just as one would draw conclusions about the happiness of Mary if given the truth of the English statement 'John made Mary happy'. But does it make sense to conclude the truth of a causal connection between 'john' and 'mary' from this sequence? Most people would say no since given the English version, it would not follow that 'John caused Mary', yet SMS would recognize a certain kind of causal connection between 'john' and 'mary' as part of its inferencing operations. Given that the system could make use of such an inference, especially as part of is nonreferentially-based operations, the reader should consider how inconvenient it would be to have to define this inference as a logical consequence. It is easy to define a notion of presence to allow a connection of this sort to be 'present' in the database based solely on syntactical considerations. What SMS would do in this situation is to produce a special kind of inference that would bear the following form:

<john <xcaused <$\theta$>> mary>

where 'xcaused' is a special causal link and '$\theta$' represents a description of the meaning of the causal link in this context. Causal links are assigned rankings of strength of presence, and 'xcaused' is one of the weakest links recognized in the system, whereas 'caused' is one of the strongest. In this example, '$\theta$' would define by description what basis there is for using a weakened link in this context. If in SMS the expression '<john <xcaused <$\theta$>> mary>' follows from sequence (41), how would one go about employing truth-functional notions to justify a description of the expression as a logical consequence of the given sequence? This sequence is not 'true' in any normal sense of truth even if it is given that sequence (41) is true. This is not to say that it would be inappropriate or impossible to assign some grade or measure of truth to the statement. A system of fuzzy logic (see e.g. Gaines, 1977; Zadeh, 1979, 1983a) that treats truth as a linguistic variable and allows values such as 'more or less true' and 'not very false' might very well be able to assign a grade of truth to the sequence; however, considering the non-truth-functional level at which SMS is defined and its orientation toward a conversational mode of expression, it is not necessary to resort to gradations of truth to enable the system to carry out its tasks.

One reason why it is difficult to employ truth-functional notions in situations such as the one being described is that the inferencing tasks are being pushed into the modal realm. Because of the avoidance of a commitment to the truth predicate, SMS avoids some of the difficulties that a truth-functional approach might encounter in these circumstances. An attempt to employ truth-functional notions in this area seemingly would cause more problems than benefits. At the very least, one might have to deal with gradations of truth to keep the many-valued approach in tact, and that in itself might raise a host of objections (but not from those fuzzy logicists who recognize gradations of truth without reservation). Some logicians have attempted to avoid this problem by employing a non-truth-functional, probabilistic approach (see Rescher, 1969, at pages 184-188), but as was revealed in section 3.5, a probabilistic approach seemingly would not be completely adequate for the tasks that SMS is to perform in a conversational environment. SMS assigns values to the derivability relation that are not traceable to truth-functional notions nor are they probabilistically based. Instead, they are defined with reference to their *utility* in a particular mode of operations that are designed to simulate human conversation and associated reasoning. The point is that some of those operations do not correspond to the preservation of semantic properties over propositional structures. It is in this respect that the approach derives the most from the informal view described earlier in section 1.1.

The reader might object to this way of doing things on the grounds that in these circumstances it would not seem that the notion of presence could fare any better than the notion of truth. It could be argued that just as one would have to resort to degrees or shades of truth to preserve the many-valued approach, one would have to do the same with the notion of presence. Is it any more legitimate to speak of degrees of presence than to speak of truth in that way? Admittedly, the use of the term 'presence' in its ordinary sense would cause problems of the sort suggested by this question. Fortunately, it is not necessary to employ the notion in this way. In fact, the notion need not be used at all as a system concept. The term 'presence' has been adopted solely for expository convenience. Technically, it should be classified as part of the metalanguage used to describe SMS. It is not fair to say, for example, that the expression '<john <xcaused

<θ>> mary>' is 'present' in the expression '<john caused <mary is happy>>' in any normal sense of the term 'presence'. The term 'presence' (or 'present') is used to prompt the reader to make familiar associations that hopefully will make the reading of this material a little easier. An otherwise meaningless expression, say 'p*ff*ent', could have been used instead of 'presence' as a descriptive term. This at least would have the advantage of drawing attention to the the real issue at hand, which is: Given that a query has been determined to be 'p*ff*ent' in the database (or perhaps 'p*ff*ent to some extent x', where x represents some gradation of p*ff*ent), how is this useful to the system or to the user? The discussions in Chapter 3 attempt to answer this question by showing that such a description can be employed advantageously in simulating the way human beings respond to one another in ordinary discourse. Section 6.3 discusses some semantical considerations that are relevant for this approach.

## 6.3 More on Semantics

For the most part, SMS has thus far been described from a syntactical point of view. The discussions now turn to the semantic foundations of the system. What do SL statements mean? This question will be answered in the context of discussing how semantic theory has been used in AI. It should be noted that the term *semantics* has no standard interpretation. Almost everyone agrees that the term is to be defined with reference to *meaning* of some sort, but there is wide disagreement about the meaning of *meaning* in this context. Whereas to a philosopher the term 'semantics' may describe the activity of searching out the very foundations of the world and the language used to describe it, to the linguist it may involve an attempt to determine how language originates as a human phenomenon and how it is used to interact with the world. In mathematics and logic, it has come to be known as the method by which meaning is assigned to the language of logic and mathematics (see e.g. Nute, 1981).

By far the most widely accepted method in logic and mathematics is the Tarskian, correspondence-based theory of semantics. The method, introduced by Tarski and later improved by Carnap, is truth-functional and model-theoretic in that the meaning of the language is defined with reference to a formal model of the world onto which functions map terms to their denotations. The theory is truth-functional in that the truth of sentences in the language depends on whether the sentences correctly describe what is true in the model. The strength of this theory is that its assertions can be written in set theory syntax, and its theorems can be proven by logically valid steps (Martin, 1987).

The Tarskian approach to semantics has become quite popular in AI, even to the point that some researchers have taken the position that they will not accept a theory that is non-denotational, at least not in an area that lends itself to an analysis in terms of denotations (McDermott, 1978). The basic idea in Tarskian-based semantics is that constant terms and predicate terms are assigned precise denotations in a formal model of the world. The 'meaning' of a constant is its denotation in the model, that is, the entity that it stands for, and the meaning of a predicate term is its extension, that is, the set of ordered n-tuples for which the predicate holds in the world model. The meaning of a one-place predicate 'F' would consist of the set of all the objects in the model for which the predicate F holds. The meaning of an n-place predicate 'G' is the set of all n-tuples in the world model, say M, for which the predicate holds. Any well-formed atomic sentence of the language, formed say by joining a constant symbol, say *a*, to a predicate symbol, say *F*, to produce the sentence *Fa*, is either 'true' or 'false' depending on whether the object denoted by *a* in M is a member of the extension of *F* in M. Logical connectives, such as conjunction, are defined for joining sentences to create complex objects whose truth-values are determined with reference to the truth-values of their constituent sentences. This brings about compositionality of meaning. The truth-value of the complex sentence '*Fa* • *Ga*,' where '•' is the connective for conjunction, is a function of the truth-values of its constituent sentences, that is, *Fa* and *Ga*. These features, coupled with the fact that quantification can be precisely defined and understood with reference to this scheme, provide a neat and powerful semantic theory for first-order systems.

The truth-functional, correspondence theory has well-known limitations, however. It is not adequate to handle statements about knowledge and belief, for example, at least not without making significant additions to the theory. The same is true with regard to modal statements. Nonetheless, the theory has been widely used as a tool for testing the semantic foundations of AI systems. Most important, perhaps, is the fact that the usefulness of the theory in the first-order context has convinced many people that it is worthwhile to attempt to specify a formal semantics for any language that purports to be a KR language. There have been numerous attempts, for example, to establish adequate formal semantics for epistemic and modal languages (e.g. Moore, 1985), many of which have adopted the *possible worlds* approach (see Hintikka, 1962) to formal semantics. By employing the possible worlds concept, one can posit worlds that *are, might be, should be, are permissible, are probable* or *are imaginable*. The possibilities seem limitless. One important benefit that can be achieved by using this approach is that a statement that is qualified by an epistemic or modal term, say the word 'ought', can be relegated to a world consisting of what 'ought to be', and there the statement can be handled by methods that correspond to the conventional methods employed in the ordinary first-order setting or by special methods designed for that particular ontological realm. As yet, no such attempt has yielded completely satisfactory results, although some of the results seem promising.

A discussion of semantic theory employed in AI need not confine itself to any particular brand of formal semantics, or to formal semantics in general for that matter. A number of researchers have questioned the necessity of providing such a formal semantics for a system as a prerequisite to its acceptability. Others have adopted 'semantic' theories that do not precisely fit the model-theoretic notion described above, yet which seem to address important semantical matters. Perhaps the best way to proceed to describe 'semantics' in general in AI is to employ some scheme that can be used to classify various theories that have been adopted. Hirst (1987) has suggested such a scheme. It seems that the theories employed lend themselves to classification based on the degree to which the linguistic objects they recognize are interpreted, that is, assigned meaning (see Hirst, 1987, at p. 34). *Procedural semantics* (e.g. Woods, 1968), in which the meaning of sentences is defined by the procedures that process them, is an example of a semantic theory that has been employed in a number of systems. Some critics of this theory claim that the procedures which manipulate the symbols do not themselves have adequate interpretations, nor do the symbols that are manipulated. The *knowledge semantics* of Tarnawsky (1982) is an example of a theory that gives interpretations to a limited set of objects, that is, sentences, by employing a knowledge base as a semantic model. The components of sentences, however, are not interpreted. *Object-oriented semantics* (e.g. Hirst, 1987), builds upon knowledge semantics by providing interpretations of the components of sentences by replacing the components with references or pointers to knowledge structures, such as frame structures or semantic nets. A system described by Hirst (1987) employs this theory through implementation of a semantic interpreter for sentences and phrases. Hirst defines 'SEMANTIC INTERPRETATION' to mean a process by which syntactically analyzed natural language is mapped to a representation of its meaning. Absity, the semantic interpreter used in the system, employs a parser and the frame-based language Frail 2.1 (Charniak *et al*, 1983), which reportedly is a development of the Frail frame language (see e.g. Charniak, 1981), to carry out the interpretation.

Within this context, how does one go about describing the semantical foundations of SL and SMS. Section 1.3 discusses how a partial specification of the semantic theory upon which the system is grounded can be accomplished using the model-theoretic approach. This can be done by considering the database of the system to be a world model. It seems reasonable to view the database in this way because for the most part it is a structure containing relations between individuated objects. The markers (cf. constants) of SL have denotations in the database, and its links (cf. predicates) have extensions. It is perhaps difficult to understand how a link like 'xcause' could have an extension in the model, but from a formal standpoint it is possible to identify a set of ordered tuples of individuated objects for which the relation holds in the database. Not only that, but it seems that the link can be given an extension in the world by mapping to causal events in the world that reflect the structures in which this kind of relation holds. After all, the link does little more than flag the fact that the subject of the link is either the sole agent or a 'participant' in an event or state that bears a causal relation to an event or state that involves the object of the link. In the last analysis, links are symbols for relations, and they can be mapped to extensions, whether in the database or in the external world. The symbol 'xcause' stands for a particular kind of relation that may hold between objects in the database. It can also be taken to stand for relations in the external world that are entailed in causal events that bear describable structures of a particular type. What might make the meaning of some links difficult to grasp is not that the relations they stand for cannot be identified or assigned extensions, but that the *significance of the relations may not be immediately appreciable* to someone not familiar with how they are to be used. But this is not a basis for questioning the semantic foundations of the system. It is really a question of *utility*. It is a question of whether these links are useful in view of the tasks to be performed by the system, but that issue is beyond the scope of the current discussion [see Chapter 4 for some discussion about why such weak relations (links) are recognized in SMS].

Another semantic issue pertains to the interpretation of the values assigned to statements. If the values are not truth-values, what are they? What do they mean? These values can be explained with reference either to the database of SMS or to the external world. They describe special relations between objects or statements in the database or between objects, states or events in the external world. Chapters 2-5 discuss some of the pragmatic justifications for using the values to describe relations between the kind of statements that occur in ordinary discourse. Later chapters will show that there is a mapping from a subset of the inference patterns of SMS into the inference patterns used in FOL and that therefore, if one really wishes to do so, a truth-preserving capability can be demonstrated for SMS. The value 'IPR' of SMS, for example, can be mapped to the value 'T' of two-valued logic. Thus, if one has difficulty with the employment of a many-valued scheme in the SMS setting, it can be argued that the difficulty is not rooted in any lack of a semantic foundation for the system, at least not within what might be considered a first-order domain. Admittedly, the semantic theory of SMS in the modal and epistemic realms is not fully defined, but the same seems to be true for truth-functional logic in these areas. As is the case with links, questions about the use of multiple values resolve into questions of utility. It might be asserted, for example, that in some cases what is done in SMS with a many-valued system could be done using a two-valued logic, but this not a basis for questioning the semantics of the system, but only its utility as compared to two-valued logic. This question of utility is beyond the scope of the present discussion but is covered in other Chapters (see Chapter 3, for example).

Before closing this chapter, something should be said about how the avoidance of the truth predicate affects the operations of the system. Section 6.4 addresses this subject.

## 6.4 Effects of Avoidance of the Truth Predicate

Although the avoidance of the truth predicate seems to produce some advantages, it causes stress to be placed on the component that is to maintain consistency in the database. Because of the absence of an ordinary theory of truth, operations that maintain consistency must be defined for a many-valued scheme. SMS uses a set of syntactically-based rules to govern what items may enter the database. It does not allow any statement to enter if it would be inconsistent with any statement already present, which corresponds to truth maintenance in other systems. This produces effects and benefits similar to those produced in systems in which database statements are assumed to be true assertions, and it also grounds the consistency-based approach to nonmonotonic reasoning that is used in the system (see section 4.8 on nonmonotonic reasoning). SMS does allow inconsistency to exist between some components that have only penumbral presence in the system, but for any component in which derivations are to be produced in a way that corresponds to ordinary inferencing, consistency is maintained in that component. Section 11.7 describes the theory behind consistency maintenance in SMS.

The task of maintaining consistency in the database is particularly difficult since SMS often must handle what corresponds to *eternal sentences*, that is, sentences that stay true forever, or false forever, independently of any special circumstances under which they happen to be written or uttered (Quine, 1986). Often that kind of sentence must be loaded with detail to distinguish the matters to which it refers from all other matters in the universe of discourse. Sentences of arithmetic and physics are generally recognized examples of eternal sentences. Ordinary assertions of fact can be converted into eternal sentences, so it seems, by supplying names and dates and by canceling the tenses of verbs. An eternal version of the assertion 'It is raining,' to use one of Quine's examples, would be 'It rains in Boston, Mass., on July 15, 1968' (Quine, 1986, at page 13).

It is well known that logical analysis is facilitated by requiring that each statement be true once and for all or false once and for all (Quine, 1980). Typically, descriptions of first-order logistic systems are made using sentences that are not eternal in this sense. It is left to the readers imagination to expand the sentences into full and eternal statements. This technique avoids the difficulty of having to represent all the associated details just to make a point, which is fine as long as the system has some way of handling those details if in fact they are represented. SL is being designed to allow statements to contain this kind of detail, which is more than can be said of some other languages. It appears that AI systems will have to be able to access expanded, eternal versions of assertions of fact to be able simulate human reasoning most effectively. Having expanded versions available dramatically increases the opportunity to do in-depth reasoning, but at the same time it seems that processing problems increase proportionally.

On the positive side, by having not made the semantic ascent to the truth predicate (see Quine, 1986 for a discussion of the importance of the semantic ascent for FOL), SMS finds itself in a position of being able to avoid existential import in its use of SL (see section 7.1). Thus, for example, a notion such as predication need not be defined as a relation between something that exists and a general concept, the relation exemplifying truth or falsity in relation to reality (cf. Strawson, 1974). Instead, such a notion can be defined merely in terms of relations between linguistic objects and their locations in spaces or realms, which somehow seems more appropriate for a formal approach (see section 7.1). However, if one wishes to do so, a more standard notion of existence can be used in the system by assigning existential import to quantifiers of the particular sort (see section 7.1).

It seems that SMS avoids a host of problems merely by failing to adopt some of the standard FOL notions of truth, existence, predication, and quantification. By avoiding the standard definition of predication, according to which a predicate is joined with one or more constants or variables to produce a sentence, SMS is able to treat terms in isolation that otherwise would have to be handled indirectly as part of the process that treats the sentences of which they are a part. This allows the derivability relation to be defined over individual terms and expressions instead of over sentences only, as is the case in FOL. The produces important benefits (see section 4.6). This is not to say that there is no correspondence between these notions and the way that symbols are manipulated in SMS, but only that it appears certain problems can be avoided by not adopting some of the standard notions.

The basic approach used in SMS is to define everything, including the derivation process, in terms of relations between spatial locations and their contents and to do so without having to deal with many of the syntactical and conceptual constraints imposed by FOL. AI researchers who have implemented reasoning systems from the ground up have likely had to do something similar to implement their systems. Since in many instances the results produced by SMS are similar to those produced by FOL, explaining things in terms of these relations often amounts to explaining aspects of FOL in those terms. SMS has unique features, however, that must be be explained and justified independently. It is not feasible to attempt to explain everything using the details of location and content. It is thus necessary to adopt some descriptive conventions to bring the discussions to a higher level. One method employed is to speak of different realms or worlds within the system and to assign familiar names and descriptions to them. Although not technically demarcated as actual regions, these realms are nonetheless indirectly appreciable and bear heavily on the derivation process. In this respect the system bears resemblance to many-sorted logic, the realms corresponding to domains of objects over which variables may range.

## CHAPTER 7

# SMS COMPARED AND CONTRASTED WITH FOL

## 7.1 FOL

Eventually it may be demonstrated that everything that can be said can be said in FOL. If methods are developed to resolve problems associated with the treatment of mental and emotional objects, adverbials, and event individuation, it would seem that FOL would be well on its way to achieving *expressive* completeness. This book takes no position on whether this will come about, but the writer's personal belief is that if FOL does not achieve full completeness, it will come so close to doing so that the lack of completeness will hardly be noticed.

The views presented in this book are offered under the *assumption* that FOL can and will achieve expressive completeness. This provides an expository environment in which it is not necessary to debate whether SL is a notational variant of FOL, since under the assumption, everything that can be said in SL can be said in FOL, and thus it seems that SL could be classified as a notational variant of FOL. It is also readily admitted that SL is less powerful than FOL in terms of generality since, at present, no claim is being made that everything that can be said may be said in SL. Having made these remarks, the scope of the following discussions can be specified. The matter at issue is whether the system SMS is better suited for certain tasks than FOL.

SMS is built upon primitive notions of sameness and otherness. A few assumptions are added to bring about the environment in which SMS can be defined. The assumption made in SMS that instances (tokens) of a sign or symbol are equisignificant (e.g Reichenbach, 1947) should not raise any eyebrows, and the extension of the categories of sign and token to include not only primitive signs and tokens but also complex ones (e.g. individuated sequences of tokens) does not appear to be cause for alarm. This allows the recognition of equisignificance to extend to complex tokens, which in turn, provides the basis for the basic derivation mechanism, which is based on *matching*. Two expressions match one another in in this sense when they are syntactically identical as defined in section 4.3. A *wfss* is derivable from an SMS database if it matches either a database statement or a legitimate transformation of one or more database statements. The familiar *modus ponens* of FOL presupposes similar notions of equisignificance since given the formulas 'p $\supset$ q' and 'p', the derivation of 'q' depends upon the two instances of 'p' being recognized as equisignificant.

The descriptions of SMS given in this book are offered in the context of a postulated spatial ordering and set of capabilities. The postulated capabilities are employed to partition the spatial ordering to accommodate particular needs. The system has recognitive, marking, numbering, remembering, accessing, copying, storing, and executory capabilities built into it, and these combine to form other operations within the system (cf. Newell, 1980; Sowa, 1984). The ability to name and recognize locations and objects, combined with an ability to access localities and transport or copy their contents, enables the executory functions ('functions' here understood in a nonmathematical sense) to carry out basic manipulations. The two basic operations are:

1) the creation of new objects (e.g. sequences, sets, sentences, equivalences, and transformations); and

2) the production of or recognition of derivations.

Although SMS has built-in capabilities and is set in a special environment, this should not prevent it from attaining status as a formal system since other formal systems, including FOL, either explicitly or implicitly make similar postulations. The notion of sequence, for example, at some point must enter the realm of mathematics. The postulated spatial ordering of SMS could be considered to be a sequence of 1, ..., n positions, where 'n' is equal to the end of the last space that may be occupied by a linguistic object in the system. On this score, at least, it seems that SMS theory has been specified within legitimate formal limits.

As mentioned in Chapter 6, the SMS approach avoids a truth-functional involvement with reality, and this brings about ontological freedom. The approach adopts the idea of using spaces (partitions) and relations between them to define and constrain symbolic manipulations within the system. Each space can be taken to correspond to an ontological category, and linguistic objects simply occur within the spaces. Occurrence within a particular space does not in itself give an object any sort of ontological precedence over any other since all categories are assumed to have the same ontological ranking. However, an ontological ranking can be assigned to the set of spaces if one wishes to do so. The version of SMS described in this book gives the space SW (Spiritual World) precedence over other spaces (see section 5.5).

The realms of SMS constitute 'reality' within the system. From this perspective, the spaces share equally in 'reality', and every concretely individuated object in the system enjoys the same existential status. This corresponds to a scheme of partitioned networks in which existential quantification is implied (see e.g. Hendrix, 1979). In other words, it is possible to define the notions of existence and quantification in this setting in a way that makes the 'occurrence' of a *concretely* individuated object in a space equivalent to 'existence' in that space. Existence in this sense can be described through use of a one-place link that has been created in SL to accommodate the notion. The expression '<ann exists>', for example, can be used to capture desired effects pertaining to the existence of 'ann'. In the current version, one may use the link 'exist', as well as its derivatives and alternative forms, to explicitly represent information about existence. This corresponds to treating 'existence' as a predicate, which has been done under some approaches (see e.g. Hobbs, 1985). The default mechanism of the system, if pressed on the matter by a query about the existence of an object, is being designed to conclude that the object 'exists' in a realm if the object is *concretely* individuated in that realm and if there is no assertion to the effect that the object does not exist in that realm.

It should be noted that although quantifiers of the particular sort are used in SMS, it is not necessary to assign existential import to them. A statement such as:

<barron likes <movie<some>>>

need not be taken to assert that there is some concrete marker $\alpha_1$ in the system such that 'barron likes $\alpha_1$'. As mentioned in section 2.3.2, the system would not concretely individuate the label 'movie' in this statement but would create a quantifier-marker for the label. It is not necessary to interpret either that marker or the expression for which it is created to mean that there is a concrete marker in the system that is related to 'barron' in the way described by this statement. Given that the statement does not assert the presence of such a concrete marker, one may not infer from this statement alone that the 'movie' exists, at least not under the interpretation of 'exists' that calls for the presence of a concrete marker. As will be described in section 10.2, under the quantification theory of SMS, a quantifier-marker names a set of objects, and one may assert explicitly that a concrete marker is a member of that set. If such an assertion is made, one may infer that the quantified object 'exists'. Otherwise, the system may not be in a position to know whether or not the set named by the quantifier marker contains a concrete marker. Sections 10.2 describes this aspect of quantification in more detail.

This having been said, it should be pointed out that there is no prohibition against assigning existential import to the particular quantifier. If it is important to be able to make statements about 'existence' in a particular implementation or application of SMS theory, one may assign existential import to quantifiers of the particular sort. When that is done, the particular quantifier is interpreted to mean that at least one concrete marker holds the relation(s) that is specified for the quantified object, and thus one may infer that the object 'exists' based on the presence of the associated quantifier. Quantifiers of the particular sort are given this interpretation in section 10.2 in order to explain the quantification theory adopted for SMS. The primary difference in effect between this approach and the one that does not assign existential import to the particular quantifier is that under the latter approach, to be able to infer that the quantified object 'exists', one must explicitly assert that a concrete marker is a member of the set referred to by the quantifier-marker. Under the former approach, the set is assumed to contain a concrete marker. Chapter 10 gives an overview of the theory behind quantification in SMS.

Since a general overview of SL has been given in previous chapters, a comparison can be made between SL and a first-order language, leaving aside for the moment the question whether the proper comparison should be with FOL or with the language of higher-order logic. FOL typically has:

1) variables (e.g. x, y, z);
2) constants (e.g. a, b, c);
3) predicates (e.g. A, B, C);
4) connectives (e.g. ~, •, →)
5) quantifiers (e.g. ∀, E)
6) functions (e.g. *f*, *g*)

Each of these components will be compared and contrasted with corresponding components of SMS.

### 7.2 Variables

All three categories of noun labels bear similarity to variables of FOL in that they stand in positions in SL sentences that correspond to the positions that variables occupy in FOL, that is, positions that names may occupy. Labels function as variables until they are individuated. All labels are individuated in some sense as they enter the DB. Those with quantifiers retain characteristics that are traditionally associated with variables of FOL, and for that reason it is proper to speak of variables when describing SL. Any noun or link label that is not *concretely* individuated because of the presence of a quantifier is assigned a *quantifier-marker* that functions as a variable (see section 10.2).

### 7.3 Constants

A strong comparison can be made between SL and FOL in the use of constants. Markers of quantifier-free labels correspond to constants in FOL.

### 7.4 Predicates

It is here that some differences between SL and FOL begin to emerge. Just as FOL employs a set of n-ary predicates, SL uses a set of n-ary *links*, and in some ways, links function as predicates do in FOL. The role of a link can be understood in part with reference to the rules for constructing wffs. These rules specify that a sequence cannot qualify as a *wfss* unless a link or link phrase occupies the second position in the sequence. A link (whether 2-place or n-place, where n > 2) connects noun labels, noun markers, *wfs*s, or a permissible combination of these linguistic objects. As is explained in section 10.5, the nature of the link forms part of the basis for individuating formalisms and events in SL. In other words, the link is taken to be a distinguishing feature of the expression of which it is a part. Another and no less important function is to serve as a basis for mapping *sentence-sequences* into related expressions such as *expansions* (section 4.9) and *normal forms* (section 4.4).

Basically, links perform the function normally connoted by the term 'link' in ordinary English. They merely link linguistic objects, a function not unheard of in the realm of the logician (see Mercier, 1912). This somewhat austere functionality allows certain linguistic objects to acquire statuses they do not hold in FOL. Predication in FOL, for example, joins predicates with constants or bound variables to form atomic sentences. In SL, links connect not only objects that correspond to constant symbols of FOL, but also linguistic objects that otherwise would be constituents of predicates. The term 'is' is a link in SL that connects two linguistic objects. The sequence '<mary is happy>' is a *wfss* that employs the link 'is' to connect 'mary' and 'happy'. By treating 'is' as a link in this way, the term 'happy' in this example is placed in the position of a noun in the sequence and thus can be treated as a noun in certain ways, one of the most important of which is to allow it to be quantified. As will be seen in Chapter 10, not only may terms such as 'happy' be quantified, but also, in certain instances, the *links* themselves. This feature pushes SL beyond FOL into the realm of higher-order languages. As desirable as it may be to extend SL in this way, it is not necessary to do so. It is possible to restrict SL in a way that requires adjectives and links to be converted into noun forms prior to quantifying over them so that they may used as names in the traditional way employed in FOL. For the moment, such a restriction will be adopted for expository purposes so that the correspondence with FOL in this regard can continue to be relied upon.

One of the most important results brought about by the use of links is that modal features can be incorporated into SMS through them. For example, links such as 'believe' and 'know' are used to introduce 'beliefs' and 'knowledge' into the system (see e.g. sections 5.8 and 4.7 for discussions on belief), and occurrences of the link 'cause' serve as focal points for the operations that deal with causality. As part of the event individuation process being developed for the system, these links can be individuated and treated as objects that may bear relations to other objects. An individuated link can be related to one or more temporal descriptions through one or more temporal links as part of the process of individuation.

The adoption of the *links* concept allows still another contrast between SL and FOL to be appreciated. Whereas the terms 'and' and 'or' are connectives in FOL, they are links in SL. A sequence that contains the link 'and' will be referred to as a *conjunctive* sequence, and a sequence that contains the link 'or' will be referred to as an *alternative* sequence. A sequence that contains both 'and' and 'or' links will be referred to as a *combinative* sequence. Links function somewhat differently in SL than do connectives in FOL. For one thing, links are not defined truth-functionally. This is not to say that there are no similarities between the roles played by links and connectives. The compound statement:

John is happy, and Mary is happy.

can be cast into the first-order form (without names):

E(x,y)(Jx • Hx • My • Hy)

where 'J' means 'has John-hood' ('John-hood' being a unique property), 'H' means 'is happy', and 'M' means 'has Mary-hood' ('Mary-hood' being a unique property). In a form appropriate for the propositional calculus the statement could be expressed as:

(P • Q)

where 'P' and 'Q' represent the constituent sentences. From this expression one may deduce 'P', for example, under the law of simplification. In SL the original statement could be represented as follows as a sequence, the first and third elements of which are sequences:

<<john is happy> and <mary is happy>>.

This sequence passes the test for a *wfss* in SL, which among other things requires that the second position in the sequence be occupied by a link. Although classified as a 'link', the term 'and' in this case operates much like the FOL connective '•' in that the sequence '<john is happy>' and the sequence '<mary is happy>' are each derivable from the given sequence under the derivation rules of SMS.

Although the derivational results produced by FOL and SMS are similar in this example, one does not have to look far to find differences between links and the connectives of FOL. The following example illustrates the point. The statement :

John or Mary is happy.

would be converted into a compound statement in FOL with the connective 'v' connecting the constituent sentences, e.g:

(P v Q)

where 'P' = 'John is happy' and 'Q' = 'Mary is happy', or into:

E(x,y)[ Jx • My • (Hx v Hy) ]

where 'J' means 'has John-hood', 'M' means 'has Mary-hood', and 'H' means 'is happy'. In SL, no such conversion takes place, and the derivations are specified in a different way. In SL, the statement would be expressed as the sequence:

<<john or mary> is happy>

and the derivations would be produced from a different perspective. Each of the following sequences is a legitimate SMS derivation:

1) <john xis happy>;

2) <mary xis happy>;

3) <john or mary>.

The first two are expressed using the *penumbral* link 'xis', a special SL link used in the qualified response component of SMS. The link 'xis' is weaker than the link 'is' and thus diminishes the strength of derivations that contain it. It should also be noted that derivation 3) above is a *wfss* in SL that is usefully employed, but the 'or' in the sequence is not a sentential connective as is the connective for disjunction in FOL. This should be obvious since in derivation 3) the 'or' connects noun labels, not sentence-sequences. In the uninterpreted environment of SMS, the sequence '<john or mary>' can be usefully employed in the syntactically-based operations of the system. The sequence, for example, could be used to help construct a syntactically determined normal form for the sequence from which it was derived, and as mentioned in section 4.2.2, that normal form could be used in semantically-based inferencing operations and in the querying process.

In FOL, predicates are joined with constants or bound variables to form atomic sentences which are either true or false. Connectives join sentences to form other sentences which also are either true or false. Thus, both n-place predicates (where $n \geq 2$) and connectives of FOL can be seen to join objects of some sort. Links also join objects and in this way are similar to predicates and connectives of FOL. But the distinction made in FOL between predicates and connectives based on the nature of the objects joined (see e.g. Thomas, 1977) is not made is SL, at least not at the syntactic level. The terms 'or', 'and', 'see', and 'give', for example, are all *links* in SL.

It should be noted that SL does not impose syntactical constraints on the use of links in the same way that FOL does for predicates and connectives. In SL, if a link does not occupy the second position in a given sequence, the sequence cannot qualify as a *wfss*, but this is not to say that links may appear only in the second position within *wfsss*. Under the syntactical rules of SL, certain links (e.g. 'and' and 'or') may appear in other positions within *wfsss* as long as the second position is occupied by an appropriate link. The following, for example, is a legitimate form for a *wfss* in SL:

<<<p1 or p2 or p3> and <p4 or <p5 and p6>>> have p7>

where p1, ..., p7 are variables that range over atomic noun markers or atomic noun labels, and 'or', 'and' and 'have' are links. The derivation process can operate on a sequence of this form even though the links of the sequence connect nonsentential objects and even though the sequence relates the link 'have' to 'or' and 'and' links. The derivation process can also perform basic operations using 'and' and 'or' that correspond to those recognized in FOL, such as the derivation of '(P • Q)' from 'P' and 'Q'. SMS thus seems to achieve useful flexibility by adopting the approach described in this section. The use of links in the derivation process is described in more detail in Chapter 11.

One might wonder why all the trouble is taken to preserve the status of 'and' and 'or' as links that may relate nonsentential objects. As mentioned above, one of the most important features of links is that their use allows modalities to be incorporated into the representational scheme. This feature is especially important in the case of 'and' and 'or' links. Although work on this part of SMS is still very much in progress, the general approach can be described by way of example. The link 'and' can be taken to represent a 'joint and several' sense of conjunction, that is, a sense in which what is said of the whole sequence of conjunctions can be said of each conjunct. Given, for example, the sequence:

< <john and mary> saw jim >

the following inferences would be appropriate in view of the joint and several sense of 'and':

1) < john <saw $\phi_1$> jim >; and

2) < mary <saw $\phi_1$> jim >

(where $\phi_1$ represents a qualifying description that flags the fact that the inference is based on the joint and several nature of the 'and' link). On the other hand, the link 'j-and' can be used to represent a joint, but not several, sense of conjunction, so that to say:

< <john j-and mary> lifted <box <the>> >;

would only permit inferences of the following form to be derived:

1) < john <lifted $\phi_2$> <box <the>> >

and

2) < mary <lifted $\phi_2$> <box <the>> >

(where $\phi_2$ qualifies the inference as being one that is derived from a mere joint sense of conjunction and thus taints the inference more than would the qualifier $\phi_1$ that was used above to indicate derivability based on a joint and several sense of conjunction). The purpose of this example is to show how convenient it is to incorporate this kind of modality into the system through links, especially when they are allowed to connect nonsentential objects.

### 7.5 Connectives and Negation

As is discussed in the preceding subsection, the links 'and' and 'or', which correspond to the connectives '•' and 'v' of FOL, are specially classified and treated in SL to achieve flexibility and notational efficiency. A similar approach is adopted for negation and for the 'if...then....' connective. Sentential negation is handled by incorporating the import of the particle into the meaning of the links intended to be affected. For example, instead of saying '~ <mary is sad>', the expression '<mary is-not sad> would be used and would be taken to establish an 'is-not' relation between 'mary' and 'sad'. The connective '→' used in FOL to represent material implication, a truth-functional notion, is not used in SL. 'If...then....' sequences are permitted in SL, but they do not have truth-values. Instead, they are specially defined to accord with the notion of 'presence' discussed previously in section 6.2 and have specially defined uses in inferencing (see section 11.4).

### 7.6 Quantifiers

The version of SMS described in this book recognizes the traditional quantifiers 'some', 'all', and 'any' as well as a set of special quantifiers such as 'some*' and 'all*' (see sections 2.3.3 and 10.2). In addition, it captures some of the effect of free logic by allowing quantifiers to range over multiple realms (see section 10.2). As mentioned in section 2.3.3, quantifiers function as operators that invoke special procedures when they are encountered. Although this version uses only commonly recognized quantifiers, the system has been designed so that new quantifiers may be introduced with convenience simply by specifying the procedures to be invoked when they are called.

## 7.7 Functions

As described in sections 2.3.3 and 10.2, SMS employs a number of special operators that produce results similar to those produced by functions in FOL. An example would be the term 'some*', which when used in a statement has the effect of mapping a set of instantial combinations for that statement into a set of quantifier-markers (see section 10.2). Many of the operations of SMS are describable in terms of functions (in mathematical sense) on sets and sequences. Chapter 11 describes some of those operations in that way.

## 7.8 Conjugation

*Conjugation* is an important notion for SMS. The notion has its roots in classical logic in which sentences are transformed into related sentences called *conjugate* sentences (e.g. Tarski, 1941). The process is accomplished by substituting quantifier words (e.g. 'any') for other quantifier words (e.g. 'some') and by negating certain components. *Contraposition* would be and example of an operation that would produce a conjugate sentence from a categorical sentence of classical logic such as 'No S is P'. The full contraposition of this sentence would be 'Some non-P are not non-S'.

Although the basic concept of conjugation in SMS is borrowed from classical logic, the notion is extended well beyond its classical definition to suit particular requirements of the system. The technique of producing conjugate sentences by substituting quantifier words and negating certain components is employed in a process that produces a set of transformations (e.g. generalizations) for the sentence being conjugated. An additional set of transformations is created by applying similar rules of negation and substitution to sentences that appear in the first set of transformations. The results are then added to the original set of transformations to produce a set of conjugate sentences for the original sentence. Any sentence that may be instantiated by the given sentence, or by one of its transformations produced by the substitution or negation process, would be included in the conjugation of the given sentence.

Just as the conjugate sentences of classical logic contain some sentences that in some way are inconsistent with the sentence conjugated (e.g. the contradiction of the given sentence is included), the conjugate sentences of SL contain sentences that are inconsistent with the conjugated sentence. This gives rise to a partition among the conjugate sentences into those consistent with and those inconsistent with the conjugated sentence. Conjugation is very important in SMS because the DB is kept consistent by not allowing any sentence to enter that has an inconsistent conjugate sentence already present in the DB. It is also employed in the derivation process since to prove the presence of an inconsistent conjugate sentence in the DB is to prove that the conjugated sentence cannot be derived from the DB. This of course corresponds to proof by way of negative assumption in FOL. A more detailed description of conjugation will be given in section 11.7.

### 7.9 Assertions

An assertion in SL is defined to be a *wfss* that contains no quantifier-markers. As result, the assertive component of the DB does not contain what corresponds to *open* sentences in FOL. The assertive component is partitioned into *object-related* assertions and *link-related* assertions. The basis for the partition corresponds to the noun/verb distinction in ordinary English and is discussed in section 9.3.

### 7.10 Enhancement of Capabilities of SMS Through Use of SL

The foregoing discussions in this chapter reveal points about SMS and SL that enable them to be used effectively in a querying system. Their capabilities in this regard will become more evident when it is shown in section 11.5 that by employing the sequence as the basic representational device, numbering and position codes can be incorporated into the inferencing scheme, which in itself produces important benefits. Nevertheless, from the foregoing discussions one can see that SMS permits links to be treated like other terms (e.g. noun components) for some purposes, yet for other purposes, they are treated differently. Given, for example, the sequence:

<<people <many>> <believe <unquestionably>> <mary has beauty>>

(which corresponds to the English sentence, "Many people unquestionably believe that Mary has beauty"), one segment of the inferencing operations of the system might take this sequence to be something like:

<< * <many>> < * <unquestionably>> < * * * >>

(where the distinction between noun and link components is not appreciated since a mere ‘*’ has replaced the nouns and links in the original sequence). This might be the case for example if the system is interested only in discovering whether terms in the sequence are modified. In such a case, the system handles links as it does other components, which in itself produces benefits defined in terms of efficiency since the same procedures handle objects that, from some perspectives, are quite different in nature. In another segment of operations, however, the system might highlight the distinction between noun and link components, say by taking the original sequence in this example to be something like:

< * believe * >

(where the link is highlighted). This might be done when the system is checking for the presence of epistemic objects. In view of the fact that it is quite useful to be able to treat noun and link components in multiple and diverse ways in inferencing, the notation used in the system should be designed to facilitate that treatment. SL has been designed to accommodate the flexibility needed to perform that kind of operation in inferencing.

CHAPTER 8

# SMS METALANGUAGE

## 8.1 Current Description

The metalanguage that has been used thus far to describe SMS consists of:

1) FOL with equality;
2) metaparlance typically used to describe FOL;
3) set-theoretic notation;
4) specially defined terminology and symbols; and
5) English.

It is convenient at this point to introduce some special symbols into the metalanguage that will be used to describe some formal aspects of quantification, instantiation, unification and the derivation process. The following subsections introduce those symbols.

## 8.2 Notation for Inclusion, Entailment and Other Relations

The symbol '$\subset$' will be used in its normal set-theoretic sense to represent the relation of inclusion; however, if the symbol has a descriptive term written under it, the symbol will represent a relation of *entailment* that conforms to whatever specifications are associated with the descriptive term. To say, for example, that a term $t_1$ is entailed as an *entry* in LEX, the lexicon of SMS, the following expression could be used:

$t_1 \underset{\text{entry}}{\subset} \text{LEX}$

where the word 'entry' describes the type of entailment involved. The most general relation of entailment will be represented by the symbol '$\underset{\text{ent}}{\subset}$', where 'ent' represents entailment in a general sense without the specification of the precise nature of the entailment. Care will be taken to explain descriptive terms as they are introduced. For the most part, the metalinguistic use of 'entailment' signifies occurrence within a specified expression or space. One expression entails another if the latter occurs within the former. A wff is entailed by an expression only if the former occurs as a wff within the latter. If a negation sign (i.e.'~') precedes the symbol, as in:

$t_1 \sim\underset{\text{entry}}{\subset} \text{LEX}$

the import of the symbol is changed to indicate that the relation of entailment does not hold between the expressions involved. Generally, a similar use of the negation sign is made throughout this book to reverse the import of symbols.

The symbol '$\subset$' is also used to describe relations that are not defined in terms of occurrence within a specified expression or space. The relation between token and sign is an example. To distinguish such a use of the symbol, the appropriate descriptive term is written above the symbol instead of below it as would be done for entailment. Schematically, the token/sign relationship can be represented as:

$\alpha \overset{\text{token}}{\subset} \beta$

where $\alpha$ is the token and $\beta$ is the sign. Similarly, the relation between a marker and a token can be represented as:

$\sigma \overset{\text{mark}}{\subset} \alpha$

where $\sigma$ is the marker and $\alpha$ is the token. Having mentioned the token/sign and the marker/token relationships, the notion of *extension* can be defined for the system. *Signs* have two types of extension within the system. One type, referred to herein as *syntactic* extension, is defined in terms of tokenhood, that is, as:

Extension of $x = \{ y \mid y \overset{\text{token}}{\subset} x \}$.

The other type, referred to as *semantic* extension, is defined more in accord with the traditional notion that the extension of a term is the set of objects to which it applies, that is, its denotation. This type of extension is defined in SMS as follows:

Extension of $x = \{ y \mid y \overset{\text{mark}}{\subset} z \bullet z \overset{\text{token}}{\subset} x \}$

where 'x' ranges over signs that are labels or markers, 'y' ranges over tokens whose corresponding signs are markers, 'z' ranges over tokens of labels or markers, and 'mark' flags the relation between a marker and its corresponding object, that is, a corresponding label or *marker-token*. A marker-token is related to itself as a marker, that is:

$\forall(x)\ (\ Mx \rightarrow x \overset{mark}{\simeq} x\ )$

where 'M' means 'is a marker token'. Any noun or link token x that appears in any $ss_i \in$ DB is individuated in two ways unless the system is told otherwise:

1) by location, each token having a unique location in the system; and

2) by marker.

Given that S is the set of signs of AW, T is the set of tokens individuated based on location, and M is the set of markers for the tokens, the following mappings can be appreciated:

$f : T \rightarrow S$ and $g : T \rightarrow M$.

Based on these mappings, the *semantic* extension of a sign $x \in S$ can be defined using a restriction of $g$ to $\{y \mid y \in T \bullet f(y) = x\}$ or $f^{-1}(x)$. The semantic extension of x is equal to the range of: $g \mid f^{-1}(x)$. It should be noted that any sign may have a *syntactic* extension, but only signs classified as labels or markers may have *semantic* extensions. This is so because not all tokens are individuated (see section 2.3.2).

### 8.3 The Consistency Relation

The notion of consistency will be particularly useful in describing SMS. The notion will be used in several related senses, so a general symbol has been provided for the general relation and descriptive terms will be added to give precising information. The symbol Ξ is used to represent the general relation of consistency, a binary relation that is reflexive and symmetrical but not transitive as used in the metalanguage. The expression:

$ss_1 \underset{cj}{\Xi} ss_2$

means that the sentence-sequence $ss_1$ is consistent with the sentence-sequence $ss_2$. The descriptor 'cj' under the consistency sign indicates that the sequences are consistent in a conjugate sense, which for present purposes should be construed to mean that neither $ss_1$ nor any inference that follows from it directly or with a degree of strength of APR is the negation of $ss_2$.

As will be seen in section 9.2, infra, ontological constraints can be placed on terms that limit their occurrence to particular realms. A member of the fictitious world (FW) cannot occur in the space that is referred to metalinguistically as the ordinary world (OW). In this sense the two worlds are said to be inconsistent with one another. The descriptor 'ont' is used to flag the inconsistency as being ontological in nature. The following are legitimate uses of the symbol to represent ontological inconsistency:

1) OW $\sim\underset{ont}{\Xi}$ FW; and

$$2)\ \forall(x)(x \underset{ent}{\subset} FW \rightarrow x \underset{ont}{\sim\Xi} OW). \qquad (42)$$

It is not convenient nor necessary to name every type of consistency that will be referred to in this book. The lexicon of SMS, for example, is consistent in the sense that it is structured and has the appropriate number of properties assigned to entries in correct order. It can also be said to be consistently related to the occurrences of its tokens in the database of SMS since it is part of the mechanism that governs those occurrences. Instead of attempting to name each type of consistency of this sort, all are categorized under the heading *general* consistency. The descriptive term 'gen' is used to flag this general consistency.

Still another use of the consistency symbol is to indicate internal consistency. A set of wffs may be free of contradiction and thus would be consistent in the conjugate sense. Internal consistency is indicated when there is no left hand term to form the ordinary binary relation of consistency. The following is an example of this kind of use:

$$\underset{cj}{\Xi}\{ss \mid ss \underset{entry}{\subset} DB\}$$

where the abstract operator defines the set of sentence-sequences in the database. An individual sequence may be consistent or inconsistent in the conjugate sense. Internal consistency of $ss_1$ would be represented by: $\underset{cj}{\Xi} ss_1$.

### 8.4 Suggestions for Reading the Metalanguage

Whenever one of the special symbols of the metalanguage is embedded within a formula, such as in (42) of section 8.3, the symbol will represent a sententially expressed binary relation. This will make the reading easier since one can envision a set of parentheses around each such relation. Also, the scope of each quantifier will demarcated by an independent set of parentheses or brackets. Formula (42), when punctuated in this way, would read:

$$\forall(x)[(x \underset{ent}{\subset} FW) \rightarrow (x \underset{ont}{\sim\Xi} OW)].$$

Sometimes a more complex mixture of special symbols and FOL is used, as in formula (43) of section 9.4, which reads as follows:

$$\forall(x,y,z)[\sim Rx \bullet My \bullet x \underset{noun}{\subset} y \bullet z \text{ is=} OW \bullet \sim Cxz \rightarrow x \underset{noun}{\subset} FW].$$

If punctuated as has been suggested, the formula would read as follows:

$$\forall(x,y,z)[\sim Rx \bullet My \bullet (x \underset{noun}{\subset} y) \bullet (z \text{ is=} OW) \bullet \sim Cxz \rightarrow (x \underset{noun}{\subset} FW)].$$

## CHAPTER 9

# TYING UP SOME LOOSE ENDS

### 9.1 Unfinished Matters

Now that the metalanguage and formation rules for SL have been introduced, some matters discussed previously in an informal way can be formalized. Section 7.8 introduced the concept of conjugation and described how a set of conjugate sentences can be produced for any SL statement. In SL a given sentence is included in its conjugation. The following thus holds for any *wfss* of SL, where $f$ ( $ss_i$ ) = { y | y is a conjugate sentence of $ss_i$ }:

$$\forall(x)[\ x \text{ is a } wfss \rightarrow E(z,w)(\ z \subset f(x) \bullet w \subset f(x) \bullet (\ z \cup w\ ) = f(\ x\ ) \bullet \forall(u)(\ u \in z \rightarrow u \underset{cj}{\Xi} x) \bullet \forall(v)(\ v \in w \rightarrow v \sim\underset{cj}{\Xi} x))]$$

where 'z' and 'w' are thus nonempty subsets of the set of conjugate sentences assigned by $f$ such that each member of z is consistent with x, and each member of w is inconsistent with x. The members of w will be referred to as the inconsistent conjugate sentences of the conjugated sentence, and the members of z will be referred to as the consistent conjugate sentences of the conjugated sentence.

### 9.2 Signs, Restrictions and Marking

As described in Chapter 1, LEX consists of a family of sequences. For each top level sequence in LEX, the first position in the sequence is occupied by another sequence that has a *sign* (also called an *entry*) as its first element. The set:

$$\{\ x \mid x \underset{entry}{\subset} \text{LEX}\ \}$$

is partitioned into the following syntactic categories, here given with assigned abbreviations: *labels* (LB), *markers* (MK), *particles* (PT) and *operators* (OP). Every primitive element y entailed in the DB has a corresponding *sign* in LEX. A function maps $\{ y \mid y \underset{elem}{\subset} DB \}$, where 'elem' is an abbreviation for 'element', into $\{ x \mid x \underset{entry}{\subset} LEX \}$. The category to which each *entry* or element of the DB belongs can be specified through the composite function *h* o (*g* o *f*), which defines the following mappings:

$$\{ y \mid y \underset{elem}{\subset} DB \} \xrightarrow{f} \{ x \mid x \underset{entry}{\subset} LEX \} \xrightarrow{g} < B_i >_{i \in \{ x \mid x \underset{entry}{\subset} LEX \}} \xrightarrow{h}$$

$$\{ \lceil LB \rceil, \lceil MK \rceil, \lceil PT \rceil, \lceil OP \rceil \}$$

where 'y' ranges over all types of linguistic objects in the DB, 'x' ranges over all entries in LEX and '$< B_i >$' is a family of sequences (indexed by the *entries* of LEX) containing properties and constraints to be associated with the entries.

Every z entailed in the DB, where z ranges over labels, markers and *wfsss*, has an assigned value indicative of the ontological realm to which it belongs. This assignment is made by a composite function (*l* o *k*) that determines the value of the syntactic category to which an entry belongs. The mappings are given below:

$$\{ z \mid z \underset{entry}{\subset} LEX \} \xrightarrow{k} < B_i >_{i \in \{ z \mid z \underset{entry}{\subset} LEX \}} \xrightarrow{l}$$

$$\{ \lceil SW \rceil, \lceil OW \rceil, \lceil FW \rceil, \lceil AW \rceil, \lceil MW \rceil, \lceil UW \rceil, \lceil NW \rceil \}.$$

The function (*l* o *k*) can be employed to define ontological restrictions in SMS. Any *entry* may be designated as a restricted *sign*, which means that all its tokens must conform to whatever restrictions are specified. A term, for example, might be restricted to FW (world of fiction) and hence would be prevented from occurring in OW. Such a restriction can be represented as:

$$R(x, FW)$$

where 'x' ranges over signs,'R' operates as the restriction, and the entire expression reads 'x is restricted to FW'. Thus,

$$\forall (x)[\ (l \circ k)\ (x) = \lceil FW \rceil \rightarrow R(x, FW)]$$

The sign 'yeti', for example, is a restricted sign if (*l* o *k*) (yeti) = $\lceil FW \rceil$. A few observations will be made at this point to assist the reader in understanding the descriptions of SMS that follow. For every member of $\{x \mid (h \circ g)\ (x) = LB\}$, a token has been placed in FW so that the sign of any label has at least one 'imaginary' instance in the 'universe' of SMS. Thus,

$$\forall (x)[\ (h \circ g)\ (x) = LB \rightarrow \text{Extension of } x \neq \varnothing\ ]$$

which means that every *label* has a nonempty extension when that extension is computed over the entire 'universe'.

It should also be noted that for any x such that $x \underset{noun}{\subset} ss_i$, where $ss_i$ is a member of DB, one of two possibilities holds:

1) $f(x) = < y >$ ; or

2) $f(x) = < y, z >$

where $f$ is a function that assigns a marker to its argument and determines whether its argument is quantified in the given sequence; 'y' is the marker so assigned; and 'z' is a quantifier of SL. It follows that every label that enters the DB can be associated with a marker, either one previously assigned to a label or one without such an assignment. It also follows that every label in the DB either does or does not bear a quantifier. The ordered pair '< y, z >' given above in example represents the case in which the label is quantified.

Marking is the process by which markers are bound to labels and locations. In the plain symbolic environment of SMS, what this amounts to is that for the $n^{th}$ encounter with any label token for which there is no previously established marker, there corresponds a sign in the *markers* category for which a marker-token is created and bound to the label token. Tokens are sequentially marked as they enter the DB, and both tokens and markers become entailed in the DB. Given S as the set of signs in LEX, T as the set of noun and link tokens individuated based on location, and M as the set of marker-tokens, the following mappings can be appreciated:

$f : T \rightarrow S$ and $g : T \rightarrow M$

The relation between marker and sign can be defined using a restriction of $f$ to $g^{-1}(z)$, where $z \in M$. Unless a marker is explicitly bound to label tokens that have different signs (in which case the marker would have more than one sign), $f \mid g^{-1}(z)$ is a constant function whose range consists of one element, that is, the sign of z.

Whenever a marker is created for a quantified label, *criteria for instantiation* are also created that govern the instantiation of the marker, which functions as a variable. A given quantifier-marker may be instantiated only by a marker that satisfies the criteria specified for the instantiation of that quantifier-marker. It follows that all variables are typed in SMS since all have criteria for instantiation associated with them. At the very least, a concrete marker must conform to the label of the quantifier-marker to be a proper instantial term for that quantifier-marker.

### 9.3 More on Assertions

In SL, each modified noun component has a corresponding set of sentence-sequences, that is:

$$\forall(x)[x \underset{\text{k-noun}}{\subset} U \bullet E(y)(y = \{z \mid z \text{ modifies } x\} \bullet y \neq \varnothing) \rightarrow$$
$$E(w)\,(w = \{<s> \mid <s> \in f\,(x,y)\})]$$

where 'U' is a wfss, 'x' ranges over noun markers and noun labels; 'k-noun' indicates that the entailed component is a *key* noun in the sequence involved, which in this case means that it occupies the first position in a sequence that occupies a top-level, noun position in U (otherwise the component must be an atom in a top-level noun position in U); 'z' ranges over modifiers and '{z | z modifies x}' is a set that includes all modifiers of x, including phrases; 's' ranges over sentence-sequences; and *f* is a function that integrates its arguments to form a set of *wfsss* (see section 11.3 for a schematic example of how a phrase-sequence can be converted into a set of sentence-sequences). It should be noted that the expression '<s>', as used here in the abstract operator, indicates that the set is a set of sequences (cf. Thomas, 1977). The sequences produced by *f*, along with the bare original sequence, that is, the original sequence with all modifiers removed leaving only the key components, become part of the realm of *object-related* assertions. The link of the given sequence is individuated and related to a marked noun form of the link. A set of *wfsss* is then generated using the marked noun form and the modifiers just as was done for the modified noun component above, only this set of sequences becomes part of the realm of *link-related* assertions. Thus, every *wfss* that contains modified components yields two types of assertions, as is diagrammed in Figure 21.

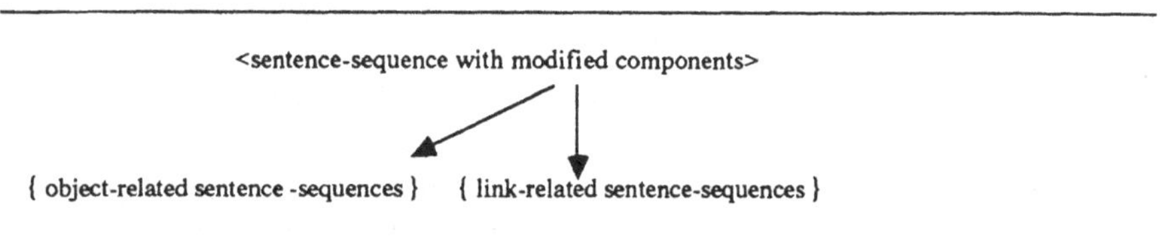


Figure 21. Sequence Types Yielded by *WFSS* Containing Modifiers

As can be deduced from the foregoing discussions, the connection between the object-related assertions and the link-related assertions is defined in terms of relations between links and their noun forms. The relation between the two realms of assertions can be defined as a function as follows:

$$g : \{O_i\}_{i \in I_1} \rightarrow \{L_j\}_{j \in I_2}$$

where '$I_1$' is an index set consisting of link markers, '$I_2$' is an index set consisting of noun form markers, '$\{O_i\}$' is a family of sets that includes the object-related assertions, and '$\{L_j\}$' is a family of sets that includes the link-related assertions.

### 9.4 Consistency Specifications for Realms

The following consistency states are *required* in SMS:

1) $\underset{cj}{\Xi}\{x \mid x \text{ is a } wfss \bullet x \in OW\}$;
2) $\underset{cj}{\Xi}\{x \mid x \text{ is a } wfss \bullet x \in FW\}$;
3) $\underset{cj}{\Xi}\{x \mid x \text{ is a } wfss \bullet x \in SW\}$;
4) $\underset{gen}{\Xi}$ AW;
5) $\underset{gen}{\Xi}$ MW; and
6) $\underset{gen}{\Xi}$ LEX.

The following consistency states are *permitted* in SMS:

1) $\underset{cj}{\Xi}\{x \mid x \text{ is a } wfss \bullet x \in NW\}$; and
2) $\underset{cj}{\Xi}\{x \mid x \text{ is a } wfss \bullet x \in ID\}$.

Thus, internal consistency obtains in all realms and components except for ID and NW, in which internal consistency is permitted but not required. In addition, the following relations hold for the current version of the system:

$$\forall(x)\ [x \underset{noun}{\subset} OW \rightarrow x \underset{ont}{\sim\Xi} FW \bullet x \underset{ont}{\sim\Xi} SW];$$
$$\forall(x)\ [x \underset{noun}{\subset} FW \rightarrow x \underset{ont}{\sim\Xi} OW \bullet x \underset{ont}{\sim\Xi} SW]; \text{ and}$$
$$\forall(x)\ [x \underset{noun}{\subset} SW \rightarrow x \underset{ont}{\Xi} OW \bullet x \underset{ont}{\Xi} FW].$$

If a key constituent of a MO (mental object e.g. belief) is not restricted through its *sign* or otherwise and if it has no known binding in OW, it is individuated in FW, that is, it is given a marker in FW that corresponds to the marker it receives in MW. By default then, such a term is relegated to FW. Thus:

$$\forall(x,y,z)[\sim Rx \bullet My \bullet x \underset{noun}{\subset} y \bullet z \text{ is}= OW \bullet \sim Cxz \rightarrow x \underset{noun}{\subset} FW] \qquad (43)$$

where '~R' means 'is not a restricted term', 'M' means 'is a mental object', '*OW*' means 'the realm of OW', '~C' means 'is not a known component of', 'noun' indicates that the object is entailed in some position appropriate for a noun, and '*FW*' means 'the realm of FW'. The symbols '*OW*' and '*FW*' have been italicized in this example to distinguish them from predicate symbols.

*Sentence-sequences* that are inconsistent in the conjugate sense may appear in MW as long as they are not bound by the same MO. Thus, for example, with respect to MW, if $ss_i \underset{cj}{\sim\Xi} ss_k$, and $\alpha_1$ and $\alpha_2$ are *believers*, the following holds:

$$\langle\alpha_1 \text{ believes } ss_i\rangle \underset{cj}{\Xi} \langle\alpha_2 \text{ believes } ss_k\rangle$$

However, given the same environment, the following holds:

$$\underset{cj}{\sim\Xi}\langle\alpha_1 \text{ believes } \langle ss_i \text{ and } ss_k\rangle\rangle.$$

The *belief-sequence* of this last example, being internally inconsistent, would be assigned a mere penumbral degree of presence in the system.

# CHAPTER 10

# QUANTIFICATION, INSTANTIATION, AND EVENT INDIVIDUATION

## 10.1 Quantifiers in SL

This section describes the theoretical basis of quantification in SMS. SL has a set of terms that serve as quantifiers, but they do so in ways that differ somewhat from the ways quantifiers are used in FOL. In SL quantification is allowed over labels, variables, sentential sequences (see section 10.3), links (see section 10.2.2) and concrete markers (see section 10.4), whereas FOL does not allow quantification over some of these objects. Two general types of quantification are recognized in the system: *universal* quantification and *particular* quantification. The term 'particular' rather than 'existential' is used to describe the second type in order to emphasize the point that it is not absolutely necessary to assign existential import to a quantifier of this type (cf. Orenstein, 1978). In section 7.1, it is mentioned that one may wish to avoid the notion of existence when assertions or questions about existence will not arise or are otherwise unimportant in a particular application or implementation of SMS theory. In such a case, the particular quantifier may be taken to be devoid of existential import, and inferencing over objects can be based on mere occurrence or presence of objects in particular realms or spaces. Alternatively, the meaning of the particular quantifier can be defined in a more conventional mode to enable it to be used to ground inferences about the 'existence' of objects. The discussions in this chapter presuppose the adoption of this last mentioned alternative so that the uses of particular quantifiers can be more readily compared with the uses of their counterparts in other languages and systems. Unless otherwise indicated, it is to be assumed that labels have at least one concrete instance in the system.

## 10.2 Instantiation, Generalization, Unification, and Quantification

As described in Chapter 2, most noun and link labels that enter the system are individuated in some sense. When a quantifier occupies the position of a modifier in a *wfss*, the modified term is not concretely individuated but is assigned a *quantifier-marker*. In the schema:

$$<< \beta_1 <\Psi>> \upsilon < \beta_2 <\Sigma>>>$$

(where $\beta$ ranges over noun labels, $\Psi$ ranges over universal quantifiers, $\Sigma$ ranges over particular quantifiers, and $\upsilon$ represents a 2-place link), neither '$\beta_1$' nor '$\beta_2$' would be concretely individuated. Instead, each noun label would be assigned a quantifier-marker that would function as a variable. This corresponds to using implicit quantifiers (pattern variables) in a first-order setting (see e.g. Charniak and McDermott, 1985). In FOL, an unbound variable in an otherwise well formed sentence formula produces an open sentence. The binding of the variable, or its instantiation by a constant, produces a sentence if no other unbound variables are present. Similarly, in the sequence given above, the quantifiers bind the labels so that the sequence qualifies as a *wfss* that may be accepted as part of the assertive component of the DB. However, a sequence produced by replacing one or more noun labels with appropriate quantifier-markers would be an *open sentence-sequence* and would not be classified as an assertion. The following is an example of a schema for an open sequence:

$$< \Psi\text{-}1 \ \upsilon\text{-}2 \ \Sigma\text{-}3 >$$

where the numbers 1, 2 and 3 individuate the symbols to which they are attached, thereby converting each symbol into a marker. The markers '$\Psi$-1' and '$\Sigma$-3' thus represent quantifier-markers. In FOL, wffs that contain only bound variables are sentences (closed sentences) and in themselves constitute deductions when they are derived from premises in which they are entailed. Sentences of this kind can be converted into propositional functions by freeing the variables from the scope of the quantifiers, a technique often employed in making proofs. Open sentence-sequences of SL correspond to such derived propositional functions of FOL. The technique employed in SMS is to create these propositional-function-like linguistic objects and then keep them around in the nonassertive component of the DB. This can be done without sacrificing too much efficiency, and the advantages produced seem to outweigh the disadvantages. For one thing, the whole process is directed since each variable is created with a defined position and relation with respect to other objects. Storage and retrieval strategies in the automated version of SMS allow the scheme to operate efficiently.

An open sentence-sequence becomes an assertion when its variables are instantiated by concrete markers or are recast into the form of a label with an attached quantifier. Instantiation of a variable (quantifier-marker) is a two step process in SMS. First, the substitution instance (marker) is tested to see whether it satisfies criteria set for the instantiation of the variable, and if not, the particular instantiation attempt is abandoned. Second, the substitution instance is substituted for the variable. Special rules govern the instantiation of each type of quantifier-marker. The rules form part of the *criteria for instantiation*. A few more symbols will be introduced into the metalanguage at this point to explain these rules. The first symbol represents a binary relation between markers and indicates that the first marker is a member of the group (set) represented by the second marker. The term 'ism' (for 'is member of') flags the nature of this relation as in the expression '$x \overset{\text{ism}}{\sqsubset} y$', where 'x' and 'y' range over markers. The second represents a relation between two signs and indicates that the first sign is a subtype of the second. The term 'isa' (for 'is a') is used to flag this relation as in '$x \overset{\text{isa}}{\sqsubset} y$', where 'x' and 'y' range over signs. The third represents a relation between a marker and a sign and indicates that the marker conforms to whatever specifications are set for the sign. The term 'm-isa' (for 'marker is a') is used to flag the relation as in '$x \overset{\text{m-isa}}{\sqsubset} y$', where 'x' ranges over markers and 'y' ranges over signs. The fourth represents a relation between two markers and indicates that they are equal. The term 'is=' (for 'is equal to') is used to flag this relation as in '$x \overset{\text{is=}}{\sqsubset} y$'. The symbol 'is=' should be distinguished form the symbol 'is≡', which is used to represent syntactical identity (see section 4.3).

With these symbols available, the aforementioned scheme of quantification can be described more formally. As stated previously, special rules pertain to the instantiation of each type of quantifier-marker. In the individuation process by which the quantifier-marker is created, the marker is bound to a label, which will be referred to as the *key* label of that marker. The rules of instantiation are defined in part with reference to relations that objects have with the sign of the key label of the quantifier-marker or with the quantification-marker itself. A universal quantifier-marker $\Psi\text{-}_i$ produced in association with the quantifier 'any' may be instantiated by any marker that satisfies 'x' in any of the following relational schemata:

1) $x \overset{\text{ism}}{\sqsubset} \Psi\text{-}_i$;

2) $x \overset{\text{m-isa}}{\sqsubset} y$ (where 'y' is the sign of the key label of $\Psi\text{-}_i$); and

3) $x \overset{\text{is=}}{\sqsubset} \Psi\text{-}_i$.

If the key label of the quantifier-marker is modified by one or more modifiers (e.g. adjectives), the criteria for instantiation would include a set of sentence-sequences that would be generated as described in section 9.3. In such a case, the key label would be flagged and thereby included in the sentence-sequences in an identifiable way. These sequences set up a test that must be passed by any marker x that is to be a proper substitution instance. To pass the test, x must occupy positions in sentence-sequences in the DB that correspond to the positions that the key label occupies in the test sequences, and in all other respects those sentence-sequences of the DB either must match or be proper instantiations of the remaining portions of the test sequences. In other words, a match must occur through unification. In addition, x must conform to a sign 'u' that bears one of the following relations to z, the sign of the key label;

1) u is= z; or

2) u $\overset{isa}{\subset}$ z.

A standard conception of unification has been adopted for SMS. Generally, to *unify* two expressions means to find values for their variables that will make the expressions identical. A *substitution* is a set of pairs, each pair containing a variable binding consisting of a variable and a value (expression) that has been assigned to it. No such variable may appear within any of the assigned values in the particular substitution. When a substitution is *applied* to an expression, each occurrence of a variable in the expression is replaced by the value assigned to it in the substitution (see e.g. Charniak and McDermott, 1985; Genesereth and Nilsson, 1987). An expression $\Phi_i$ subsumes another expression $\Phi_j$ if there is a substitution $\theta_i$ that, when applied to $\Phi_i$, produces a result identical to $\Phi_j$. Expressions may subsume one another, and if $\Phi_i$ subsumes $\Phi_j$, then $\Phi_j$ follows from $\Phi_i$.

### 10.2.1 Using Quantification, Instantiation and Generalization in Simple Statements

In section 4.4, a *simple sentence* was described as a sentence-sequence that contains only atoms as elements. This conception will be broadened slightly at this point to include sentence-sequences that contain atoms with attached quantifiers or special operators, such as 'the' and 'c*'. Thus, a simple sentence will be taken to be a sentence-sequence that does not entail another sentence-sequence as a *wfss*, as was the case before, but now the elements in the sequence may have quantifiers or operators, or both, attached to them. Under this conception, the sequence '<jane saw nancy>' would qualify as a simple sentence, whereas the sequence '<brian caused <mimi is happy>>' would not be a simple one because it contains the *wfss* '<mimi is happy>'. This notion of a simple sentence can be usefully employed in explaining how quantifiers affect the meaning of the SL expressions of which they are a part. When a quantifier is attached to a label in expression, reference is being made to one or more members of the extension of that label, and in this regard, the quantifier governs what kind of reference is being made. The quantifier 'any', for example, indicates that the reference is to each and every member of the extension of the label associated with the quantifier. The following discussions describe how quantifiers affect meaning in *simple statements*. Section 10.2.2 will describe how quantifiers affect meaning in *complex statements*. A complex statement is one that contains another statement as a *wfss*. The statement about 'brian' and 'mimi' given above qualifies as a complex statement.

In explaining the operation of quantifiers and the notion of sentential instantiation defined in section 10.3, it will be useful to employ the notion of a *proper instantial combination* for an SL statement. Such a combination $c_i$ for a given SL statement $\Phi_i$ consists of a sequence of terms that correspond to $\Phi_i$ in a precise way in which each component of $c_i$ must be a proper instantial item for the term that bears the corresponding position in $\Phi_i$. Also, each and every term in $\Phi_i$ must have a corresponding and appropriately positioned instantial term in $c_i$. Under these specifications, $\Phi_i$ subsumes $c_i$ since there is a substitution in which the quantifier-markers in $\Phi_i$ are bound to corresponding values that appear in $c_i$, and the application of that substitution into $\Phi_i$ produces a result that is identical to $c_i$. This can be illustrated by the following example in which temporal information has been omitted for the sake of simplicity. Given that $\Phi_i$ is:

<<logician <any>> likes <logic <any>>>

and that 'ue-l1' *isa* 'logician' and that 'ue-log1' and 'ue-log2' each qualify as a 'logic', each of the following would be a proper instantial combination of $\Phi_i$:

<ue-l1 likes ue-log1>; and

<ue-l1 likes ue-log2>.

This is so because 'ue-l1' is a proper instantial term for '<logician <any>>' (individuated say to 'uqe-15') and because both 'ue-log1' and 'ue-log2' are proper instantial terms for '<logic <any>>' (say individuated to 'uqe-16').

The notion of a proper instantial combination is thus defined in terms of the notion of a proper instantial term. What may qualify as a proper instantial term for a given quantifier-marker is determined by special rules, such as those set forth previously for the universal quantifier-marker and those presented in the following discussions that cover quantifier-markers of the particular sort. An independent set of rules have been specified to govern the instantiation of each type of quantifier-marker. Section 10.4 defines an extended notion of instantiation by which a concrete marker may be replaced by another expression. In these examples and the ones that follow, temporal representations have been omitted from the notation for the sake of simplicity, and syntactically identical links are to be assumed to be proper instantial terms for one another.

The theory behind the use of quantifier-markers in SMS lends itself to a set-theoretic description. Whenever a quantifier is used in a *simple statement* $\Phi_i$, the system creates a quantifier-marker that names a set M that can be taken to consist of one or more markers of the concrete type or of the quantifier type, depending on the type of quantifier used. The meaning of the quantifier is defined with reference to the relation between M and C, a set consisting of the proper instantial combinations of $\Phi_i$, each such combination bearing the original quantifier-marker (the one that names M) at the appropriate location within that combination. The following discussions describe this relation and show how it can be used to distinguish one type of quantifier from another.

In one sense, the ground-level meaning of a *simple* sentential sequence $\Phi_i$ that contains one or more quantifier-markers can be taken to be the set of proper instantial combinations of $\Phi_i$. At any given point in database construction, the system may not be able to determine that set in its entirety because it may not know who or what is a member of a particular set named by a quantifier-marker. This can be seen to be the case for a quantifier-marker of the particular sort produced by the quantifier/operator 'some'. The quantifier 'some' may be taken to mean 'at least one', and thus for an expression of the form <$\beta_i$ <some>>, where $\beta$ ranges over labels, the individuation process would produce a marker of the form pqe-$_i$ that would be bound to the label $\beta_i$. The result, expressible as '<pqe-$_i$ isa $\beta_i$>', corresponds to the expression 'at least one x is a $\beta_i$'. The marker pqe-$_i$ can be taken to name a set M as described previously. For the quantifier 'some', the set M is a *unit* set that contains its name. The significance of the set being a unit set of the form {pqe-$_i$} is defined with reference to the fact that a mapping is to be established from the set of proper instantial combinations of $\Phi_i$ into M. The mapping determines which marker(s) in M is to replace the corresponding quantifier-marker(s) in the instantial combination(s) to produce one or more inferences. If M is a unit set, each instantial combination will be mapped to the same element in M. Schematic examples of the use of the quantifier 'some' given later on in these discussions will define this significance more clearly.

Any open sentential object of SL that contains a quantifier-marker determines a set of relations that hold between the quantifier-marker and the other markers in the sentence. With that in mind, a quantifier-marker of the particular sort can be taken to name a subset, and normally a proper subset, of the extension of its key label. As mentioned in section 10.1, in the version of SMS being described, quantifiers of the particular sort are assumed to have existential import in the sense that they imply the presence of at least one concrete individual. The *stipulated* meaning of a particular quantifier-marker of the form pqe-$_i$, when used in an SL statement $\Phi_i$, is that the relations held by pqe-$_i$ in any proper instantial combination of $\Phi_i$ are held by each and every member of pqe-$_i$ and that there is at least one member of pqe-$_i$. Thus, for example, the sequence '<<logician <any>> likes <logic <some><c* 1>>>' (where say the subject term individuates to 'uqe-5' and the object to 'pqe-2', so that the statement reads '<uqe-5 likes pqe-2>') means that there is a relation named 'likes' that holds between any 'logician' and any member of pqe-2. There may or may not be more than one member of the set pqe-2.

One of the major benefits that results from the employment of quantifier-markers is that they may be incorporated into other statements by reference. Using the previous example involving 'pqe-2' and assuming that the name 'john' is bound to a particular concrete marker in the system, the statement '<john studies <logic <c* 1>>>' would individuate to '<john studies pqe-2>' because of the cross-reference operator 'c*' (see section 2.3.3). Unless otherwise indicated, reference to a previously created quantifier-marker of the particular sort is taken to be a reference to *any* member of the set named by that marker (see section 10.2.2). Thus, in this example, the reference via the operator 'c*' would carry with it the assignment of an implicit universal quantifier to 'pqe-2', so that for *any* member of pqe-2, it would follow that the 'studies' relation holds between 'john' and that member. If, in addition, the system somehow were to be given that '<ue-log1 ism pqe-2>' and that '<ue-log2 ism pqe-2>' and that both 'ue-l1' and 'ue-l2' are 'logicians', the relations diagrammed below would hold (where each arrow indicates that the relation 'likes' holds between the objects connected by the arrow):

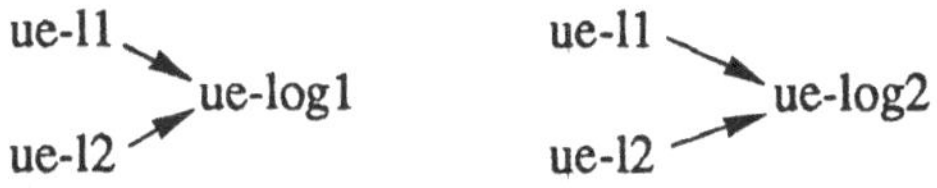

ue-l1 → ue-log1 ← ue-l2

ue-l1 → ue-log2 ← ue-l2

The constraints on what may qualify as a proper instantial term for pqe-2 are indeed very strict. Any particular quantifier-marker of the form pqe-$_i$ may be instantiated only by a marker that satisfies 'x' in one of the following schemata:

1) $x \overset{ism}{\subset}$ pqe-$_i$; and

2) $x \overset{is=}{\subset}$ pqe-$_i$.

The operation of the quantifier 'some*' lends itself to a set-theoretic description partly in terms of what has been specified above for the quantifier 'some'. The default procedure for the *some** operator is for the system to create a quantifier-marker of the form psome*-$_i$ for any expression of the form <$\beta_i$ <some*>> (where $\beta$ ranges over labels or markers). The quantifier-marker names a set M of newly created particular quantifier-markers, each of which bears an *isa* relation to $\beta_i$ when $\beta_i$ is a label and an *ism* relation to $\beta_i$ when $\beta_i$ is a marker. Given any simple sentential sequence $\Phi_i$ that contains a marker of the form psome*-$_i$, there is a *one-one* and *onto* function *f* that maps the set C, consisting of the proper instantial combinations of $\Phi_i$, into M, so that $f(c_i) = m_i$. The mapping is specified for the marker psome*-$_i$ so that $m_i$ stands for the marker that will replace the marker psome*-$_i$ in $c_i$ to produce an inference. Thus, the *some** quantifier differs from the *some* quantifier in that the mapping for the latter is defined as a constant function, that is, each proper instantial combination is mapped to the same quantifier-marker. The difference between the two can be illustrated by contrasting example. Instead of the statement '<<logician <any>> likes <logic <some><c* 1>>>' that was used to illustrate the use of the *some* quantifier, the statement:

<<logician <any>> likes <logic <some*><c* 1>>>

(in which the term 'some' has been replaced by 'some*') will be used. This statement would be individuated to, say, '<uqe-5 likes psome*-2>', where psome*-2 is the *some** quantifier-marker. This marker names a set such that for any proper instantial combination $c_i$ for the statement, where $c_i$ bears the form

'<ue-$l_i$ likes psome*-2>', there corresponds a marker of the form pqe-$_i$ that may replace psome*-2 in that combination, which in this schematic example would produce '<ue-$l_i$ likes pqe-$_i$>'. For a different instantial combination, say of the form '<ue-$l_k$ likes psome*-2>', a different corresponding marker, say pqe-$_k$, would be created to produce the result '<ue-$l_k$ likes pqe-$_k$>'. Thus, schematically speaking, for the *some* quantifier, the mapping would be from C into the unit set {pqe-i}, whereas for the *some** quantifier, the mapping would be from C into {pqe-$_i$, ..., pqe-$_n$}.

Obviously, inferencing over quantifier-markers must be carefully controlled. The primary reason for using markers of this type is to enable the system to deal with the marker instead of having to deal with each and every member of the set named by that marker. In some instances, what holds for the quantifier-marker may be taken to hold for each member of the set it names, whereas in other instances it would not be appropriate to draw such a conclusion. One important difference between the 'some' and 'some*' quantifier-markers that must be recognized in inferencing can be illustrated using the examples developed thus far. Given that '<ue-log1 ism pqe-2>' in the example above for the quantifier 'some', one may infer that for any logician ue-$l_i$, the following holds: <ue-$l_i$ likes ue-log1>. The reason that this is a valid inference is because the set M that would be created as previously described would be the unit set {pqe-2}, with the result that the value for each element of C under the mapping from C into M would be 'pqe-2'. Since, by stipulation, what holds for 'pqe-2' in any $c_i \in$ C also holds for any member of pqe-2, it follows that the 'like' relation would hold between 'ue-$l_i$' and 'ue-log1'. In contrast, given that '<ue-log1 ism psome*-2>' in the example using the quantifier 'some*', one may not validly infer that '<ue-$l_i$ likes ue-log1>'. The term 'psome*-2' names a set of particular quantifier-markers, so technically, it is not correct to say that 'ue-log1' is a member of that set. The system, however, interprets the statement to mean that 'ue-log1' is a member of some element of the set psome*-2 (heretofore represented as M), but the identity of that element is left unspecified. Until a mapping, say by the function *g*, is specified between psome*-2 and L, where L is the set of concrete markers for 'logics', the correspondence between C and L is unspecified. To the extent that a mapping is specified between a subset of psome*-2 and L, a composite mapping can be specified for any $c_i \in$ C whose value under *f* falls within that subset of psome*-2. If the mapping between psome*-2 and L is complete, the composite function (*g* o *f*) would assign a value in L to any $c_i \in$ C, and that value would replace the marker 'psome*-2' in $c_i$ to produce an inference. Under this scheme, the inference '<ue-$l_i$ likes ue-log1>' would be valid if the system had information of the following form available:

*f* (<ue-$l_i$ likes psome*-2>) = pqe-$_i$ (where pqe-$_i \in$ psome*-2)

and

$g$ (pqe-i) = ue-log1.

It may be that a particular value for ($g$ o $f$) can be derived from other information in a given case, but if not, the system cannot produce inferences of the concrete sort for that situation.

Given the SMS world situation diagrammed below:

```
ue-l1 ———→ ue-log1

ue-l2 ———→ ue-log2
          ↗
ue-l3         ue-log3
```

(where the world consists of exactly three 'logicians' and exactly three 'logics', and where each arrow represents a 'likes' relation that holds between a 'logician' and a 'logic', the following is a valid statement:

<<logician <any>> likes <logic <some*><c* 1>>>

This statement asserts that for any 'logician' there corresponds at least one 'logic' such that the 'likes' relation holds (as called for by the statement) between that logician and that 'logic'. Simple inspection will reveal that this is a valid assertion for this world situation. The following assertion, however, would not be valid in the same situation:

<<logician <any>> likes <logic <some><c* 1>>>

This asserts that there is at least one 'logic' that is liked by every logician. Simple inspection reveals that this last assertion is not valid because there is no 'logic' that every logician likes. The precise meaning of the statement is controlled by the fact that the mapping for the 'some' quantifier is into a unit set. In other words, the mapping from the set of 'logicians' is into a unit set containing the particular quantifier-marker, which means that all the 'logicians' are related to the same individual.

When a quantifier appears in the antecedent of an 'If ...., then ....' expression or in an expression that will constitute all or part of the criteria for instantiating a quantifier-marker, that quantifier is given special treatment. As mentioned previously, the creation of a quantifier-marker by the system is accompanied by the establishment of criteria for instantiating the marker. The criteria take the form of test sequences, and for a marker to be a proper instantial term for the quantifier-marker, it must be *present* in one or more proper instantial combinations that unify with the test sequences. Sometimes a quantifier will have to be replaced by another quantifier when the test sequences are generated. This can be illustrated by example. Given the expression '<owner<any><of <house<some*>>>>', which corresponds to the English expression 'any owner of some house', the individuation process might produce the quantifier-marker 'uqe-777' to name a set of unspecified owners, each of whom owns a house. The test for whether an individual is a member of 'uqe-777' would be whether that individual is an owner of some house. It could be *any* house as far as this test is concerned. For that reason, the test sequence would be something like '<<owner<any>> v-of <house<any>>>', so that any 'owner' that bears a corresponding relation in a sequence that is subsumed by this test sequence would pass this part of the test for the instantiation of 'uqe-777'. The fact that quantifiers must be specially treated when they appear in antecedents or under negation is well known by those who Skolemize first-order formulas for use in clausal databases (see e.g. Charniak and McDermott, 1985). In SMS, quantifiers are given similar treatment in similar circumstances.

The following principles pertain to generalization. If a concrete marker for an individual is quantified, the quantifier has no effect and may be ignored. Thus, for example, where $m_i$ is such a marker, $m_i \vdash <m_i<any>>$, and $<m_i<any>> \vdash m_i$. If $\beta_i$ is a label of $m_i$, the following holds: $m_i \vdash <\beta_i<\Sigma>>$, where $\Sigma$ ranges over quantifiers of the particular sort. The relation $m_i \vdash <\beta_i<\Psi>>$, where $\Psi$ ranges over universal quantifiers and x ranges over concrete markers, holds if the following holds: $\forall(x)[\ x \text{ isa } \beta_i \rightarrow x \text{ is= } m_i\ ]$. One may infer that a relation holds for $<\beta_i<any>>$ if by checking concrete markers, it can be determined that the relation holds for every member of a set of concrete markers M such that $\forall(x)[\ x \text{ isa } \beta_i \rightarrow x \in M\ ]$, where x ranges over concrete markers.

Just as a set of proper instantial combinations can be produced for a given SL statement, a set of proper generalizations can be produced for that statement using the generalization rules just described. It thus becomes possible to assign each simple statement of SL an *inference-set* consisting of all the proper instantial combinations and generalizations that can be produced from the statement under the aforementioned rules. The inference-set and other direct inferences of the statement constitute the *core* of the inferences that can be drawn from the statement (see section 4.2.2). If a query matches a member of the *core* inferences of a statement that is present in a given database, the query is derivable from that database. It can thus be said the the inference-set of a statement points to a set of queries that are satisfiable by that statement. Since generalizations are implicitly present in the concrete information from which they are produced, the *core* of an *inference-set* of a given statement can be taken to be the concrete instantial combinations of that statement. For the most part, the theory of inference-sets can specified with reference to core segments of inference-sets because the effects of generalizations are defined in terms of the effects of core inferences.

The theory behind the creation of an inference-set for a *simple* statement is specified with reference to the theory of creating an inference-set for a nonsentential object. As is described in section 4.6, the concept of derivability is extended in SMS to include nonsentential objects so that it becomes meaningful to speak of relations such as $\beta_i \vdash \beta_k$ even when $\beta$ ranges over atoms and phrases. Some of the more important and frequently used nonsentential inferencing patterns are given below in schematic form in which $\beta$ ranges over labels and $\alpha$ ranges over concrete markers. Given that the concrete marker $\alpha_1$ *isa* $\beta_i$, the following pattern is valid:

<$\beta_i$ <any>>

---

<$\beta_i$ <some>>

$\alpha_1$

Likewise, given that $\beta_i$ *isa* $\beta_j$ and that $\beta_k$ *isa* $\beta_i$, and assuming that $\alpha_1$ *isa* $\beta_k$, the following nonsentential patterns are accepted:

<$\beta_i$ <any>>

---

<$\beta_j$ <some>>

<$\beta_k$ <any>>

<$\beta_k$ <some>>

and

<$\beta_i$ <some>>

---

<$\beta_j$ <some>>

However, in conformity with the prohibition against inferring the presence of a particular individual from mere reference to the presence of some otherwise unidentified individual, as in the reference 'some person', the following pattern is *not* accepted:

<$\beta_i$ <some>>

---

$\alpha_2$

where $\alpha$ ranges over concrete markers, each of which bears an *isa* relation to $\beta_i$.

As will be discussed in section 11.5 on querying, given a query component that bears the form of one of the conclusions in one of the valid inference patterns, that query component is satisfiable in a database that conforms to the corresponding premise. In this respect, querying amounts to theorem proving. Inference patterns of this kind are used to determine membership in inference-sets and to determine what expressions are proper instantial terms or combinations of other expressions. The *inference-set* of a nonsentential expression $\theta_i$ can be defined to be the set of all proper generalizations and instantiations that can be produced for $\theta_i$ under the instantiation and generalization rules of the system.

The *inference-set* of a *sentential* object is specified with reference to inference-sets of nonsentential objects. The construction of an inference-set for a simple statement can be described as a two-step process. First, inference-sets are created for the individual components of the statement. Second, the components of the inference-sets created in the first step are related to one another through the components of the inference-set created for the link of the statement. Each element of an inference-set of a sentential object is itself a sentential object and constitutes what will be referred to herein as a *line of correspondence* in which objects are related to one another through links. Each element of such an inference-set constitutes a separate line of correspondence that may be related to one or more lines of correspondence of another inference-set, thereby producing one or more new lines of correspondence. The process can be illustrated by example. For the sake of simplicity, links will not be treated in this example. It should be noted, however, that inference-sets can be created for links just as they are for noun components. Given an expression of the form:

<<$\beta_1$<any>> likes <$\beta_2$<some>>>

(where $\beta$ ranges over labels), an inference-set could be produced for this statement by creating inference-sets for '<$\beta_1$<any>>' and '<$\beta_2$<some>>', and then casting the elements of the former into relations with the elements of the latter using the link 'likes'. Each such relation would constitute a line of correspondence. The total set of these related components would constitute the inference-set of this simple statement; however, to produce such a total set, the system must have some way of knowing how the elements of one inference-set are to be related to the elements of another. In SMS, the relations between elements of inference-sets of the components of *simple* statements are postulated in advance based on the type of quantifiers that may appear in combination within such a statement. Although postulated, the relations seem to conform to what a person might understand them to be, at least this appears to be so for commonly recognized quantifiers such as 'any' and 'some'. To give the reader some idea of what kind of rules have been postulated for the creation of inference-sets, some of the rules for a 2-place simple statement are given below. The rules are explained in terms of some of the more common combinations of quantifiers that may occur in such a statement. The quantifiers are listed in pairs. The first member of each pair is to be taken as the quantifier of the subject of the statement, and the second member is to be taken as the quantifier of the object. The arrow represents the link that relates the subject and object. For each combination of quantifiers, there is a corresponding rule that determines how the members of the inference-set of the subject are to be related to the members of the inference-set of the object.

Using the letters S and O to represent the inference-sets of the subject and object respectively, the relations between the members of S and O are determined as follows:

> any → any combination --- Each member of S is related to every member of O.
>
> any → some combination --- Every member of S is related to each member of O, which is usually a unit set.
>
> any → some* combination --- Each member of S has a different, corresponding member of O.
>
> some* → any combination --- Each member of S is related to a different, corresponding member of O.
>
> some → any combination --- Each member of S, which is usually a unit set, is related to every member of O.
>
> some* → some* combination --- Each member of S is related to a different, corresponding member of O.

Using rules of this kind, an inference-set can be generated for any 2-place simple statement, and what can be done for a 2-place simple statement can be done for any other simple statement. Now that an explanation has been given of how the rules of quantification, generalization and instantiation can be used to produce inference-sets for *simple* statements, an explanation will be given of how these rules can be used in *complex* statements to produce corresponding effects. Such an explanation is given in section 10.2.2.

### 10.2.2 Using Quantification, Instantiation and Generalization in Complex Statements

Since quantifiers, through their quantifier-markers, name sets of objects, and since statements in SL cast those sets into relationships with one another through links, an understanding of SL requires that one become familiar with how the relations between those sets are determined. Section 10.2.1 described how the relations are handled for simple statements. The discussions will now focus on complex statements. Quantifiers are used in complex statements to specify what relations hold between the members of the inference-sets of the components of those statements, whether those components be sentential or nonsentential objects. An inclusive inference-set for a complex statement can be created by creating an inference-set for every nonsentential object and simple statement within the complex statement and by relating the results through links using rules similar to those described in section 10.2.1. A *sentential* element of an inference-set may be related to an element of another inference-set just as may be done for a nonsentential element of an inference-set. The process of creating inference-sets and relating their components can be continued within a complex statement until an inference-set is created for the entire statement. Each element of the inclusive inference-set is itself a sentential object and constitutes a line of correspondence in which objects have been related to one another through one or more links. As described in section 10.2.1, for *simple* statements, the relations between inference-sets are specified with reference to the quantifiers attached to the noun components of the statements. For *complex* statements, the relations between inference-sets are specified with reference to quantifiers associated with the *primary links* of the statements that appear within the complex statements. The primary link of a sentence-sequence is the root of the expression that occupies the second position in that sentential sequence. Before discussing how *link* quantifiers affect meaning, the special quantifier 'all*' will be introduced and used in an example to show how a *noun* quantifier can affect the meaning of a complex statement.

The quantifier 'all*' is used to impose a group effect on the reference to a given set of objects or individuals. Suppose, for example, one wishes to say that a person named Mary is delighted by the fact that John likes any and all dogs. It would be a mistake to represent this in SL as '<<john likes <dog<any>>> delights mary>' because, given that 'fido' is a 'dog', the inference '<<john likes fido> delights mary>' would follow from it, yet this inference would not follow from the original idea because what delights Mary is the fact that John likes any and all dogs, not the fact that he likes any particular dog. To capture this idea, SL provides the special quantifier 'all*'. This quantifier creates a quantifier-marker of the universal sort that bears the form all*-$_i$ and invokes special procedures that affect inferencing. When used in an assertion, the term 'all*' is assigned a *scope* within which it will have the same effect as the quantifier 'any'. The scope can be set conventionally in the SL notation by using the operator 's*', which will be discussed a little further on, but if the scope is not so fixed, it is taken to be the smallest *wfss* that contains the quantifier. Hence, if the quantifier is used in a sentential sequence within another sentential sequence, the former sequence marks the scope of the quantifier by default. For any inference drawn from information that is totally within that scope, the quantifier is taken to be the quantifier 'any', and the quantifier-marker produced therein may be instantiated by any marker that bears an *isa* relation to the key label of the quantifier marker. If, however, an inference is to be drawn from information that includes information beyond the scope of the quantifier, the instantiation rules for the 'any' quantifier are not applicable. Instead a restriction is imposed that allows the quantifier-marker produced for the 'all*' quantifier to be instantiated only by itself or by a marker semantically equivalent to it. The example above involving John, Mary and the dogs can be used to illustrate these effects. The original idea in that example can be represented as:

<<john likes <dogs<all*>>> delights mary>.

Since there is no 's*' operator associated with the quantifier 'all*', its scope, by default, is the expression:

<john likes <dogs<all*>>>

which qualifies as a direct inference (see section 4.2.1) and thus has the same strength of presence as the sequence from which it is derived. This direct inference would be interpreted in a special way. The quantifier 'all*', for example, would be taken to be the quantifier 'any'. The result of this interpretation would read '<john likes <dog<any>>', which, in turn, would be individuated to say to '<john likes any-24>', where 'any-24' is an ordinary universal quantifier-marker that may be instantiated by any marker or name, including 'fido', that conforms to its key label 'dog'. As result, the inference '<john likes fido>' follows as a valid inference not only from this direct inference, but from the original sequence also. It should be noted that the portion of the original sequence pertaining to the delightment of 'mary' is beyond the scope of the quantifier 'all*'. Consequently, if an attempt were to be made to derive an inference based on all or part of that information, the restrictions associated with 'all*' would be imposed. Given that the expression '<dogs<all*>>' would be individuated to 'all*-7', so that the original sequence would be individuated to '<<john likes all*-7> delights mary>', the quantifier-marker 'all*' could not be instantiated by 'fido' under these restrictions to produce the inference '<<john likes fido> delights mary>.

The operator 's*' is used to set the scope of a quantifier. Like the operator 'c*' it is used in an expression of the form '<s* #>', where # ranges over numbers. When an 's*' expression appears in association with a quantifier, the scope of the quantifier is set by an identical 's*' expression that is associated with another term as a modifier. The smallest well formed sentential expression that contains this second instance of the 's*' expression is taken to be the scope of the quantifier that is marked by the first 's*' expression. Generally, the second instance of the expression is associated with a link. The effect is that within that scope, the quantifier 'all*' will operate as the quantifier 'any' as was previously described. Given the statement:

<<<john likes <dogs<all*><s* 1>>> <delights<s* 1>> mary>

causes

<jim is happy>>

the scope of the quantifier 'all*' would be:

<<john likes <dogs<all*><s* 1>>> <delights<s* 1>> mary>

and hence the inference '<<john likes fido> delights mary>' would be valid because the quantifier 'all*' would be taken to be the quantifier 'any' within this scope and thus would not be constrained by the aforementioned limitations.

As mentioned previously, relations between inference-sets of sentential objects that appear within complex statements are specified with reference to the quantifiers that are attached to the primary links of those sentential objects. The quantifiers attached to the links thus operate on inference-sets of statements rather than on extensions of labels as they do when the quantifiers are associated with terms other than links. Given that $C_1$ is the inference-set of a simple statement $\Phi_1$ and that $C_2$ is the inference-set of another object $\Phi_2$, whether sentential or not, a complex statement that relates $\Phi_1$, say as the subject of the statement, to $\Phi_2$, say as the object of the statement, through some link $\delta_i$ would have a corresponding inference-set that would be constructed by relating the members of $C_1$ to the members of $C_2$ through the link $\delta_i$. The rules that govern the relationship between $C_1$ and $C_2$ are specified with reference to the quantifiers that are attached to the primary links of $\Phi_1$ and $\Phi_2$, assuming here that both $\Phi_1$ and $\Phi_2$ are sentential objects. The rules operate like the rules described in section 10.2.1 that relate inference-sets between nonsentential objects. Thus if the primary links of both $\Phi_1$ and $\Phi_2$ bear the quantifier 'any', which would produce an 'any $\rightarrow$ any' combination, each member of $C_1$ would be related to every member of $C_2$ through the link $\delta_i$. The resulting set of inferences would be the inference-set for the complex statement $<\Phi_1\ \delta_i\ \Phi_2>$.

By being able to control the type of quantifiers that are attached to the noun and link components of simple and complex statements, one acquires a significant amount of control over expression. If, for example, a complex statement $\Phi_j$ relates the statement $\Phi_i$ to a statement $\Phi_k$ through the link $\delta_i$, and the quantifier 'all*' is attached to the primary link of $\Phi_i$, the inference-set for $\Phi_i$ would be treated as a unit, so that if the quantifier associated with the primary link of $\Phi_k$ happened to be 'any', the relevant quantifier combination would be 'all* $\rightarrow$ any'. Under this combination of quantifiers, the entire inference-set of $\Phi_i$ (being taken as a unit because of the quantifier 'all*') would be related to each member of the inference-set for $\Phi_k$ through the link $\delta_i$ to produce an inference-set for the complex statement. Thus, under this scheme, the statement:

<<<logician<some>> <likes<all*>> <logic<any>>>

causes

<<philosopher<any>> <is<any>> <delighted<some*>>>

would mean that the entire inference-set for '<<logician<some>> <likes<all*>> <logic<any>>>' (in which the 'logician' referred to would be related to each and every 'logic' through the link 'likes') would be related to each and every member of the inference-set generated for the statement '<<philosopher<any>> <is<any>> <delighted<some*>>>'. The inference-set of this last statement would relate each 'philosopher' to a different state of being 'delighted'. It should be noted that what delights any 'philosopher' under the original statement is the fact that the 'logician' likes any 'logic', not any particular 'logic'. Hence, given that 'john' is a 'philosopher' and that 'logic-24' is a 'logic, the inference:

<<<logician<the>> likes logic-24> causes <john is delighted>>

would not be included in the inference-set of the original statement and thus could not be derived from it on that basis. This is because of the effects produced by the quantifier 'all*'. As a notational convention adopted to reduce the number of quantifiers used in SL notation, a link implicitly carries the quantifier 'any' unless otherwise indicated. Under this convention, the use of the quantifier 'any' to quantify the link 'is' in the statement '<<philosopher<any>> <is<any>> <delighted<some*>>>, as was done in the example above, constitutes a redundant use of that quantifier.

From this last example one can see that the quantifier 'all*', when associated with a link, can produce effects similar to those produced by that same quantifier when it is associated with a noun label. Drawing upon previous examples, under the rules described thus far in this chapter, the effects that would be recognized for the statement:

<<john likes <dogs<all*>>> delights mary>

would be very similar to those that would be recognized for:

<<john <likes<all*>> <dog<any>>>
delights
mary>.

SL provides a special quantifier to enable one to specify that the relation between members of two inference-sets is to be a *one-one* and *onto* relation. The quantifier 'some*' produces that kind of relation, but since it does not necessarily cover all members of the extension or set upon which it operates, it would not be appropriate for use in representing a relation in which *all* elements of a set are being referred to and are to be cast into a one-one and onto relation with members of another set. Therefore the special quantifier 'any*' has been introduced into SL to enable one to produce the desired effects. Thus, for the statement:

<<teacher<any>>
causes
<<student<some*>> <reads<any*>> <book<some*>>>>

the inference-set of the object would be created as usual so that each element of the inference-set of the expression '<student<some*>>' would be related (through the link 'reads') to a different element of the inference-set of the expression '<book<some*>>'. The quantifier for the resulting inference-set O would be the quantifier 'any*', which is the quantifier attached to the link of the object of the complex statement above. Taking S to be the inference-set of the expression '<teacher<any>>', the elements of S would be related to the elements of O using rules specified for the quantifier combination 'any → any*'. Those rules are defined to establish a one-one and onto mapping, and each member of S would be assigned a different member in O. What this amounts to is that a member of O is created for each member of S.

Before leaving the subject of how quantifiers affect the meaning of SL statements, something should be said about how the operators 'c*' and 'the' can be used to make reference to previously created quantifier-markers. Since one of the effects of using a quantifier is to designate a set named by the associated quantifier-marker, care must be taken when reference is to be made to a previously created quantifier-marker. SMS has a set of default rules that govern references to previously created quantifier-markers. Under those rules, whenever the 'the' or 'c*' operator is used to cast a previously created set into a relation with some other object or set, previous correspondences are inherited unless explicitly overridden. What this amounts to is that once a member of a set is associated with a member of another set, the two continue to be bound to one another when the two sets are again related to one another through use of the operator 'c*' or 'the'. If the expression '<logician<some*>>' is used in expression and causes the members of the set named by the assigned quantifier-marker to be cast into one-one and onto lines of correspondence with members of another set, and if through use of the 'c*' or 'the' operator, a reference is subsequently made to the set named by the quantifier-marker, unless otherwise indicated in expression, that reference by default will attach to each line of correspondence. In other words, when one makes reference in an SL statement to a previously created quantifier-marker, it is as if one is speaking of an arbitrarily selected member of the set named by that quantifier-maker, and what is being said of that member is being said of the other members of that set. To represent the idea that 'any church has a steeple, and the steeple has a bell', where the intended meaning is that each church has a different steeple, and each steeple has a different bell, the following SL statements could be entered into an SMS database:

1) <<church<any>> has-possess <steeple<some*>>>

2) <<steeple<the>> has-possess <bell<some*>>>.

The reference in the second statement to 'steeple' is a reference to the quantifier-marker that, because of the quantifier 'some*', would have been created for the label 'steeple' in the first statement. The second statement asserts that each 'steeple' referred to in the first statement has a 'bell'. As far as the system knows, each 'steeple' has a different 'bell' since under statement 2, an independent 'bell' marker would be created for each corresponding 'steeple' marker, and under statement 1, an independent 'steeple' marker would have been created for each 'church' marker.

Taking another example, suppose one wishes to represent a situation in which any man likes some woman and the woman likes the man. The ideas involved could be brought to presence in a database using the following statements:

1) <<man<any>> likes <woman<some*>>>

2) <<woman<the>> likes <man<the>>

Assuming that the subject and object of statement 1 individuate to 'any-7' and 'psome*-12' respectively, and taking these markers to name sets, a one-one and onto mapping from any-7 into psome*-12 would be recognized. Statement 2 employs the 'the' operator to cast the sets psome*-12 and any-7 into another relationship, and since there is a previously defined correspondence between the sets, that correspondence is preserved. Thus, given that 'john' is a 'man', under the mapping in statement 1, a newly created particular quantifier-marker, say 'pqe-24', would be assigned to 'john' to represent the 'woman' that corresponds to 'john' in the 'likes' relation. This correspondence would be preserved in the second statement, which relates the set psome*-12 to the set any-7. In other words, pqe-24 would be bound to 'john' in the relationship established in statement 2. To put this another way, when a 'c*' or 'the' operator is used to refer to a set whose members are bound in correspondence with members of another set, the reference, by default, attaches to each member of the first set and honors previous bindings associated with that member.

In closing out this section, the point should be stressed that SL provides basic quantifiers to enable one to produce varying effects in expression. New quantifiers and operators can be introduced as needed to produce additional effects. The only practical constraint seems to be that the number of operators, quantifiers included, should not be allowed to become unmanageably large. At this point in the development of SMS, it appears that the number of operators can be held within reasonable limits.

### 10.2.3 Realms and Quantifiers

Unless otherwise indicated, a quantifier is bound to the realm of OW, which constitutes the ordinary world of SMS. Quantifiers for particular realms are created by concatenating the symbol for that realm to the quantifier. Thus, the quantifier 'somefw' would be bound to the realm of FW, the world of fiction. Quantifiers operate in the realms to which they are bound as do their counterparts in the realm of OW. Whenever the intent is to have the quantifier range over all the realms of SMS other than NW, the letter x is concatenated to the end of the quantifier, as in 'somex'. Since the realm NW operates as a receptacle for inconsistencies, it is handled separately, and only quantifiers that end in 'nw' operate within that realm. Under this scheme, the statement '<<person<somex>> flies>' asserts that in at least one realm of SMS, some individual 'flies' and is bound to the label 'person'. It should be noted that the argument:

<<<person<somex>> flies> IPR>

---

<<<person<some>> flies> IPR>

is not valid because what is present in one realm is not necessarily present in another, and here the 'some' quantifier of the conclusion is limited to the ordinary world, whereas the 'somex' quantifier of the premises ranges over all realms except for the realm NW. In order to allow the range of a quantifier (operator) to extend over more than one realm, but not all, the default quantifier can be given arguments, as in '<some ow fw>', which sets the range of the quantifier to the realms of OW and FW. By allowing quantifiers to range over multiple realms, SMS captures some of the effects produced under free logic (see e.g. Bencivenga, 1986; LeBlanc and Thomason, 1968; and Cocchiarella, 1966).

### 10.2.4 Cluster-Entities (CEs) and Quantifiers

As discussed in section 2.5, when an unquantified, plural form of a label is used in expression, it is individuated into a CE marker that names a subset of the objects that conform to the sign of the singular form of that label. Thus far, to keep matters simple, singular forms of labels have been used in the examples of the production of inference-sets. References to groups or CEs (cluster-entities) are more difficult to handle because in the first round of creating inference-sets, inferences containing CE markers are produced. The problem is that each CE marker represents a group, so to produce a complete set of inferences, the members of each group must be cast into proper relationships with other objects. This section describes the general approach being used to established those relationships.

Inference sets for statements that contain CEs are created by methods similar to those described in sections 10.2.1 and 10.2.2, which for the most part deal with statements that contain singular forms of labels. For simple statements that contain one or more CEs, none of which are quantified, the relations between the members of the CEs are postulated as is done for relations between inference-sets of quantified UEs of simple statements. An important difference is that the relations for CEs are specified with reference to a special set of modifiers or operators rather than with reference to various combinations of quantifiers. The set of CE operators has been created so that the operator that is to be associated with individual CE markers can be distinguished from the quantifiers that are to operate on sets that contain the CE markers. The operator 'blk', for example, when associated with a CE, causes that CE to be treated as a unit in much the same way that the operator 'all*' causes the set upon which it operates to be treated as a unit. In the absence of a special CE operator, the CE will be treated as if the quantifier 'any' is associated with it so that each and every member of the CE will be cast into the relation called for by the original statement. The simple statement:

<women saw men>

contains two labels that are plural forms and are not quantified. The inference-set for this statement would consist of a set of inferences in which each member of the group of 'women' would be related through the link 'saw' to each and every member of the group of 'men'. This is because the default rule mentioned above would be invoked. If the operator 'blk' had been attached to the label 'women' in this statement, a different effect would have been produced. The entire group of 'women', taken as a unit, would have been related to each and every man in the group of 'men'. As result, one would not be able to infer that any particular member of the 'women' 'saw' any particular member of the 'men'.

Another operator that is used on CEs is the term 'diff*', which is used to cause the system to assign a *diff*erent (hence the 'diff' in 'diff*') value to each member of a set. As is the case for the 'some*' and 'any*' operators, the 'diff*' operator causes a one-one and onto mapping to be recognized between sets. For the statement:

<churches have-possess <steeples<diff*>>>

the effect of the operator 'diff*' would be to cause each member of the group of 'churches' to be assigned a different 'steeple'. It should be noted that this statement is *not* asserting that *all* 'churches' have 'steeples'. To make that statement, quantifiers would have to be used. What the statement asserts is that a group of 'churches' is related to a group of 'steeples' through the link 'have-possess'. The relations between the members of the groups are determined by the CE operators that are explicitly or implicitly present.

The aforementioned set of special CE modifiers has been created in SL to enable one to capture effects produced by both CE operators and ordinary SL quantifiers. When an ordinary quantifier is attached to a plural label, the set named by the quantifier-marker consists of CE markers, and those CE markers are then cast into relations with other objects. Each relation so produced has an inference-set of its own. In order to enable one to control how such an inference-set will be related to other objects, SL allows one to attach both a quantifier and a CE operator to a plural label. In such a case, the quantifier is invoked first to produce a quantifier-marker that names a set of CE markers, and the CE operator is then associated with each CE marker in that set. A conventional exception is made for the quantifier 'all*'. This quantifier may quantify a plural form of a label without the reference being construed as one to a set of CE markers. The reason for this is that the reference otherwise would be construed as being to all groups that could be distinguished within the extension of the label, the set of groups being taken as a unit. Seemingly, such a reference would not be any more useful than a reference to all members of the extension of the label taken as a unit.

The scheme for combining quantifiers with CE operators can be illustrated by example. For the statement:

<<logicians<some*><blk>> like <formula<any>>>

which may be taken to assert that for any 'formula', there corresponds an independent group of 'logicians' who, *as a group*, like that 'formula'. The quantifier 'some*' of the subject of the statement would be called on first to create a quantifier-marker, say psome*-7, that would name a set consisting of markers for CEs. As usual, under the rules specified in section 10.2.1 for the 'some* → any' combination, each 'formula' would be associated with a different member of the set psome*-7 in the way called for by the statement. This would create an inference-set in which each member would bear the form <ce-i likes ue-i>, where ce-i would be a CE marker and ue-i would be some 'formula'. The process of generating inference-sets would continue, however, because each CE marker names a set or group that bears a relation to a 'formula'. How the members of a particular CE set would be related to the associated 'formula' would be determined by the implicit or explicit CE operator associated with the plural form of the label that is bound to the CE markers. In this example, the label is 'logicians', and the CE operator 'blk' is explicitly given. The operator, by default, would attach to each CE marker in psome*-7. The result would be that instead of bearing the form '<ce-i likes ue-i>', each member of the inference-set would bear the form '<<ce-i<blk>> likes ue-i>'. At this point, an inference-set could be generated for each inference that bears this form using the rules postulated for this combination of CE operators, one of them being explicitly given and one of them being implicitly given. The result for each such inference would be that the group of 'logicians' named by the CE marker in the inference would be related, as a unit, to the 'formula' in that inference.

Using methods such as those described above, an inference-set can be created for a *complex* statement by methods very similar to those described in sections 10.2.2 for statements that do not contain CEs. As is done for those statements, relations between the inference-sets of components are determined by the quantifiers associated with the primary *links* of the statements that appear within the complex statements (see section 10.2.2).

### 10.3 Sentential Quantification and Instantiation

Sentential quantification in SL involves quantification over *wfsss*. The symbol '∇' will be used to indicate that a quantifier is a sentential one. The symbols Ψ and Σ introduced in section 10.2 for the schematic representation of the universal and particular quantifiers will be used again in that way to represent sentential quantifiers when the symbol '∇' is prefixed to them, as in '∇Ψ' and '∇Σ'. The following is an example of a legitimate schema for a *wfss* that employs a sentential quantifier:

$$< <\Phi <\nabla\Psi>> \delta \beta >$$

where $\Phi$ ranges over *wfsss*, $\delta$ ranges over 2-place link atoms or link phrases, and $\beta$ ranges over noun phrase-sequences. The expression $<\Phi <\nabla\Psi>>$ in this schema is interpreted to mean that for any proper instantial combination $c_i$ of $\Phi_{ind}$ (where $\Phi_{ind}$ represents $\Phi$ in an individuated form such as an open sentence containing one or more quantifier-markers), the following holds: $< c_i \delta \beta >$.

Just as the presence of an individual quantifier causes the individuation process to create an individual quantifier-marker for the associated key label, a sentential quantifier causes the process to create sentential quantifier-marker for the key sentential sequence (e.g. $\Phi$ in the schema above) that is associated with the sentential quantifier. The original quantifier attaches to the set of proper instantiations of the key sentential sequence. A proper instantiation of the key sentential sequence requires that each component of the key sequence be properly instantiated by the corresponding component of the instantial sequence. The process is described in section 10.2. That section explains how the process works for components that are quantifier-markers in open sentences, but a special explanation is in order for components that are not quantifier-markers, such as concrete markers. Although not instantiation in a standard sense, since a variable is not being replaced by a constant or another variable, the replacement of a concrete marker by another linguistic object is nonetheless classified as instantiation in SMS. The process is described in the next subsection.

Given that the sentential quantifier-marker names a set of proper instantiations for the key sentential sequence, if the quantifier 'any' is the original quantifier, all instantial sequences for the key sequence are included in the set named by the sentential quantifier-marker, whereas if the quantifier is of a particular sort, the set of instantial sequences is dealt with accordingly. If the original quantifier is 'some', then the meaning is that at least one member of the instantial set is being referred to, but which one is not specified. If the 'some*' quantifier is the original quantifier, the same subset of instantial sequences is being referred to, but again the subset is not specified, so new markers would have to be created to represent that set. The set of new markers would be handled in a way that conforms to the way the corresponding set would be handled for individual quantifier 'some*'.

### 10.4 Instantiation of Concrete Markers

The concept of instantiation is broadened in SL to include not only variables but concrete markers as well. Although it is not necessary to broaden the concept in this way, it is convenient to do so in connection with sentential instantiation. As stated in section 10.3, to instantiate an open sentence-sequence, each component of the instantial sequence must instantiate the corresponding component of the sentence-sequence being instantiated. Since sentence-sequences contain some components that are not variables, one either has to ignore those components in the instantiation process or allow them to be instantiated. In SL the latter approach is adopted but as a restricted operation that allows a concrete marker to be instantiated only by a marker that is syntactically identical to it or else bears an explicitly given relation of equality with it, such a relation being represented by the symbol is= (see sections 10.1 and 4.3). Thus given the concrete noun markers 'ue-1', 'ue-2', and 'ue-3', and given the concrete link marker 'v-5', and also given that 'ue-1 is= ue-2', the sentence-sequence:

< ue-1 v-5 ue-3 >

may instantiate:

< ue-2 v-5 ue-3 >

since 'ue-1' is explicitly cast into a relation of equality with 'ue-2' and since the two token instances of the sign 'v-5' are syntactically identical as are those of the sign 'ue-3'.

## 10.5 Event and State Individuation

The question of how one should go about individuating situations, states and events has been of conscious concern for logicians for decades (see e.g. Quine, 1986, for pertinent comments). This section will describe the general approach being employed in SMS in this area and will introduce some of the principles that are guiding the development of this component of the system.

In SMS, events and states are individuated as part of the same process. The discussions will focus on principles of event individuation, but the principles described are also applicable to states. When events are individuated and marked, inferencing processes that operate on event descriptions can perform part of their operations over atoms, that is, on the markers that have been assigned to those events. It has been noted on occasion (e.g. Moore, 1982) that first-order logic does not place limits on what may be taken as an object. Expressions, times, states, and events, even worlds, may be considered to be logical individuals. Section 6.3 mentions that the links (relations) of SL can be given extensions in the database of SMS. It is easy to understand how relations between individuals that correspond to persons and things of the world can be given extensions since each individual can be assigned a marker in the system. Thus, for any point in time recognized in the system for which a relation holds between one or more individuals, the relation can be assigned a set of individuals or ordered tuples that constitute its extension. The two-place relation *love* would have an extension consisting of all ordered pairs of individual markers between which the relation holds. It is more difficult to understand how relations between states and events can be given extensions.

In one sense, it is a simple task to individuate an event. One can simply assign a marker to the event. Given the event description:

<alvin saw lisa>

a marker, say 'e-100', could be assigned to the event sequence, thereby individuating it to some extent since at least it now has a name. The marker 'e-100' can be used to refer to the event, but the event *description* has not been individuated in the sense that it can be matched or distinguished *semantically* from all other event descriptions in the system. Given another event sequence consisting of the same terms, that is, '<alvin saw lisa>', how would the system go about determining whether this sequence is identical with the event marked by 'e-100'? The point is that for an event description to be matched with or distinguished from other descriptions in the system, sufficient information about the event must be available for that purpose, including temporal specificity and other denotata. In a nutshell, the problem to be resolved is how does one determine whether two statements are identical in a sense that would cause them to receive the same marker. It may be that the test for semantic identity between statements will have to be conducted at the atomically normalized level by methods of the sort described in sections 4.9 and 4.4.

Event individuation has proven to be troublesome problem in FOL, although some progress appears to have been made (e.g. Hobbs, 1985; Davidson, 1967). The problem is so difficult that it may be some time before SMS will be able to individuate events at an acceptable level of efficiency, but the wait seemingly will be far outweighed by the resulting benefits, a point discussed in more depth at the end of this section. In these discussions the meaning of *event* is to be construed broadly to include both states and events so that as far as SL representations are concerned, any sentence-sequence is to be taken as an event description. Three important reasons for individuating events are:

1) to enable them to be related to other expressions through links (which corresponds to allowing events to be predicated);

2) to enable them to be quantified; and

3) to enable instantiation, unification, inferencing and resolution processes to operate more efficiently.

Event marking presupposes an ability to mark atoms and phrases since each of these objects may appear in an event sequence. The approach used in SMS is to individuate events based on the denotata of their noun and link components. For the event to be individuated, each key component of the event-sequence must be individuated. By definition, a sentence-sequence contains at least one link or link phrase, and for a link to be individuated, temporal specificity must be complete just as would be the case for an ordinary description of an act in English. The individuation of the sentential sequence '<john saw mary>' would require that the denotation of 'john' and 'mary' be set and that the act of seeing be determined.

Acts are individuated by their related denotata, which in this case would consist of the denotations (markers) of 'john' and 'mary' and of the denotation of the particular act of seeing involved, which would consist of the marker assigned to the link 'saw'. Temporal specificity is determined by temporal markers, and one or more temporal markers are assigned to each link.

Temporal specificity is of crucial importance in the event individuation process of SMS. There are a number of temporal descriptors available in SL that can be used to describe aspects of time, including points and intervals. Temporal descriptors are introduced into SL as phrase sequences that have temporal prepositions as their root terms. The temporal preposition 't-at', for example, is used to introduce points in time, whereas the preposition 't-for' is used to introduce points or complete intervals. A complete interval is a segment of time demarcated by a starting point and an ending point and which includes all intervening points. In other words, a complete interval is conceived of as an unbroken series of temporal points. Complete individuation of any segment of an event requires that the segment be assigned a complete interval that covers the entire segment and requires that the interval be bound on the time scale of the system. The time scale is being designed to correspond to a world calendar.

The following factors are among those that are pertinent to event individuation: 1) who or what objects participated in the event; 2) when and where did the event occur; 3) to what extent did it occur; 4) at what measure, speed or intensity did it occur; 5) what attitudes, emotions, or intentions did the participants have when it occurred; 6) how well and efficiently was it done; 7) what means were used to bring it about; 8) does it take place incrementally; 9) if an end-state is involved, did that end-state come into being over a period of time or suddenly; 10) if subevents are involved, how are they related; and 11) what temporal intervals are involved and how are they related to one another. This listing of factors is by no means exclusive. It is presented to make the point that if a given event can bear these features, how can one determine whether another event that bears one or more of these features is that same event?

The general approach being developed for SMS is to categorize the features and to specify rules for each category that can be used in comparing event descriptions to determine whether they are semantically identical. The crucial factors seem to be time, location and participants. A set of default rules is being developed to operate when information is lacking. One of the ground rules is that two events cannot be matched (made equivalent) unless the temporal information matches, which means that if temporal information is left unspecified, the events should not be assumed to be the same. If the participants and the links are the same in the two events and the temporal descriptions are semantically identical under specially run tests, the presumption is that the events are the same *unless* differentiating factors in the form of modifiers or qualifiers are found to be present.

It should be noted that some factors are not comparable for distinguishing events. A few examples can illustrate some of the considerations involved. Temporal information has been omitted for the sake of simplicity, but the reader should assume that complete temporal information has been given for each pair of statements and that the temporal information has been found to be the same for each statement. The reader should also assume in each example that the statement given first is already present in the database and that the statement given second is an entering statement about which the system must decide whether it is to be assigned the same marker as the first statement. The statements are numbered accordingly to remind the reader of this assumption. The statements 1) ‘<john <ran<fast>>>’ and 2) ‘<john <ran<slow>>’ would not be taken to be the same event because of the differentiating modifiers ‘fast’ and ‘slow’, which are comparable. The statements 1) ‘<john <saw<bmo<john use telescope>>> mary>’ (where ‘bmo’ is to be read ‘by means of’) and 2) ‘<john saw mary>’ would be assumed to be the same event because the ‘seeing’ in the second statement is not particularized by modifiers and thus is construed in a general sense. The two ‘seeings’ referred to in the statements are thus not taken to contain differentiating qualifiers. Likewise, the statements 1) <john <saw<bmo<john use telescope>>> mary> and 2) ‘<john <saw<clearly>> mary>’ would not be deemed to contain differentiating qualifiers since ‘<bmo<john use telescope>>’ and ‘<clearly>’ can be classified as noncomparable, nondifferentiating modifiers. On the other hand, the statements 1) ‘<john <saw<bmo<john use telescope>>> mary>’ and 2) ‘<john <saw<bmo<john use eyeglasses>>> mary>’ would not be considered to be the same event because the terms ‘telescope’ and ‘glasses’, being comparable and different, would be assumed to be differentiating qualifiers.

One can begin to appreciate the enormity of the problem of the determination of semantic identity between statements when one considers the number of relevant factors and the seemingly limitless number of ways that they can be combined in expression. To complicate matters, the problem of having to test for consistency may enter the picture. In an election, for example, a political candidate might ‘run strongly’ in Baton Rouge, yet ‘run weakly’ statewide, all during the same time interval. Assuming the system would know that Baton Rouge is in Louisiana and would have some sense of what ‘run’ means in this context, it would face the task of having to analyze a situation that could be taken to involve an event/subevent relationship between the events of running weakly in Louisiana and of running strongly in Baton Rouge. It would also face the task of having to decide whether the opposites ‘strongly’ and ‘weakly’ create and inconsistency in this situation. Opposites such as this can create inconsistences when included within descriptions that map to the same event marker, and this is relevant for resolution. An event description, the presence of which is given as a mere alternative possibility for example, would be eliminated as a possibility if another event description is present that maps to to the same event marker and bears some comparable qualifier that makes the descriptions inconsistent. Given, for example, that the database contains the sequence '<<john <ran<fast><t-for tr-1>>> or <john <walked<quickly><t-for tr-2>>>>', where 'tr-1' and 'tr-2' are separate intervals, if the sequence '<john <ran<slowly><t-for tr-1>>>' were to be entered, the sequence '<john <walked<quickly><t-for tr-2>>>>' could be deduced by resolution based on the assumption that any reference to a 'running' by 'john' for the entire interval 'tr-1' is reference to the same event. That being so, the presence of 'slowly' in the new event description would serve to cancel the corresponding alternative possibility.

The hope is that the scheme of default rules and methods of handling adverbials through generation of link-related assertions as described in section 9.3, along with special notational conventions that will allow one to override the default rules, will enable a satisfactory theory of event individuation to be specified for the system. Although early results seem promising, the sheer magnitude of the problem discourages any confident prediction of near-term success in this area. That having been said, something should be said about the benefits that could be brought about by the development of an adequate system of event individuation. The remaining discussions in this section explain why less emphasis is being placed in this book on a description of unification, inferencing, and resolution methodologies than otherwise might have been the case.

A weakness of many AI systems, which is sometimes glossed over in descriptions of some FOL-based systems, is that they are not really equipped to handle fine descriptions of the states and events with which they are to deal. Often such a system operates on a clausal database that does not capture all the temporal and other specificity that may be associated with a given event, yet the system is described as if it has the capability of recognizing when two events are the same without difficulty. Powerful resolution and unification methodologies are specified for the system, but they operate on descriptions that on close inspection may be found to be less than adequate for reasoning about the domain within which the system is designed to operate. For a system to operate effectively at the level of specificity at which SMS is being designed to function, it must be able to determine when complex event descriptions are semantically identical. One can imagine the potential of such a system. Suppose, for example, that such a system were to be given an alternative list of event descriptions in which each description would average 20 sentences in length. The system could assign an event marker to each description and set up a procedure to determine whether, when confronted by a new description of any length or complexity (letting the imagination go a bit here), it should assign one of those same markers to the new description. With the addition of the ability to detect inconsistencies between descriptions of that kind, it would know when it was given a description that would cancel one of the descriptions on the alternative list. The operations could be conducted over event markers (atoms), with the result that benefits in storage and retrieval efficiency would increase quite significantly. If currently available resolution, unification and inferencing methodologies were to be used in such an environment, they would achieve far greater results than they currently achieve because of the specificity that would be carried in the event markers. It is these enticing prospects that are prompting the development of event matching capabilities in SMS that will maximize the benefits that can be realized through use of currently available methodologies. Section 11.8 describes how the most basic resolution technique can be employed effectively in an environment of event markers.

CHAPTER 11

# CORRESPONDENCE AND INFERENCING

## 11.1 Preliminary Remarks

The derivation process in SMS depends upon a host of functions that define crucial correspondences within the system. The approach used is to postulate a set of SL formalisms to be accessed in building the DB component. The mechanics of proof depend in large measure upon the correspondences described in this section. The following notation will be used schematically to describe those correspondences:

1) the symbols 'ss, $ss_1$, ..., $ss_n$' will continue to stand for sentence-sequences;

2) the symbols 'sf, $sf_1$, ..., $sf_n$' will continue to stand for sentence-sequence formalisms;

3) the letter 'S' will stand for the set of all well formed sentential sequences;

4) the letter 'F' will stand for the set of all well formed sentential formalisms.

By taking schemata to be formalisms, the closure of SL formalisms can be defined by the schemata presented in section 2.3.2 for the closure for well formed sentence-sequences, but the reader should recall that descriptions pertaining to type have been omitted from those schemata.

## 11.2 WFSSs, WFSFs and Their Penumbras

As explained in sections 4.2.1-4.2.2, a set of direct inferences and a set of penumbral inferences can be produced for each SL statement. For convenience of discussion, the notion of penumbra will be redefined here to include direct inferences as well as penumbral inferences so that for any SL statement, the penumbra of that statement will include all the direct and penumbral inferences that can be generated from it. In the discussions that follow, the letter 'P' will be used to represent penumbras. Subscripts will be attached to the letter to identify the sequence to which the penumbra belongs. Thus, $P_{ss1}$ would stand for the penumbra of the sentence-sequence $ss_1$. An italicized P will be used to represent families of penumbras, and subscripts will be attached to the letter to identify the particular family. Thus '$P_F$' represents the family of penumbras of all *wfsfs*, and $P_S$ represents the family of penumbras of all *wfsss*.

As stated previously, the derivation process depends on the defined correspondence between components of SMS. This section describes the scheme of correspondence between *wfsss*, *wfsfs*, and their penumbras. The scheme can be explained in terms of the functions:

$$f : \{ x \mid x \text{ is a wfss} \} \rightarrow \{ y \mid y \text{ is a wfsf} \};$$

$$g : F \rightarrow P_F; \text{ and}$$

$$h : S \rightarrow P_S.$$

The correspondence between $P_S$ (the family of penumbras for sentence-sequences) and $P_F$ (the family of penumbras of formalisms of sentence-sequences) can be specified using the restriction:

$$( g \circ f ) \text{ to } h^{-1} (y),$$

where $y \in P_S$. Thus, for any $y \in P_S$, the corresponding penumbra z in $P_F$ is determined by:

$$( g \circ f ) \mid h^{-1} (y).$$

## 11.3 Intrasentential Inferencing

This section describes the theoretical basis of intrasentential inferencing in SMS. The inferencing patterns will be described for an environment in which statements carry assigned values of presence as described in sections 1.3 and 4.2. It should be kept in mind that for a given SMS implementation, it may be possible to specify the sets F (the set of sentential formalisms of SL) and $P_F$ (the family of penumbras of the sentential formalisms) in advance if the demand for expressive power is not too great. A relatively small number of formalisms can suffice to represent a significant amount of general information (see section 12.1). By being instantiated with appropriate linguistic objects taken from the vocabulary of SL, the formalisms of F can be converted into sentence-sequences. Perhaps the easiest way to understand the scheme of intrasentential inferencing is to regard the formalisms as axioms, each of which is associated with an independent rule of inference. Such a rule of inference might take the form:

$$<\beta_{i\text{-}ti} \text{ cause } < \beta_{j\text{-}tj} \text{ has-emot } \beta_{k\text{-}tk}>$$

---

$$<\beta_{j\text{-}tj} \text{ has-emot } \beta_{k\text{-}tk}>$$

$$<\beta_{i\text{-}ti} \text{ mcause } \beta_{k\text{-}tk}>$$

$$<\beta_{i\text{-}ti} \text{ xcause } \beta_{j\text{-}tj}>$$

where $\beta$ ranges over concrete markers and '$_{ti}$', '$_{tj}$' and '$_{tk}$' represent constraints on type. The premise and conclusion segments of this valid argument formalism can be instantiated uniformly by proper instantial terms to produce sentence-sequences that bear the relation to one another that is indicated by the argument form. For a term to qualify as a proper instantial term, it would have to meet the type requirements specified for the variable it replaces.

An alternative conception of the scheme is possible in terms of the 'if ...then ....' construction. An expression of the form '$<\text{if } \Phi \text{ then } \Delta>$', in which $\Phi$ is the antecedent and $\Delta$ is the consequent, means that if $\Phi$ is present, then $\Delta$ is also present. If the argument forms of the sort given previously were to be expressed in 'if ...then ....' constructions, so that $\Phi$ would range over the premises and $\Delta$ over the conclusions of those argument forms, only a single inference rule would be required to produce the same effects produced under the previous conception. The inference rule would correspond to *modus ponens* of FOL and would take the form:

$$<\text{if}\Phi \text{ then } \Delta>$$

$$\Phi$$

---

$$\Delta$$

Although this conception is as valid as the previous one, the former conception will be used to describe the intrasentential inferencing scheme to stress the point that each formalism is given special recognition and treatment in building SMS (see e.g. section 4.2.2). The idea of there being a special rule for each formalism seems to place proper emphasis on this point.

The effect of having a special inference rule for each sentential formalism is that a penumbra consisting of direct and penumbral inferences can be generated for each formalism, which amounts to postulating a penumbra for each formalism. The conclusion segment of the inference pattern constitutes the penumbra of the premise in the pattern. Each formalism/penumbra combination can be saved as a stored relation so that when an SL sentence is entered into the system, the formal structure of that sentence can be coded and associated with the appropriate formalism/penumbra combination, which, in turn, can be instantiated to produce a penumbra for that sentence. The penumbras of the formalisms can be related to one another in precise ways that can be recognized in inferencing. One formalism, for example, may entail another as a direct inference. Each component of the entailed formalism has a named position within that entailed formalism, and it will also have a named position in the inclusive formalism. SMS recognizes the relation between the two named positions and, if necessary, can move from the consideration of one position to another when attempting to satisfy a query. If the query bears the structure of the entailed formalism, that query may be satisfiable in a database statement that bears the structure of the inclusive formalism even when it is not satisfiable in a top-level database statement that bears the structure of the entailed formalism. The point is that SMS knows about the pertinent relations in advance and thus knows what type of structures it should search and where in those structures the search should be conducted.

In addition to the inference rules postulated for each formalism, the instantiation and generalization rules described in Chapter 10 and the intrasentential patterns and rules of replacement listed below are all employed in intrasentential inferencing. Unless otherwise explicitly given, each expression implicitly carries the value IPR. The value $V_{tainted}$ signifies tainted presence. Where appropriate, correspondence with patterns or principles of the propositional calculus is indicated.

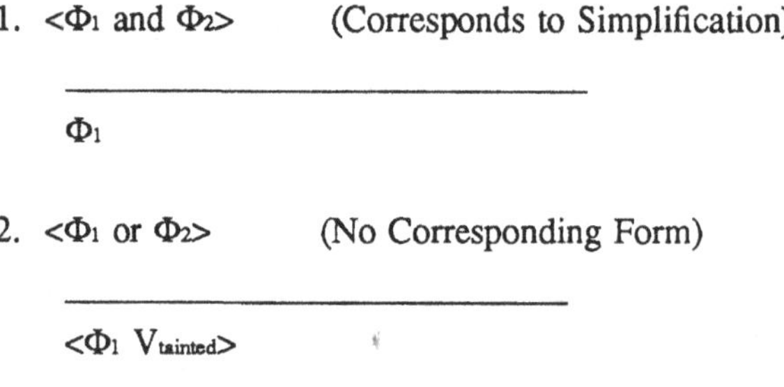

1. <$\Phi_1$ and $\Phi_2$> (Corresponds to Simplification)

   ---

   $\Phi_1$

2. <$\Phi_1$ or $\Phi_2$> (No Corresponding Form)

   ---

   <$\Phi_1$ $V_{tainted}$>

3. <<$\Phi_1$ or $\Phi_2$> is= <$\Phi_2$ or $\Phi_1$>> (Corresponds to Commutation)

4. <<$\Phi_1$ and $\Phi_2$> is= <$\Phi_2$ and $\Phi_1$>> (Corresponds to Commutation)

5. <<$\Phi_1$ or <$\Phi_2$ or $\Phi_3$>> is= <<$\Phi_1$ or $\Phi_2$> or $\Phi_3$>> (Corresponds to Association)

6. <<$\Phi_1$ and <$\Phi_2$ and $\Phi_3$>> is= <<$\Phi_1$ and $\Phi_2$> and $\Phi_3$>> (Corresponds to Association)

SL statements that bear the form '<If $\Phi_1$ then $\Phi_2$>' do not indicate the presence of either $\Phi_1$ or $\Phi_2$. The presence of $\Phi_2$ can be derived if the presence of $\Phi_1$ is given, and <$\Phi_1$ NPR-IC> can be derived if the presence of $\sim\Phi_2$ is given (see section 11.4). In addition, <If $\Phi_1$ then $\Phi_2$> $\vdash$ <<$\Phi_1$ NPR> or $\Phi_2$> (see section 11.8). The following pattern is also recognized in SMS:

$$\frac{\langle \text{If } \Phi_1 \text{ then } \Phi_2 \rangle \qquad \text{(No Corresponding Form)}}{\langle \text{If } \langle \Phi_1\ V_{tainted\text{-}i} \rangle \text{ then } \langle \Phi_2\ V_{tainted\text{-}i} \rangle \rangle}$$

where $V_{tainted}$ ranges over values indicative of tainted presence.

Now that mention has been made of some of the more important intrasentential principles and inferencing patterns, the general scheme for conducting this kind of inferencing can be described. Given that $\Gamma_{SS}$ is a set of sentence-sequences of SL and that $\Gamma_{SF}$ is a set of sentential formalisms that correspond to $\Gamma_{SS}$, a formalism $sf_i$ is present in $\Gamma_{SF}$ from an intrasentential perspective if $sf_i$ matches any top level formalism in $\Gamma_{SF}$ or any formalism in the penumbra or inference-set (see sections 10.2.1 and 10.2.2) of a member of $\Gamma_{SF}$. Similarly, a sentence-sequence $ss_i$ is present within $\Gamma_{SS}$ from this perspective if it matches a sentence-sequence either at the top level in $\Gamma_{SS}$ or in the penumbra or inference-set of a member of $\Gamma_{SS}$. The mapping from sentence-sequences to formalisms is an *onto* mapping. For any $sf_i \in F$ and $P_{sfi} \in P_F$, the following holds:

$$\text{If } \Gamma_{SF} \vdash^{IPR} sf_i$$
$$\text{then } \Gamma_{SF} \vdash^{IPR} P_{sfi}$$

It also holds that:

$$\text{If } sf_i \in P_{sfk} \text{ and } sf_i \notin \langle sf1, \ldots, sfn \rangle \text{ and } sf_k \in \langle sf1, \ldots, sfn \rangle$$
$$\text{then } \langle sf1, \ldots, sfn \rangle \vdash^{IPR} sf_i.$$

The strength and validity of the derivation process is perhaps best understood through an explanation of its subprocesses, such as the process by which a sentence-sequence containing at least one phrase-sequence (i.e. a sequence consisting of a root term and one or more modifiers; see section 2.3.1) is converted into a set of *bare* sentence-sequences, that is, sentence-sequences that do not contain any modifiers other than quantifiers and special operators. The sequence '<john saw <person <tall>>>' is not a bare sequence because the label 'person' is modified by the adjectival label 'tall', whereas the sequences '<john saw person>' and '<person is tall>' qualify as bare sentence-sequences because none of their components have modifiers. The process by which bare sentence-sequences are produced will be illustrated herein by schematic example since the formalisms and sentence-sequences of SL are infinite in number and have an infinite number of structural differences. The first step in the process consists of converting each top level phrase-sequence into a set of independent sentence-sequences leaving only the root terms (atoms) of the phrase-sequences as constituents of the original sequence. The process continues recursively for each member of the set of independent sentence-sequences, and the results, including the bare version of the original sequence, are joined to form a single set. The process is schematically outlined below.

The process by which a phrase-sequence is converted into a set of sentence-sequences will be explained first. Given *f* as a function that converts a preposition into a link by prefixing 'v-' to the preposition (e.g. the preposition 'at' would be converted into 'v-at', where the prefixed 'v-' indicates that the term has the status of a link), and given a phrase-sequence of the form:

$< p_1 < pr_1\ p_2 > < pr_2\ p_3 > >$

where '$p_1$', '$p_2$' and '$p_3$' stand for noun labels, and '$pr_1$' and '$pr_2$' stand for prepositions, the following sentential sequences would be produced:

1) $< p_1$ v-$pr_1\ p_2 >$ ; and

2) $< p_1$ v-$pr_2\ p_3 >$.

In other words, the root term of the phrase-sequence has been related to the objects of the prepositions by links constructed from the prepositions by the function *f*.

Given that any phrase-sequence can be converted into a set of sentential sequences using operations similar to those described above for prepositional phrases, it is easy to define the function *h* that assigns a set R to a sentence-sequence containing modifiers, where R is a set of bare sentential sequences produced as described above. Thus, for example, given a sentential sequence of the form:

$< \theta_1\ \delta_1\ \theta_2 \ldots \theta_n >$

where $n \geq 2$, $\delta_1$ is an n-place link or link phrase, and $\theta$ ranges over phrase-sequences, the corresponding set R would consist of:

$\{< \alpha_1\ \upsilon_1\ \alpha_2 \ldots \alpha_n >\} \cup h(\theta_1) \cup h(\delta_1) \cup h(\theta_2) \cup \ldots \cup h(\theta_n)$

where '$\alpha_1\ \alpha_2 \ldots \alpha_n$' represent the root terms of $\theta_1$, $\theta_2$, and $\theta_n$ respectively, and $\upsilon_1$ is the root link of $\delta_1$.

It should be noted that the derivation process employs special procedures when a conjunctive, disjunctive, or combinative sequence (see section 7.4 for the meanings of these terms) is involved either as a premise or as a conclusion to be proved. Section 4.6 gives examples of some of those procedures. Given that no such sequence is involved, the process for determining whether one sentential sequence $ss_i$ can be derived intrasententially from another $ss_j$ can be delineated stepwise as follows.

1)the set $R_1$ is determined by $h(ss_i)$;

2) the set $R_2$ is determined by $h(ss_j)$; and

3) an attempt is made to match each $ss_k \in R_1$ with a member of $R_2$ or with a member of the penumbra or inference-set of a member of $R_2$.

If the attempt in step 3 fails, $ss_i$ cannot be derived from $ss_j$ as an untainted intrasentential derivation under the rules of SMS. It is possible that a penumbral match could be made, in which case $ss_i$ would follow from $ss_j$ in a penumbral sense.

### 11.4 Intersentential Inferencing

This section describes the theory behind intersentential inferencing in SMS. Again, the inference patterns will be specified for an environment in which statements bear assigned values of presence as described in section 1.3 and 4.2, which means that the rules recognize the strength of presence of the statements over which they operate. As described in sections 1.2 and 2.2, one builds an SL database in a manner similar to the way one builds a database of English text. Sentences are entered individually in sequence, and just as English sentences have stylistic constraints imposed upon them (e.g. sentences should not be too lengthly or complex), similar constraints are imposed on SL statements. Statements that contain two or more independent, sentential expressions connected by conjunctive links should be expressed as separate statements, each statement corresponding to one of the independent sentential expressions. This constraint amounts to a stylistic requirement that sentential conjuncts be entered separately. For expository convenience, the term 'statement' will be used in this section to refer to sentential expressions of SL that meet this requirement.

Section 11.3 describes the theory behind intrasentential inferencing, that is, the derivation of direct and penumbral inferences from statements on an individual basis. Intersentential inferencing, on the other hand, deals with deriving conclusions from two or more independent SL statements by using special inferencing patterns. Intersentential inferencing is thus defined over sentential expressions connected by 'and' links. At the sentential level, it corresponds to the use of syllogistic and other rules of inference in the propositional calculus. Some of the basic inference patterns used in SMS are given below. Correspondence to patterns of the propositional calculus is indicated where appropriate. The letter 'V' will be used as a variable ranging over the set of values {IPR,APR,SPR,WPR,FPR,NPR,NPR-IC}, which are the measures of strength given in section 3.3. The symbol $V_{tainted}$ will be used in an abstract mode to indicate presence that is tainted in some way and thus in each instance will represent some unspecified value drawn from the set of values {APR,SPR,WPR,FPR}. The Greek letter $\Phi$ will be used as a variable to range over well formed sentential expressions of SL. In this section the symbol $\sim\Phi$ will stand for an expression that is inconsistent with $\Phi$. Section 11.7 will define this sense of inconsistency in detail, but for present purposes all the reader need understand is that under SMS theory, $\Phi$ and $\sim\Phi$ cannot both be *present* in the same database. Since statements are entered sequentially, once $\Phi$ is entered into the database, $\sim\Phi$ will not be allowed to enter that database and hence cannot be present in it. The value of $\sim\Phi$ under the many-valued scheme in such a case would be NPR-IC. Although $<\Phi_i$ NPR-IC$>$ $\vdash$ $<\Phi_i$ NPR$>$, the reverse does not hold because the mere fact that $\Phi_i$ is not present in a database at a given point does not mean *necessarily* that it could not be present. Another point worthy of note is that any object present in a strong sense is also deemed to be present in a weak sense. Thus, $\Phi_i \vdash <\Phi_i$ $V_{tainted}>$. The reverse, of course, does not hold. As usual, the value IPR will be the default value for an expression if no other value is explicitly given. The patterns given below should be read to allow unification to produce appropriate results in addition to those specified. In other words, where formulas unify with the premises through some substitution $\theta_i$, the result of applying $\theta_i$ to the conclusion also follows as a conclusion. The basic pattern that determines the effect of the inconsistency mentioned above is:

$\Phi_1$

---

$<\sim\Phi_1$ NPR-IC$>$

This basic principle by which consistency is maintained validates the inference that if $\Phi_1$ is present, $\sim\Phi_1$ cannot be present and thus has the value NPR-IC. The following are basic intersentential inferencing patterns:

1. $<$If $\Phi_1$ then $\Phi_2>$ (Corresponds to Modus Ponens)

   $\Phi_1$

   ---

   $\Phi_2$

2. $<$If $\Phi_1$ then $\Phi_2>$ (Corresponds to Modus Tollens)

   $\sim\Phi_2$

   ---

   $<\Phi_1$ NPR-IC$>$

3. $\langle \Phi_1 \text{ or } \Phi_2 \rangle$ (Corresponds to Disjunctive Syllogism)
   $\sim\Phi_1$

   ___

   $\Phi_2$

4. $\Phi_1$ (Corresponds to conjunction)
   $\Phi_2$

   ___

   $\langle \Phi_1 \text{ and } \Phi_2 \rangle$

5. $\langle \text{If } \Phi_1 \text{ then } \Phi_2 \rangle$ (Corresponds to Hypothetical Syllogism)
   $\langle \text{If } \Phi_2 \text{ then } \Phi_3 \rangle$

   ___

   $\langle \text{If } \Phi_1 \text{ then } \Phi_3 \rangle$

Patterns of the following sort, here created by substituting indicators of tainted presence for implicit IPR values in pattern 1 above, are also accepted in SMS:

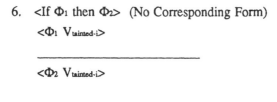

6. $\langle \text{If } \Phi_1 \text{ then } \Phi_2 \rangle$ (No Corresponding Form)
   $\langle \Phi_1 \; V_{\text{tainted-i}} \rangle$

   ___

   $\langle \Phi_2 \; V_{\text{tainted-i}} \rangle$

7. $\langle \text{If } \langle \Phi_1 \; V_{\text{tainted}} \rangle \text{ then } \Phi_2 \rangle$
   $\Phi_1$

   ___

   $\Phi_2$

8. $\langle \text{If } \langle \Phi_1 \; V_{\text{tainted-i}} \rangle \text{ then } \Phi_2 \rangle$
   $\langle \Phi_1 \; V_{\text{tainted-i}} \rangle$

Patterns too numerous to list here can be created in a way similar to that done to produce patterns 6 - 8 by substituting, when and where appropriate, indicators of tainted presence for implicit IPR values in the inference rules that have counterparts in the rules of the propositional calculus, such as the Constructive Dilemma and the Hypothetical Syllogism just to name two.

An important use of 'If ... then ....' statements is given in pattern 5 above, which is used for the production of inferences by standard forward chaining operations. The forward chaining operations in SMS are defined for 'If ... then ....', causal, and other transitive relations. A causal chain is defined as a relation between any two sentential objects that conform to the pattern:

9. $<<\Phi_1 \text{ cause}_i \ \Phi_2>$

and

$<\Phi_2 \text{ cause}_j \ \Phi_3>>$

where 'cause' ranges over the link 'cause' and its alternate forms and derivatives, including those that carry only penumbral strength. With reference to this pattern, the following inference pattern is used for forward chaining over causal relations:

10. $<\Phi_1 \text{ cause}_i \ \Phi_2>$

$<\Phi_2 \text{ cause}_j \ \Phi_3>$

---

$<\Phi_1 \text{ cause}_k \ \Phi_3>$

where '$\text{cause}_k$' represents a causal link that is tainted, perhaps only slightly, because of the remoteness of $\Phi_1$ from $\Phi_3$ (i.e. $\Phi_2$ stands between the two in the causal chain) and perhaps because of penumbrality that might be associated with either '$\text{cause}_i$' or '$\text{cause}_j$', or both, for some other reason. The principles of forward chaining that operate over transitive relations are referred to collectively in this book as 'transitivity principles'. It should be noted that SMS is being designed to keep track of causal chains that are created within its database. Section 11.5 describes some basic theory behind querying in SMS and gives an overview of the proof theory adopted thus far for the system, including the theory that has been adopted for causal chains.

## 11.5 Querying and the Process of Proof

For a first-order knowledge base (KB), a query can be defined to be any formula of FOL. A query of this form is answered by consulting the provability relation $\vdash$ to determine what does and does not follow from the KB (e.g. Levesque, 1984). In SMS, a query is any *wfss* of SL, and answerability is defined with reference to the derivability relation $\vdash^{P}$ . The posing of an SL query to SMS amounts to asking the system whether the query can be derived from the DB. The system attempts to satisfy the query by employing the inference patterns and principles described in sections 11.3 and 11.4. The following subsections describe the theories of query preparation and employment that have been adopted thus far for use in the system.

### 11.5.1 Querying

SMS employs functions that transform sequences that contain modifiers into *bare* sequences for convenient handling. A *bare* sequence is one that does not contain modifiers other than quantifiers and special operators. Each query is transformed into a sequence of subqueries, each of which is a bare sentential sequence, and the system attempts to satisfy each subquery by matching or unifying the subquery with a database object. Given that *f* is a function that assigns a query a sequence of bare sentential subqueries, the query:

A large green block is heavy?

could be assigned the following sentential sequences through application of the function *f*:

<<block is large> <<block<the>> is green> <<block<the>> is heavy>>.

The article ‘a’ in the original sentence would be interpreted as a request to the system that it find any instance of a block that satisfies all three sequences. For a query to be satisfied, each subquery, taken in the order in which it appears in the sequence, must be satisfied. It should be noted that the sequences produced by the function *f* contain appropriate cross-indexing operators so that, to the extent that the query is satisfiable by finding substitution instances for one or more of its components, appropriate substitutions can be applied uniformly throughout the subqueries. Thus, if the system finds an instance of the label ‘block’, say ‘block-7’, that is ‘large’, thereby satisfying the first subquery, the value ‘block-7’ would become bound in a substitution to the label (cf. variable) ‘block’ of the first subquery and, as result, would be substituted for ‘block’ in the other subqueries based on the presence of the cross-referencing operators. Each resulting subquery would have to be satisfied to satisfy the original query based on this instance of 'block'.

It would be nice if everything was as simple as described in these examples. The truth is that matters are vastly more complicated than these examples might lead one to believe. Temporal relations, causality, quantification and other complex factors and operations frequently become relevant in the querying process, and each presents unique problems. Nonetheless one can gain a general understanding of what is involved through consideration of this simple example. The following notation will be used to give schematic descriptions of of what is involved:

(1) $\beta$ will range over items in the vocabulary of SL that correspond to the parts of speech of ordinary English (e.g. nouns and verbs), and these items will be referred to as *atoms*;

(2) $\alpha$ will range over properties that have been assigned to the atoms mentioned in (1) above;

(3) $\theta$ will range over position codes representative of precise structural positions in the sentential expressions and formalisms of SMS;

(4) $\sigma$ will range over lists of indices for sentential expressions that constitute a database of assertions in SMS;

(5) $f$ and $g$ will range over functions; and

(6) $\Phi$ will range over sentential expressions.

Numbers will be attached to the Greek letters to differentiate occurrences.

As explained previously, each query can be expanded into a sequence of subqueries (by application of the function $f$), and each subquery must be satisfied in the database. Just as the function $f$ can be defined to assign a sequence of subqueries to a given sentential sequence, the function $g$ can be defined to assign a sequence of *atoms* to any subquery in the sequence produced by the function $f$. In addition, the function $g$ can be defined to assign a structure and position code, a quantifier (if present), and one or more special operators (if present) to each atom in the sequence it produces. The scheme for a bare sequence that does not contain quantifiers or operators is discussed below.

Given $\Phi_i$ and that $f(\Phi_i) = Q$

the following holds for any $\Phi_k \in Q$:

$$g(\Phi_k) = \langle\langle \alpha_1\ \theta_1\rangle, \ldots, \langle \alpha_n\ \theta_n\rangle\rangle$$

Thus, any element of the sequence Q can be mapped to a sequence of ordered pairs, each pair consisting of an atom and its structure/position code. The satisfaction of each $\Phi_k$ of Q requires that each atom $\alpha_i$ of $\Phi_k$ be matched in the database in a way that accords with whatever structure/position code is associated with that atom. A complete match requires that each atom in the subquery bear an index in common with the other atoms in the subquery. A separate match results for each common index found. One can see how this theory of query satisfaction can be implemented for a database of frames or property lists without much difficulty because each atom of each sentential sequence stands alone and can be assigned a frame or property list. Quantifiers of database atoms can be converted into symbols for properties or slots. An atom quantified by 'any', for example, can be assigned an 'any' slot or an 'any' property that will receive or be assigned values consisting of indices for instances of the atom that are quantified by the term 'any'. Each atom can be associated with structural codes, indices, and other information that relate the atom to other objects present in the database. A database designed for the querying process is schematically represented in Figure 22. In the database scheme, exactly one list of properties exists, and that list is repeated for each atom.

---

$$<< \beta_1 < \alpha_1 << \theta_{1,1,1} \quad \sigma_{1,1,1} > \; < \theta_{1,1,2} \quad \sigma_{1,1,2} > \ldots < \theta_{1,1,m_{1,1}} \quad \sigma_{1,1,m_{1,1}} >>>$$

$$\vdots$$

$$< \alpha_n << \theta_{1,n,1} \quad \sigma_{1,n,1} > \; < \theta_{1,n,2} \quad \sigma_{1,n,2} > \ldots < \theta_{1,n,m_{i,n}} \quad \sigma_{1,n,m_{1,n}} >>>>$$

$$< \beta_2 < \alpha_1 << \theta_{2,1,1} \quad \sigma_{2,1,1} > \; < \theta_{2,1,2} \quad \sigma_{2,1,2} > \ldots < \theta_{2,1,m_{2,1}} \quad \sigma_{2,1,m_{2,1}} >>>$$

$$\vdots$$

$$< \alpha_n << \theta_{2,n,1} \quad \sigma_{2,n,1} > \; < \theta_{2,n,2} \quad \sigma_{2,n,2} > \ldots < \theta_{2,n,m_{2,n}} \quad \sigma_{2,n,m_{2,n}} >>>>$$

$$< \beta_k < \alpha_1 << \theta_{k,1,1} \quad \sigma_{k,1,1} > \; < \theta_{k,1,2} \quad \sigma_{k,1,2} > \ldots < \theta_{k,1,m_{k,1}} \quad \sigma_{k,1,m_{k,1}} >>>$$

$$\vdots$$

$$< \alpha_n << \theta_{k,n,1} \quad \sigma_{k,n,1} > \; < \theta_{k,n,2} \quad \sigma_{k,n,2} > \ldots < \theta_{k,n,m_{k,n}} \quad \sigma_{k,n,m_{k,n}} >>>>>$$

---

Figure 22. Database Scheme

If a bare subquery contains quantifiers, those quantifiers must be taken into account when satisfying components of the subquery. Special rules govern how quantifiers affect the process of query satisfaction. The rules are specified with reference to various classifications of query components. A component that is an atom is either a marker or a label and is either quantified or not. If such a component is not quantified, the general rules for interpreting it for query-satisfaction purposes can be stated as follows:

a) if the component is a marker, it is interpreted as a request to the system to prove that the database contains a marker that is syntactically or semantically identical to that component or that the database contains an expression that subsumes it.

b) if the component is a label, it is interpreted as a request to prove that the database contains either an instance of the label or an expression that subsumes the component.

The structural and position code information associated with the component must also be satisfied in the database, as is the case for all the types of query components mentioned in this section.

The rules for quantified components of bare subqueries are specified with reference to quantifier type. Each quantifier type is governed by one or more special rules. Basically, the rules conform to the rules given in Chapter 10 that define the various quantifiers. For the quantifier 'any', for example, the request to the system is interpreted as one to prove that each and every member of the quantified object bears the relation called for by the subquery. One way for the system to proceed in an attempt to satisfy the request is to search for an identical object in the database that is quantified by 'any', whether explicitly or by way of permissible derivation from an instance in which the object is quantified by one of the special universal quantifiers (e.g. 'all*'). Another way to satisfy the request is to find that the database contains a subsuming expression. Still another way to satisfy it is to search out each member of the quantified object and determine that it holds the relation called for by the subquery. Sometimes the system can identity all the members of the object quantified and thus is in a position to proceed in this way.

A subquery component that is quantified by 'some*' or 'some' is interpreted as a request to prove that the database contains an instance of the quantified object, an identical component, or an expression that subsumes the subquery component. The component '<student<some>>', for example, may be satisfied by any database marker created for 'student', '<student<some>>' or '<student<some*>>'. It may also be satisfied by an expression that subsumes any of these, such as the expressions '<student<any>>' and '<being<any>>'. When the system is called upon to prove that multiple relations hold for the subquery component, if the quantifier of that component is 'some', the system must find that all the relations hold for the same instance or marker, whereas if the quantifier is 'some*', it need only show that each relation holds for some instance or marker that satisfies the component.

As a last resort, for a bare subquery containing one or more quantifiers, the system can interpret the subquery as a request to prove that each element of the *core* of the *inference-set* of that subquery is provable from the database. Under such an interpretation, the system would treat each element of the core of the inference-set as a separate subquery.

Combinative, conjunctive and alternative sequences are specially treated in the querying process. Given a conjunctive sequence of the form:

<$x_1$ and ... and $x_n$>

where $n \geq 2$ and '$x_1$ ... $x_n$' range over atoms, phrase sequences and sentential sequences, one can see that the greater the length of the sequence, the greater becomes the number of sequences that can be produced by manipulating the positions of the conjuncts within the given sequence. Each such sequence produced is equal to the original sequence in the derived sense sense of equality described in section 4.3 and can be considered to be a derivation that follows from the original sequence. This corresponds to the rule of Commutation in FOL. Since the larger 'n' becomes, the greater becomes the number of syntactically unique derivations that follow from the sequence, a special technique had to be developed to handle the combinatorial problem that would be faced in the derivation process. Section 4.6 describes one way of addressing the problem. Another method consists of reducing the conjunctive, alternative or combinative sequence to its normal form before processing it (see section 4.4). One can see how this technique can be used in the querying process of SMS, which employs syntactical matching procedures. The query would first be reduced to its normal form, and the system would attempt to satisfy each element of that normal form in the DB. Without this technique and the methods described in section 4.6, the system might have to search out the whole combinatorial range of possibilities to satisfy the query.

The querying scheme described in this section is based on matching terms and structure/position codes at the atomic level. These processes ground important higher level processes, such as those that produce qualified responses to queries and those that engage in modal inferencing. They also provide the demarcation of an appropriately segmented environment that can be analyzed in bottom-up fashion with a view toward bringing concurrent processing to bear on some of the more difficult processing problems.

### 11.5.2 The Proof Process

This section gives an overview of the proof theory that has been adopted for SMS. The proof process will be explained by schematic example involving a query that contains a 2-place link. In this example, it is to be assumed that all subqueries are also expressible in terms of 2-place links. Given a query $\Omega_i$ that has been assigned, as described in section 11.5.1, a sequence of subqueries of the form < <$\Phi_i$ $\delta_i$ $\Delta_i$>, . . ., <$\Phi_n$ $\delta_n$ $\Delta_n$> >, where $\Phi$ and $\Delta$ range over atoms and bare sentential objects, the process of proof will be explained by describing how '<$\Phi_i$ $\delta_i$ $\Delta_i$>' would be handled. To satisfy (prove) the inclusive query, each subquery, or the result of applying an appropriate substitution to that subquery, must be satisfied. The proof processes that are applicable to one subquery in this example are applicable to all.

The first step in the process is to attempt to satisfy the first subquery '$<\Phi_i\ \delta_i\ \Delta_i>$' (herein also to be represented as $\Omega_{sub-1}$) under the *intra*sentential inferencing scheme described in section 11.3. As part of that process, an attempt can be made to satisfy $\sim\Omega_{sub-1}$ by intrasentential methods, where $\sim\Omega_{sub-1}$ represents a sentential object that is inconsistent with $\Omega_{sub-1}$. If $\sim\Omega_{sub-1}$ is satisfiable, then $\Omega_{sub-1}$ is not satisfiable. With reference to the subquery '$<\Phi_i\ \delta_i\ \Delta_i>$', which is now the object of attention, it should be noted that if $\delta_i$ does not represent a transitive connection through which relations with other objects may be inherited or passed on, the failure to satisfy $\Omega_{sub-1}$ intrasententially implies that it cannot be satisfied under the rules of the system unless it can be derived through backward or forward chaining over 'If ... then ....' or causal structures or through resolution over disjunctive sequences. If, for example, the query '<john saw mary>' is not provable intrasententially or in one of the other ways mentioned, the system has no way of extracting 'john' from one statement and 'mary' from another and then casting them into a 'saw' relationship with one another. The link 'saw' does not invoke transitivity mechanisms under the proof rules, and the system does not allow proof by uncontrolled extraction of components from statements for the purpose of casting them into relationships that meet the specifications set by the query. Under the current rules of the system, such a procedure is allowed only in the special cases mentioned in the following discussions.

If '$<\Phi_i\ \delta_i\ \Delta_i>$' cannot be proven by intrasentential methods, an attempt is made to prove it by *inter*sentential methods. One way to proceed is by use of standard chaining and resolution methods described frequently in the AI literature (e.g. see Genesereth and Nilsson, 1987; Charniak and McDermott, 1985). In *backward chaining*, for example, an attempt is made to appropriately unify the subquery with the consequent of an 'If ... then ....' expression through some substitution $\theta$, and if that succeeds, the substitution $\theta$ is applied to the corresponding antecedent of the expression, and the resulting substitution instance is invoked as a subquery to be satisfied. If the resulting substitution instance is satisfied, the original subquery is satisfied. In SMS, these methods are employed in a standard way, but it should be pointed out that they are invoked in an environment of sentential markers, which is like invoking them for expressions of the propositional calculus. The effects of the predicate calculus are incorporated into the scheme by employing unification and instantiation operations over event markers. One sentential marker is a proper instantial term for another marker of that type when the statement represented by the former is a proper instantial combination for the statement represented by the latter. As discussed in section 10.5. the sentential marking system is not yet complete, but the theory seems to work, at least at the level it is being implemented. FOL-based systems also are typically implemented at selected levels of complexity that enable them to operate efficiently. Some systems use clausal form databases, for example, and employ resolution methods on expressions that match one another at the normalized level at which only ground literals exist. Temporal and other information that would suffice to completely individuate sentences is lacking in many of those systems. The point is that it is a quite common practice to implement a theory at a practical level of complexity at which it can handle the kind of problems it is likely to encounter.

In addition to the standard methods mentioned above, the following approach is employed in intersentential inferencing. First, an attempt is made to prove $\Phi_i$. If $\Phi_i$ is an atom, an attempt is made to find an instance of that atom that has a structure/position code that satisfies the structure/position code called for by the query (see section 11.9 for pertinent discussion on the use of structure and position coding). If $\Phi_i$ is a sentential object, the proof process is invoked recursively on $\Phi_i$. If $\Phi_i$ cannot be satisfied under any of the methods mentioned in this section, then $\Omega_{sub-1}$ is not provable under the proof mechanisms of SMS. If $\sim\Phi_i$ is provable, the the value to be assigned to $\Omega_{sub-1}$ is NPR-IC.

If $\Phi_i$ is proven, an attempt is made to prove $\Delta_i$ using the same methods described for $\Phi_i$, and the same results occur if $\Delta_i$ cannot be proven. If both $\Phi_i$ and $\Delta_i$ are proven, an attempt is made to prove the *connection* between the two, that is, the relation represented by $\delta_i$ or one of its penumbral derivatives. The process by which this is done will be illustrated by an example involving the link 'cause' and its alternative and derivative forms. Taking $\delta_i$ to be the link 'caused', the next step in the process is to attempt to establish a connection between $\Phi_i$ and $\Delta_i$ through the link 'cause' or one of it derivatives. As mentioned in section 11.4, SMS is being designed to keep track of the causal relations and chains that are created in its database. A causal chain conforms to pattern 9 given in section 11.4. A cross-indexing scheme is being developed that relates objects to the causal chains of which they are a part. Given that the structure of a causal chain $C_i$ is:

$<\theta_1$ and-cc $\theta_2$ and-cc . . . and-cc $\theta_n>$

(where $\theta$ ranges over sets of objects, whether atomic, phrasal or sentential, where 'and-cc' is a special conjunctive link used to represent causal chains and where n > 2), to satisfy the subquery in this example by applying transitivity rules to causal chains, it must be found that $\Phi_i$ is equal to or is part of an object that is a member of some $\theta_i \in C_i$, and that $\Delta_i$ is equal to or is a part of an object that is a member of some $\theta_k \in C_i$. It must also be found that the position of $\theta_i$ in $C_i$ precedes that of $\theta_k$ in $C_i$. If those specifications are met, the following holds:

$<\theta_i$ cause$_i$ $\theta_k>$

where 'cause$_i$' is a penumbral derivative of the link 'cause' and represents taintedness based on remoteness (see pattern 10 in section 11.4). At this juncture, the precise connection between $\Phi_i$ and $\Delta_i$ can be determined using the intrasentential rules of the system. This is so because $\theta_i$ and $\theta_k$ are, in respective order, expressible in SL as the subject and object of the link 'cause$_i$'. As result, a penumbral connection of a particular sort can be recognized and an appropriately qualified response can be generated for the query.

It should be noted that the proof processes specified above for intersentential inferencing is applicable to any sentential object that is inconsistent with the original query so that proof by negative assumption may also be invoked as needed. An additional proof technique is described in section 11.8 on resolution.

### 11.6 Many-Valued Approach Appreciable at the Atomic Level

The many-valued approach used in SMS depends upon the ability of the system to generate a response value for any ordered pair of SL atoms. As is described in section 11.5, any query $\Phi_i$ is transformable into a sequence of subqueries, each of which must be satisfied to satisfy the original query. Each of those subqueries can be transformed into a sequence of ordered pairs of atoms and structure/position codes, the sequence bearing the form:

$$< <\alpha_1, \theta_1>, ..., <\alpha_n, \theta_n> >$$

(where $n > 1$, $\alpha$ ranges over SL atoms, and $\theta$ ranges over structure/position codes). An attempt is made to match each atom of the transformed subquery with a database component. The many-valued approach is grounded on matches made at this atomic level. Each atom $\alpha_i$ of the transformed subquery is assigned a set of relevant atoms $\{\alpha_i, ..., \alpha_n\}$ so that for any member of the set that is matched in the database, an associated and predetermined response can be given for the atom $\alpha_i$. The result is that a response value can be returned for each ordered pair in the transformed subquery. In other words, the elements of the sequence $< <\alpha_1, \theta_1>, ..., <\alpha_n, \theta_n> >$ can be mapped into a set of response values $\{v_1, v_2, v_3, . . . v_n\}$, where $n \geq 3$. Thus, each ordered pair of the sequence can be assigned a response value, so that a corresponding *sequence of response values* can be assigned to the original subquery. A function can then assign the sequence of response values a single value, which in turn, can be assigned to the original query. What this amounts to is that the response values that are assigned to atoms determine the responses values that are assigned at the sentential level of the subquery. The whole process is defined to proceed in a bottom-up manner.

It is at the atomic level that the basis for the many-valued approach first becomes appreciable. Each atom in the vocabulary of SL is related to every other atom in the system in one or more ways. Atoms are related to one another in a general way based merely on the fact that they are part of the same system. Type/subtype relations (defined through links) and singular/plural relations are examples of more specific relations that hold between atoms. Given any of these relations and any two atoms, a function can be defined to determine whether the relation holds between the atoms. Thus, given any atom and any relation, a set can be defined to consist of all the atoms, if any, that bear the given relation to that atom. Schematically speaking, given the atom $\alpha_i$ and the set $\{\alpha_j, ..., \alpha_n\}$ as consisting of those atoms that bear the relation R to $\alpha_i$, the set A can be defined to consist of the set of ordered pairs that have $\alpha_i$ as the first element and a member of $\{\alpha_j, ..., \alpha_n\}$ as the second element. A function *g* can then be defined as follows: $g : A \rightarrow \{v_1, ..., v_n\}$, where $n > 1$ and '$\{v_1, ..., v_n\}$' is a set of response values. In other words, a specific response value can be assigned to every pair that satisfies the relation as described above. Section 3.5 also describes this aspect of the approach.

## 11.7 Maintaining Consistency

This section describes the theoretical basis of consistency maintenance in SMS. As discussed in section 8.3, the consistency relation may hold between any types of objects in SMS, whether atomic or sentential. One of the most basic relations of inconsistency at the atomic level is the relation between a link and its negation. A link is negated by concatenating the expression '-not' to the link, but if the link already ends with '-not', the link is negated by removing that expression from the link. Thus, for example, the links 'is' and 'is-not' are negations of one another and are inconsistent in this sense. A broader notion of inconsistency between links can be specified by employing the derivability relation at the atomic level. Given that $\delta$ ranges over links and that '~' flags the negated form of a link, any link $\delta_i$ is inconsistent with:

(1) $\sim\delta_i$;

(2) $\sim\delta_j$ (where $\delta_j$ is a synonym of $\delta_i$); and

(3) $\sim\delta_k$ (where $\delta_i \vdash \delta_k$).

As to (3), if the derivability relation holds at the atomic level between $\delta_k$ and $\delta_i$, so that $\delta_k$ is provable from $\delta_i$, it follows that $\delta_i$ is inconsistent with $\sim\delta_k$. Thus, if *walk* were to be defined in terms of *move*, so that *walk* $\vdash$ *move*, the link 'walk' would be inconsistent with the link 'move-not'.

Inconsistency defined at the atomic level can be extended to include inconsistency at the sentential level. Given that $\Phi$ ranges over bare sentential objects that do *not* contain quantifiers, the most basic type of inconsistency that is defined for such an object is that between the sentence and its negation, which is formed by negating the primary link of the sentence. The primary link is the root of the expression that occupies the second position in the sentential sequence. Unless otherwise indicated, in these discussions the negation of such a sentence will be represented by prefixing the symbol ~ to whatever symbol represents the sentence, as in $\sim\Phi_i$. This contrasts with the usage in section 11.4 in which an expression of the form $\sim\Phi_i$ is used in a general way to represent any expression that is inconsistent with $\Phi_i$, not just the negation of $\Phi_i$. Taking the form $\sim\Phi_i$ to represent the negation of a bare and quantifierless sentence, such a sentence $\Phi_i$ is inconsistent with:

1) $\sim\Phi_i$;

2) $\sim\Phi_j$ (where $\Phi_j$ is a direct inference of $\Phi_i$ or is an inference that follows from $\Phi_i$ with a degree of strength of APR); and

3) $\sim\Phi_k$ (where $\Phi_j$ or $\Phi_j$ is a proper instantial combination of $\Phi_k$).

[Note: A sentence covered by $\Phi_k$ may or may not contain one or more quantifiers.]

Under this scheme, if the following relation holds:

($\beta_1$ loves $\beta_2$) $\vdash$ ($\beta_1$ has-emot emot-pos$_1$)

(where $\beta$ ranges over concrete atoms and 'emot-pos' ranges over 'positive emotions') then the following also holds:

($\beta_1$ loves $\beta_2$) $\sim\Xi$ ($\beta_1$ has-emot-not emot-pos$_1$)

(where $\sim\Xi$ is the symbol for the relation of inconsistency).

Inconsistency between bare sentences that contain quantifiers is defined with reference to the relations between sentences and their conjugations. As discussed in section 7.8, any SL sentence $\Phi_i$ has a conjugation that is partitioned into sentences that are consistent with $\Phi_i$ and those that are not. Given that the set $C\text{-}_{\Phi i}$ contains the inconsistent conjugate sentences for $\Phi_i$, the basic principle by which consistency is maintained in SMS can be stated as follows:

> $\Phi_i$ is consistent with any SMS database $DB_i$ if no member of $C\text{-}_{\Phi i}$ is present in $DB_i$ and if, for any $\Phi_k$ that is either a direct inference of $\Phi_i$ or an inference that follows from $\Phi_i$ with a degree of strength of APR, no member of $C\text{-}_{\Phi k}$ is present in $DB_i$.

An extended notion of conjugation has been adopted for SMS. The theory behind conjugation can be explained with reference to a transformation process that is defined to operate on SL sentences to produce conjugations. The process proceeds in a bottom-up manner by applying specially defined rules of transformation. The transformation of an SL sentence is constructed by first applying appropriate rules of transformation to the components of the sentence and by then relating the constituents of the resulting transformations to one another using other rules. The process is similar to the one used to create *inference-sets* for sentential objects (see sections 10.2.1 and 10.2.2). The transformation process treats atoms, as well as labels with attached quantifiers or operators, as *basic units* and creates transformations for each basic unit. The transformation of a basic unit will be referred to herein as an *atomic transformation*. Thus, an expression of the form:

$<\beta_i <\psi_i>>$

[where $\beta$ ranges over labels (e.g. 'person') and $\psi$ ranges over quantifiers (e.g. 'any')] would qualify as a basic unit that would have an atomic transformation consisting of the set of all expressions that can be produced under the following rules by substituting markers for labels or labels for markers, or by substituting labels for labels or quantifiers for quantifiers, or both:

1) any label or quantifier may be replaced by itself;

2) $\beta_i$ may be replaced by $\beta_j$ if one of the following relations holds:

(a) $\beta_j$ *isa* $\beta_i$; or

(b) $\beta_i$ *isa* $\beta_j$;

3) any quantifier may be replaced by another quantifier;

4) any label may be replaced by any member of its extension; and

5) any marker $\alpha_i$ can be replaced by itself, by any label $\beta_k$ such that $\alpha_i$ *isa* $\beta_k$, or by a marker $\alpha_k$ such that '$\alpha_i$ is= $\alpha_k$'.

The set from which no new expressions can be produced under the recursive application of these rules would constitute the atomic transformation for $<\beta_i <\psi_i>>$. The atomic transformation of '<man <any>>', for example, would include expressions such as '<man <some>>' and 'ue-777' (where 'ue-777' *isa* 'man') as well as expressions such as '<person <any>>' and '<person <some>>' (where 'man' *isa* 'person').

By using the atomic transformations of the basic units that are comprised by a given SL sentence, a *sentential transformation* for that sentence can be produced by combining, in appropriate order, elements drawn from the atomic transformations. Given a finite number of markers, labels, quantifiers, and a determined set of *isa* relations and extensions for the labels, the recursive application of the transformation process for an SL sentence $\Phi_i$ can be made to reach a fixed point at which no new expressions can be created by application of the combinatory rules. Given that $T_t$ is the set of transformations produced for $\Phi_i$ under the process described thus far, a complete conjugation in the broadest sense defined for the system could be produced for $\Phi_i$ by creating negations of the sentences in $T_t$ and by employing a function $\Omega_t$ that produces transformations by replacing, as appropriate, noun and link components of SL sentences with their corresponding negations. Given, for example, that the range of recognized states of happiness and unhappiness is {happy neutral-emot unhappy}, the following would hold:

$\Omega_t$( <mary is happy> ) = { <mary is-not unhappy>, <mary is-not neutral-emot>, . . . . }

A complete transformation of $\Phi_i$ would be created as follows:

1) the set $T_{tn}$ would be created to consist of the negations of the sentences in $T_t$, the negations being formed by negating the primary links of the sentences.

2) the set $T_{\Omega t}$ would be created by applying $\Omega_t$ to the elements of: $T_t \cup T_{tn}$.

The complete conjugation $T_c$ for $\Phi_i$ would consist of:

$$T_t \cup T_m \cup T_{\Omega t}.$$

A set of special transformation rules can be specified to produce a subset of $T_c$ that consists only of sentences that bear particular relations to the conjugated sentence $\Phi_i$. Just as inference patterns can be employed at the nonsentential level to produce inference-sets (see section 10.2.1), the special transformation rules can be applied at the nonsentential level to determine which expressions are to be included in the atomic transformations of basic units. The rules can be used to create a subset of $T_c$ that, in turn, can be converted into a set of inconsistent conjugate sentences for $\Phi_i$ in a straightforward manner, as the following example illustrates. To keep matters simple, this example will not cover negations of *noun* components, and thus $T_c$ will be restricted to sentences that contain positive rather than negative noun components. In other words, a positive noun like 'planet' will be used instead of a negative form like 'non-planet'. Given a version of SMS that recognizes only two quantifiers, say 'any' and 'some', and that the only labels recognized other than proper names are 'person', 'planet', and 'thing', and where 'john' *isa* 'person' and is concretely individuated, 'mars' *isa* 'planet', and a 'planet' *isa* 'thing', and given the sentence:

<john likes <planet <any>>> (44)

the set $C_{\sim cj\text{-}44}$, consisting of the inconsistent conjugate sentences of (44), can be constructed as follows. First, a set of consistent conjugate sentences can be created for (44) using the previously described rules of substitution and combination. Given that the set $A_{john}$ is the atomic transformation of 'john' and that the set $A_{<planet<any>>}$ is the atomic transformation of the expression '<planet<any>>', the set of consistent conjugate sentences $C_{cj\text{-}44}$ for sentence (44) would include all sentences of the form $<\theta_i$ likes $\theta_j>$, where $\theta_i \in A_{john}$ and $\theta_j \in A_{<planet<any>>}$. Thus, $C_{cj\text{-}44}$ would include sentences such as:

<<person <any>> likes <thing <any>>

<<person <any>> likes <thing <some>>

. . .

<<person <some>> likes <thing <any>>

<<person <some>> likes <thing <some>>

. . .

<<person <any>> likes <planet<any>>

<<person <any>> likes <planet <some>>

<<person <any>> likes mars>

. . .

<john likes <thing <any>>

<john likes <thing <some>>

. . .

<john likes <planet <any>>>

<john likes <planet <some>>>

<john likes mars>

. . . .

In order to create $C_{\sim cj\text{-}44}$ [i.e. the inconsistent conjugate sentences for (44)], the set $B_{cj\text{-}44}$, where $B_{cj\text{-}44}$ is a subset of $C_{cj\text{-}44}$, would be created first. The set $B_{cj\text{-}44}$ can be distinguished as a subset of $C_{cj\text{-}44}$ by restricting membership in the atomic transformations $A_{john}$ and $A_{<planet<any>>}$. This can be done by applying special transformation rules. The rules are set forth below in a schematic form in which $\alpha$ ranges over concrete markers and $\beta$ ranges over labels. An expression to the left of an arrow will represent the type of expression for which the transformation is to be constructed, and the expressions to the right of an arrow will represent the members of the transformation.

1) $\alpha_i \rightarrow \alpha_i$; $\alpha_k$ (where $\alpha_k$ is= $\alpha_i$); and <$\beta_i$ <any>> (where $\alpha_i$ *isa* $\beta_i$).

2) <$\beta_i$ <some>> $\rightarrow$ <$\beta_i$ <any>>; <$\beta_k$ <any>> (where $\beta_i$ *isa* $\beta_k$).

3) <$\beta_i$ <any>> $\rightarrow$ $\alpha_i$ (where $\alpha_i$ *isa* $\beta_i$); <$\beta_i$ <some>>; <$\beta_i$ <any>>; <$\beta_k$ <any>> (where $\beta_i$ *isa* $\beta_k$); <$\beta_j$ <any>> and <$\beta_j$ <some>> (where $\beta_j$ *isa* $\beta_i$).

By constructing atomic transformations for the expressions 'john' and '<planet <any>>' using these rules and by then relating the components of the results as was explained previously for the complete conjugation of sentence (44), the sentences so produced would constitute a subset of $C_{cj\text{-}44}$. The sentence:

<<person <any>> likes <thing <any>>> (45)

is a member of $C_{cj\text{-}44}$ and would also be a member of $B_{cj\text{-}44}$ under the rules of restriction given above. On the other hand, although the sentence:

<<person <some>> likes <thing <some>>> (46)

is a member of $C_{cj\text{-}44}$, it would not qualify for membership in $B_{cj\text{-}44}$ because the expression '<person <some>>' would not be a member of the restricted version of $A_{john}$. Also, '<thing <some>>' would not be a member of the restricted version of $A_{<planet<any>>}$. The set $B_{\sim cj\text{-}44}$, consisting of inconsistent conjugate sentences of sentence (44), can be created simply by negating the primary links in the sentences contained in $B_{cj\text{-}44}$. Thus, sentences such as the following would be included in $B_{\sim cj\text{-}44}$:

<<person <any>> like-not <thing <any>>>

. . .

<<person <any>> like-not <planet <any>>>

<<person <any>> like-not <planet <some>>>

<<person <any>> like-not mars>

. . .

<john like-not <thing <any>>>

<john like-not <planet <any>>>

<john like-not <planet <some>>>

<john like-not mars>

. . . .

The relation between each member of $B_{\sim cj\text{-}44}$ and sentence (44) is defined to be one of inconsistency.

From the foregoing discussion, one can see that for sentence (44) to be consistent with a given SMS database $DB_i$, at the very least, no member of $B_{\sim cj\text{-}44}$ may be present in $DB_i$. Fortunately, there are short-cut methods that can be employed to run the test for this sort of consistency for a given $DB_i$. Every SL sentence $\Phi_i$ has a corresponding set of inconsistent conjugate sentences $B_{\sim cj\Phi i}$, and $B_{\sim cj\Phi i}$ has a corresponding minimum set of queries $Q_q$ such that if any member of $Q_q$ is satisfiable in $DB_i$, then $DB_i \vdash x$, where $x \in B_{\sim cj\Phi i}$. In other words, if a member of $Q_q$ is derivable from $DB_i$, then $\Phi_i \sim\Xi\ DB_i$. This system of testing for consistency is somewhat easy to implement. A function, call it $\Omega_\Xi$, can be defined to produce $Q_q$ for any SL statement $\Phi_i$ so that $Q_q$ can be presented to the system as a set of queries to be tested. Sentence (44) can be used as an example. To test the consistency between sentence (44) and a given $DB_i$, the function $\Omega_\Xi$ would be employed to produce $Q_q$ for sentence (44). The principles under which $\Omega_\Xi$ operates are based on general principles to the effect that any general assertion may be disproved by proving a contrary instance either of that assertion or of one of its direct inferences, and that any concrete assertion may be disproved by proving its negation or the negation of one of its direct inferences. To disprove that '<john likes <planet <any>>', the system need only find that 'john' does not like some 'planet', and thus, the the following sequence would be an element of $Q_q$ for sentence (44):

<john like-not <planet <some>>>

Under the querying rules of SMS, when the quantifier 'some' is used in a *query* in an expression of the form <$\beta_i$ <some>>, the quantifier is taken as an instruction to the system to find either an instance of $\beta_i$ or an expression from which <$\beta_i$ <some>> can be derived, such as the expression <$\beta_i$ <any>>. Thus, for example, if the system were to determine that 'mars' is an instance of 'planet' and would find that the database contains the assertion '<john like-not mars>', the original statement (44), which reads:

<john likes <planet <any>>>

would be inconsistent with this database.

For a *complex* statement $\Phi_i$ to be consistent with a given database $DB_i$, it must be shown, using the methods described in this section, that:

1) $\Phi_i \Xi DB_i$; and

2) $\Phi_k \Xi DB_i$ (where $\Phi_k$ is a direct inference of $\Phi_i$ or is an inference that follows from $\Phi_i$ with a degree of strength APR).

This discussion of consistency maintenance in SMS is intended to give the reader an idea of the basic approach being used in this area to develop the system. These techniques are not adequate to handle some of the more difficult problems of consistency maintenance. The system as described could not detect, for example, that an assertion to the effect that John is a college professor of English is very likely inconsistent with an assertion to the effect that John does not read English. Nonetheless, the techniques described are the basic ones that would be employed in attempting to detect inconsistency between these two assertions. To handle this sort of inconsistency, more information, such as a description of the skills of a typical professor of English, would have to be available to the system. A detection of the likelihood of inconsistency in such a case would depend on the ability of the system to transform and manipulate the available information into a state in which one of the types of consistency described in this section could be detected. In a given case, the inconsistency may be detectable only at the level of the system that contains the atomically normalized version of the available information. To say the least, some very difficult consistency problems can be presented by quite ordinary discourse about quite ordinary matters. Although the results on the less difficult problems described in this section have been promising, there is much work still to be done in the development of SMS to enable it to operate usefully at higher levels of problem difficulty. The hope is that the basic techniques described herein can be extended to meet the task.

## 11.8 Using the Resolution Principle

The resolution principle developed by Robinson (1965) has been used extensively in AI systems as a proof mechanism. A formula that is provable from a given set of logically consistent premises can be shown to follow from those premises by negating the formula, adding it to the premises, and then deducing a contradiction by resolution. The basic idea is that formulas can be resolved against one another to produce new formulas that are valid. Formulas are first transformed into clauses and then cast into conjunctive normal form. Any two clauses x and y may be resolved against one another if clause x contains a disjunct that is the negation of a disjunctive literal of clause y. The resolvent is produced by removing those disjuncts from the clauses and combining the results into one clause. The clauses removed are the ones that are the negations of one another. One can see that the process produces valid results by taking the familiar hypothetical syllogism and simply transforming each premise and the conclusion into disjunctive form under the rule for material implication so that:

$$p \supset q$$
$$q \supset r$$
$$\overline{\qquad\qquad}$$
$$p \supset r$$

becomes:

$$\overline{\qquad\qquad}$$
$$\sim p \vee r$$

(where the bidirectional arrow points to the disjuncts that are eliminated). In other words, the resolution principle applied to '(~p v q) • (~q v r)' produces the resolvent '(~p v r)'. Powerful resolution techniques have been developed over the years to make the resolving process efficient. The process is effective both in the propositional calculus and in the first-order predicate calculus. The details about how the process works will not be discussed here since those details have been given on frequent occasion in the AI literature (e.g. Stickel, 1988; Genesereth and Nilsson, 1987; Wos *et al*, 1984; and Robinson, 1965). Instead, the discussion will focus on the most basic resolution principle employed in the system to demonstrate how an adequate system of event individuation can be employed to make resolution strategies operate effectively at the level of event markers (see comments in section 10.5).

At the level of event markers, resolution techniques can be employed as the database is built. Each entering statement can be resolved against database statements, where appropriate, so that the database is maintained in an optimized state. For every disjunctive sentence-sequence that is entered, a corresponding set-theoretic structure can be created for that sentence-sequence. Section 4.6 describes how a disjunctive sentence-sequence can be converted into a data-set structure consisting of the disjuncts of the sequence. The data-set is bound to marker which, in turn, is bound to a modal qualifier that flags the fact that the data-set has been derived from a disjunctive sequence. Such a qualifier prevents the application of normal set-theoretic principles to the data-set. Given, for example, that a statement of the form:

< $\Phi_i$ or $\Phi_j$ >

has been entered into the database, a corresponding and marked data-set structure would be created in conformity with the scheme diagrammed below.

| Data-Set | | Marker | | Qualifier |
|---|---|---|---|---|
| { $\Phi_i$ $\Phi_j$ } | <---> | AS-1 | <---> | alt |

Here 'alt' (for alternation) represents a qualification on the marker that is bound to the data-set. If subsequently the statement $^{\sim}\Phi_j$ were to be entered, where $^{\sim}\Phi_j$ represents a statement that is inconsistent with $\Phi_j$, one can see that $\Phi_i$ would be present to degree 'IPR' because at the IPR level there is a direct mapping to the disjunctive syllogism of the propositional calculus (see section 11.4). In the current implementation of SMS, every time a statement is entered, any statement that is inconsistent with the entered statement is removed from every disjunctive data-set that contains the inconsistent statement. By assigning event markers to the statements, the efficiency of the process can be optimized because operations can be made to operate over markers instead of sentential expressions. In this example, for instance, if $^{\sim}\Phi_j$ were to be entered, $\Phi_j$ would be removed from the disjunctive data-set structure { $\Phi_i$ $\Phi_j$ } to produce { $\Phi_i$ }, which the system would take to be a unit data-set structure. Any disjunctive data-set structure reduced to a unit structure yields the presence of its single element. Thus, in this example, the full presence of $\Phi_i$ would be recognized. This simply amounts to the following: Given that at least one member of a list of alternatives is present in the database and that all the alternatives on the list except one are not present, it follows that the one excepted is present in the database. SMS is being designed to assign event markers to statements as they enter the database and to optimize, by resolution, all disjunctive data-set structures containing event markers so that if any set is reduced to a unit set, the element of that set is given full presence in the database.

As mentioned in section 11.3, the following holds: <if $\Phi_i$ then $\Phi_k$> $\vdash$ <<$\Phi_i$ NPR> or $\Phi_k$>. When given a statement of the form <if $\Phi_i$ then $\Phi_k$>, the system creates a disjunctive data-set structure to accommodate the inference <<$\Phi_i$ NPR> or $\Phi_k$> so that the resolution rules can produce proper results for the 'if ... then ....' construction. Thus, for example, the expression <$\Phi_i$ NPR> would be subject to being eliminated from that data-set based on relations of inconsistency such as:

$\Phi_i$ $\sim\Xi$ <$\Phi_i$ NPR>

and

$\Phi_i$ ~Ξ <$\Phi_i$ NPR-IC>.

In other words, if $\Phi_i$ were to become present in the database, <$\Phi_i$ NPR> would be eliminated from the data-set based on its inconsistency with $\Phi_i$, and the presence of $\Phi_k$ would be yielded under the rules described in this section.

A sequence of the form < $\Phi_i$ or $\Phi_j$ > presented as a conclusion to be proved from the database is, by default, taken to be a request to the system to succeed in doing at least one of the following:

(1) prove the presence of $\Phi_i$;

(2) prove the presence of $\Phi_j$; or

(3) prove the presence of < $\Phi_i$ or $\Phi_j$ >.

It is easy to explain the strategy behind requests (1) and (2): a disjunctive conclusion is proved if any one of its disjuncts is proven. The idea behind request (3) requires a little explanation. A request given in the form of an alternative sequence to be proven is taken as a request to the system to show that this sequence, or one semantically equivalent to it, is present in the database. Instead of showing that one of the disjuncts of the sequence can be proven, the system is called upon to show that the alternative sequence itself, or one semantically equivalent to it, is present.

The basic procedure used to implement requests (1) and (2) is to show that the requested sequence is present or is derivable by the strategies described in sections 11.3 and 11.4. The same procedure is applicable to request (3), but in addition, standard resolution strategies, modified appropriately for the SMS environment, may be invoked in an attempt to satisfy the request. The system is being designed so that the standard methodologies can be implemented over event markers.

## 11.9 Implementing SMS Theory

The SMS theory described in this book has not been specified with reference to any particular mode of implementation. The intent is to leave open the possibilities in this regard. Because SMS theory is defined in a bottom-up manner so that what holds at the atomic level determines what holds at the sentential level (see sections 11.5 and 11.6), a number of possible modes of implementation are available and feasible, including object-oriented approaches. Each atom of an SL statement, including each link, bears precise relations to other atoms in the system and can be treated in isolation. Links can be assigned properties and structure/position codes like any other object. Frames or property lists can be built for atoms and accessed in querying. Figure 22 in section 11.5.1 describes an abstract database structure that could be implemented in frames or property lists.

The prototype of SMS was written in Franz LISP and employed property lists. The hope is that parallel processing, and perhaps neural nets, will make possible some implementations that are not currently being considered. The system has been defined from the atomic level upward in hopes that advances in hardware and software development will produce better methods of taking advantage of the kind of *atomized* environment within which SMS operates so that the system can reach its full potential.

As described in sections 11.5 and 11.6, querying can proceed quite straightforwardly for an implemented database that captures the features of the database described in Figure 22. It should be noted that each atom in that database is used only once regardless of how many times the atom appears in the SL input, and that makes storage tasks less burdensome than they otherwise might be. Each label can be assigned a frame or property list that can serve as a receptacle for information about any instance of the label that appears in individuated SL input. In other words, the label itself serves as a basic indexing mechanism. Each label bears independent intrasentential and intersentential information about position and structure, and this information can be incorporated into the frames or property lists and itself perform an indexing function. The abstract database structure given in Figure 22 is designed to receive this kind of information and to employ it in this way. Information in the form of sentential structure codes and intrasentential position codes can be effectively employed to minimize search area. The system need not search a part of the database that is indexed by a particular atom, structure code or position code, for example, if the information associated with the query atom does not bear one or more recognized relations to that database information. One of the most important benefits that results from this approach is that since atoms carry all the information necessary for them to be treated in isolation, related atoms need not be stored in close proximity to one another in the statements that introduced them into the database. The practical constraint here seems to be that the system must be capable of finding an atom in a reasonable amount of time when called upon to do so in querying.

By defining relations between abstract structures and their components as has been done for the sentential formalisms of SL, relations between actual statement components can be determined with reference to the relations between their abstract counterparts. This is the theory behind the intrasentential methods described in section 11.3. The approach being employed is to provide the system with as much abstract information in advance as possible and feasible and to develop methods by which concrete information can be converted into abstractions in an efficient way so that it can be treated with the knowledge that the system already has available. The results thus far seem promising, but it appears that to develop and implement SMS theory to its full potential, a significant amount of success must be realized in achieving the goals set forth in section 10.5 event individuation.

## CHAPTER 12

# SMS IN ACTION

### 12.1 A Session with SMS

This section will describe a brief session with original version of SMS to illustrate some of its underlying theory. The version described is being enhanced to meet the goals set forth in the previous chapters. As mentioned in section 11.3, a set of sentential formalisms is processed in advance and saved as stored relations to be accessed by SMS when statements are entered into the database. The processing consists of constructing penumbras for the formalisms and of relating those penumbras to one another in precise ways. If an entering sentence bears a structure that matches a processed formalism, the sentence is accepted, but if not, the system pauses and processes the new structure before accepting the sentence into the database. Any subsequent entry bearing that structure does not have to be processed again and thus would not cause the system to pause.

The session described in this section uses a small set of basic sentential formalisms that conform to the patterns given in figure 23. Although few in number and simple in form, the formalisms can be employed to capture more information than perhaps one might first imagine. Much of the theory that has been described in the foregoing chapters has been implemented in SMS. The system knows SL syntax and knows how to individuate complex sentential expressions that contain modifiers by breaking them down into sets of more basic expressions that can be individuated more efficiently. With the exception of proper names, terms used in this session are entries in the lexicon of the system. A proper name need not be in the lexicon to be used (see section 2.3.4). Plural and singular forms of links are taken to be synonymous, whereas the same does not hold for terms other than links, such as nouns.

---

(?a is ?b)
(?a ism ?b)
(?a isa ?b)
(?a has ?b)
(?a has-own ?b)
(?a has-possess ?b)
(?a has-emot ?b)
(?a v-of ?b)
(?a v-l-from ?b)
(?a v-n=i ?b)
(?a or ?b)
(?a and ?b and ?c)
(?a cause (?b has-own ?c))
(?a likes ?b)
(?a v-bmo ?b)

---

Figure 23. Basic Sentential Patterns

One builds a database in SMS by using the command '(stdb)' and by then entering database statements written in SL. The following descriptions of database construction are written in uppercase letters. Brackets are used sometimes to make the reading easier. In the actual program, everything is written in lowercase letters, and parentheses instead of square brackets are used in punctuation. The system is menu-driven and prompts the user to enter statements or queries one at a time. To save space, the menu and prompts are sometimes omitted from the session described below. Comments to the right of the semicolons either describe the corresponding command or give an English interpretation of the corresponding SL statement. The comments have been inserted for the convenience of the reader and are not part of the session. In the first part of the session, some simple statements are entered into the database, and a few queries are processed to illustrate the system of qualified response. The session begins when the user types:

(STDB); The command to build a database.

The system responds by prompting the user for a statement, and statements are entered as shown below.

Please enter statement at arrow or type q to quit

```
***> (OWNERS HAVE LAND)            ; Some owners have
                                     some land.

(LESSEE HAS LEASE)                 ; Some lessee has a
                                     lease.

[(OWNERS(BLK)) HAVE LAND]          ; Some owners (in a
                                     joint sense)
                                     have some land.

[PERSON (IS(T-AT TR-1)) HAPPY]     ; Some person
                                     is happy at
                                     a particular time.
```

The modifier 'BLK' (for *block*) means that the term modified is to be taken as a unit. A session ends when the user types 'q' to quit. When that is done, the system is prepared to respond to queries. It should be noted that the system recognizes the sequential order in which statements are entered and assigns numbers to those statements as part of its indexing mechanism. A complex statement yields a set of statements (see sections 9.3 and 11.3), and each member of the set is assigned a different number.

One asks questions in SMS by using the command '(stqq)' and by entering queries written in SL when the system prompts for them. The description of the querying process given below for the most part is written in lowercase letters for convenient contrast with the description of database construction. The system responds to queries by giving qualified responses where appropriate. This version of the system uses four values (MB, SPMB,SPNO, and NO) to describe tainted presence. The value YES is used to indicate full presence. The value NO indicates that the query cannot be satisfied as stated but that if appropriate changes were to be made in the modifying phrases entailed in the query or if particular information were to be made available, the query would be satisfiable to some degree. If the system cannot find information that is sufficiently relevant to a query, it responds by saying that it could not satisfy the query. The values YES, MB, SPMB, SPNO, and NO (listed here in decreasing order of strength) roughly correspond to the values IPR, APR, SPR, WPR and FPR that are defined in Chapter 3. The querying session begins when the user types:

```
(stqq)   ; The command to start a querying session.
```

The system prompts the user to enter a query, and queries are entered as shown below:

Please enter query at arrow or type q to quit

***> (owner has land) ; Some owner has some land?

The system responds as follows:

MB-response-The following statements perhaps satisfy your query:

(1 (owners have land))

SPNO-response-Although the following statements do not match your query, they may be of interest to you:

(3 ((owners(blk)) have land))

At this point the system is ready for another query. By default, the system assumes that when either an unmodified term or a term modified by 'some' appears in a query, the system is to find any instance of the term in the database that bears the relations specified the query. Note that the system gave a dual response to the first query. The first response is qualified slightly because the query contains the word 'owner, whereas the database contains the plural form of that word. This response however is quite strong since the value MB is almost as strong as the value YES. The second response is weaker because in the third statement that was entered into the database, the modifier 'blk' was used to indicated that the 'owners' were to be taken as a unit. In other words the relation described in the statement holds for the 'owners' in a joint sense but does not necessarily hold for any one of them. The value SPNO flags part of the taintedness involved.

Now that an example of a query/response combination has been given, the prompt will be dropped and the word 'QUERY' will flag the query in each example. The session continues as follows:

QUERY: (lessees have lease) ; Some lessees have some lease?

SPMB-response-The following statements may be of interest to you because they fit your query in some respects:

(2 (lessee has lease))

Again a tainted response is given because a singular term does not match a plural form, as was the case in a previous example in which an MB response was given. In the previous case, however, the plural term was in the database and the singular one in the query, but here the reverse is true, and for that reason, a weaker response is in order and is implied by the value SPMB.

QUERY: (person is happy) ; Some person is happy?

YES-response-Your query is satisfied by statements:

(5 (person (is(t-at tr-1)) happy))

Having no temporal information in it, the query is interpreted as asking whether this relation can be found to hold for any time interval, and hence statement 5 satisfies the query. The session continues:

QUERY: (person (is(t-at tr-2)) happy) ; Some person is happy at time 'tr-2'?

NO-response-The following statements do not match your query because of qualifiers or needed information:

(5 (person (is(t-at tr-1)) happy))

This time the query cannot be satisfied as called for because of the temporal information it contains. The response indicates that but for the temporal qualifiers, the statement could be satisfied by a statement that has been indexed by the system as statement 5.

Now that some simple illustrations have been given of how the system qualifies its responses to reflect the strength of its conclusions, some examples that contain more complexity will be presented. First, the system will be given the background information that 'mary' is a 'person', and that 'baton-rouge' and 'boston' are cities. It will also be told that any 'owner' owns 'property'. This information would be entered as described above using the following SL sentences:

[(CITY(N=I BATON-ROUGE)) AND (CITY(N=I BOSTON)) AND (PERSON(N=I MARY))]

[(OWNER(ANY)) HAS-OWN (PROPERTY(SOME*))]

With this preliminary information available, some facts will be entered that are intended to conform the the English description below:

> Some owner named Paul gave Mary a car. Mary also owns a house. Some lessee of Mary's car is rich, and if anyone holds the status of being the lessee of Mary's car, that individual is this rich lessee. A lessee from Baton Rouge named John has a lease, and a lessee from Boston named Sam is a lessee of Mary's car and also owns some land.

The following SL statements are entered in an attempt to capture the meaning of these sentences:

[(OWNER(N=I PAUL)) (CAUSE(VBMO GIVE)) (MARY HAS-OWN CAR)]

(MARY HAS-OWN HOUSE)

[(LESSEE(OF (CAR(THE)))(D*)) IS RICH]

[(LESSEE(L-FROM BATON-ROUGE)(N=I JOHN)) HAS-OWN LEASE]

[(LESSEE(N=I SAM)(L-FROM BATON-ROUGE)(OF (CAR(THE)))) HAS-OWN LAND]

The term 'VBMO' is used in SL to indicate that the verb associated with the term describes the type of act that was done to 'cause' the result that is given in the statement. In this case the verb is 'GIVE', which in this example is to be assumed to bestow the status of 'owner' on the recipient of the thing given. The term 'THE' binds the label it modifies to the marker that has been assigned to a previous instance of that label (see section 2.3.3). These facts are specially tailored to illustrate particular capabilities of the system. The following queries and responses are intended to reflect those capabilities.

QUERY: (john has-own lease)

YES-response-Your query is satisfied by statements:

(17 ((lessee(l-from baton-rouge)(n=i john)) has-own lease)

QUERY: (sam has-own lease)

sorry -- could not satisfy your query

QUERY: (sam is rich)

YES-response-Your query is satisfied by statements:

(17 ((lessee(of (auto(the)))(d*)) is rich))

Note that although a statement was entered into the database that identified 'sam' not only as a 'lessee', but as the 'lessee' of the 'car' owned by 'mary', the system did not learn that 'sam' has a 'lease' because it does not know that being a 'lessee' implies that one has a 'lease'. It knows that 'john' has a lease because it was told so explicitly in a statement. It did detect, however, that because 'sam' is the 'lessee' of the 'car', 'sam' is the rich 'lessee' referred to in the database. This results from effects produced on the label 'LESSEE' by the special operator 'D*' (see section 2.3.3), which sets up a test to determine whether an object is a particular individual already referred to in the database. To cure a problem of lack of knowledge of what effects follow from having a status like being a lessee, the system has to be taught that information. The immediate problem could be solved by entering the following statement into the database at this point:

[(LESSEE(ANY)) HAS-OWN (LEASE(SOME*))] ; Any lessee has a lease.

Now the following results would occur:

QUERY: (sam has-own lease)

YES-response-Your query is satisfied by statements:

(23 ((lessee(any)) has-own (lease(some*))))

With the addition of a few more assertions to the database, some additional features of SMS can be demonstrated. The system will be told that either 'john' or 'mary' is 'happy' and that any 'person' likes at least one 'lessee'. It will also be told that there is at least one 'owner' who is liked by all people, and that 'paul' qualifies as 'at least one owner who is liked by all people'. Lastly, it will be told that 'john' is one of the lessees referred to who is liked by at least one 'person'. The following SL statements are employed to capture these ideas:

[(JOHN OR MARY) IS HAPPY]

[(PERSON(ANY)) LIKES (LESSEE(SOME*)(C* 1))]

[(PERSON(ANY)) LIKES (OWNER(SOME)(C* 2))]

[PAUL ISM (OWNER(C* 2))]

[JOHN ISM (LESSEE(C* 1))]

The term 'C*' operates as a cross-referencing mechanism to bind expressions to the same marker (see section 2.3.3). The system responds as follows to the queries given below:

QUERY: (john is happy)

SPNO-response-Although the following statements do not match your query, they may be of interest to you:

(24 ((john or mary) is happy)

Here the the value SPNO is assigned because of taintedness based on the presence of a mere alternative possibility.

> QUERY: ((person(some)) likes john)
>
> YES-response-Your query is satisfied by statements:
>
> (25 ((person(any)) likes (lessee(some*)(c* 1))))

Since it is given that 'john' qualifies as a member of a class of 'lessees', each of which is liked by some 'person', it follows that at least one 'person' likes 'john', but it is not given which 'person' likes 'john'. The following query/response brings out the latter point:

> Query: (mary likes john)
>
> NO-response-The following statements do not match your query because of qualifiers or needed information:
>
> (25 ((person(any)) likes (lessee(some*)(c* 1))))

This response is generated because it was given that 'mary' is a 'person', and the statement indexed by the number 25 indicates that any 'person' likes some 'lessee', so it follows that 'mary' likes some unspecified 'lessee'. Because it is possible that 'john' is that 'lessee', a NO response was given. One might wish to have the system under these conditions simply indicate that it could not satisfy the query. The system can be adjusted to give such a response when taintedness of this sort is found. The following query/response situation gives a different result:

> QUERY: (mary likes paul)
>
> YES-response-Your query is satisfied by statements:
>
> (26 ((person(any)) likes (owner(some)(c* 2))))

Here the system is able to deduce that the query can be satisfied because it knows that 'paul' is a member of a set, possibly a unit set, such that all people like each and every member of that set, and since 'mary' is a person, it follows that 'mary' likes 'paul'. These effects result because of the way the quantifier 'some' operates, a matter discussed in section 10.2. The quantifier 'some*' that was used in the statement 25 in the preceding example produced a different result. The operation of the quantifier 'some*' is also discussed in section 10.2. The response given to the query '(mary likes john)' would change if the system were to be informed that any 'person' who likes a 'lessee' also likes 'john', as in:

[(PERSON(ANY)(WHO LIKES (LESSEE(SOME*)))) LIKES JOHN].

If this assertion were to be added to the database, the system would respond to the query about whether 'mary' likes 'john' as follows:

QUERY: (mary likes john)

YES-response-Your query is satisfied by statements:

(29 ((person(any)(who likes (lessee(some*)))) likes john)

Since it is given that 'mary' is a 'person', it follows from the statement indexed by the system as number 25 that 'mary' likes some 'lessee', and that is sufficient to qualify 'mary' for membership in the class referred to by the expression '(PERSON(ANY)(WHO LIKES (LESSEE(SOME*))))'. This leads to the conclusion that 'mary' likes 'john' under the statement indexed by the system as number 29. As described in section 10.2, membership of an individual in such a class is determined by whether that individual passes the test for membership in that class. The test, expressible as a set of sentential sequences, specifies a set of relations that must be satisfied by a proper set of instantial combinations. In this example the test could be expressed as a unit set containing the sequence:

[(PERSON(ANY)) LIKES (LESSEE(ANY))]

The test is set up so that for any instantial combination that is subsumed by this test sequence, the object in the subject position of that instantial combination passes the test for membership in the corresponding class. In this example, the instantial combination would be '[MARY LIKES (LESSEE(SOME*))]'.

This ends the description of the session. This brief description of a session with SMS was offered to show that some of fundamentals of SMS theory have been implemented as basic features of the system. The system has many features that are not described in this session, such as its ability to explain why a particular response has been qualified and an ability to indicate how it has arrived at a particular response based on one or more generalizations. It should be noted that as discussed in section 4.6, the system produces an internal description of the basis for each type of response returned, so that if the user wishes to know the reason why a qualified response was given, the system has sufficient information available to give a fine point analysis of the qualified response. It keeps track of the paths it traverses and of each encounter along the path that causes the line of reasoning to be tainted.

## 12.2 System Limitations

The capabilities of SMS are limited in a number of areas that present particularly difficult problems. Event individuation, reasoning in epistemic and modal realms, detection of remote inconsistencies, default reasoning, and reasoning within an incomplete environment are well known problem areas that plague AI systems in general. Some of the problems SMS faces in these areas have already been described in previous sections of this book. For some of those areas, the progress made in SMS thus far amounts to the mere establishment of a perspective from which to operate in addressing problems.

Normally, at any given point in database construction, the database constitutes what might be considered to be a partial view of the SMS universe. Even so, statements that are fully present hold for the entire universe of the system because a statement that is inconsistent with the constructed database will not be allowed to enter that database. It is obvious that the system would not be able to give a yes or no answer to many queries because although formulas that evaluate to NPR-IC do not hold for the entire universe of SMS, formulas that evaluate to NPR may or may not hold for that universe. One problem is that the entire universe for a particular application may never be appreciable. In this respect, the system has features in common with what has been described as an *open system* (see Hewitt and de Jong, 1984). Whenever a formula evaluates to NPR in such a case, it means that the statement is not present in the part of the universe that is known to the system at that time. Assuming that the system knows that 'john', 'mary' and 'jim' are 'persons' and that the only database statements present in it are:

<john likes mary>

<jim saw mary>

the query '<<person<any>> likes mary>' would receive the value NPR because to deduce this conclusion, even for just this database, the system would have to find that each and every instance of 'person' likes 'mary'. It could not reach this conclusion because it would not be able to find that 'jim' likes 'mary'. It should be noted that it could not disprove the conclusion because it would not be able to find that a person 'likes-not mary'. As result, the query would be assigned the value NPR. Even if the system were to be given that '<jim likes mary>', it nonetheless would not be able to deduce this conclusion for the entire 'universe' because it has not been given that the 'persons' named are the only 'persons' in the universe. Thus, the system would have to qualify its response to indicate that its answer is based only on information known at the time. Problems of this kind described above are well known to AI researchers (see e.g. Levesque, 1984).

For databases that contain large numbers of objects, it may be difficult or even impossible to find and test all the possibilities that would be needed in a given case to reach a particular conclusion. If for instance there is no equal or general statement in the database from which the system could conclude that some individual named 'john' likes any 'number', the query '<john likes <number<any>>' could not be satisfied no matter how many times the system discovers that particular numbers are liked by 'john'.

Another problem area is consistency maintenance. A statement may be entered in database construction and be consistent with the database at that point, yet when additional information is input, the statement would cause an inconsistency if this new information were to be accepted into the database. A problem may arise because previously accepted information may have to be reconsidered just to detect the inconsistency. This can be illustrated by example. The database:

1) <<logician<any>> likes <logic<any>>> ; Any logician likes any logic.

2) <<person<n=i john>> isa <logician<cl*>>> ; John is a logician.

3) <john like-not system> ; John does not like some system.

(where English versions of the SL statements appear to the right of the semicolons) is consistent at this point, but if an attempt is made to enter the statement:

4) <<system<the>> isa <logic<cl*>>> ; The system that John doesn't like is a logic.

the system should reject the statement because it would cause an inconsistency. This is so because the statement '<john likes <logic<any>>>' follows from statements 1 and 2, and the statement '<john likes-not <logic<some>>>' is provable from statements 3 and 4. To detect this inconsistency, the system would have to compute the effects of statement 4 on the database, which in this case would require it to test all relations that entail the 'system' referred to in order to see whether they will admit of that 'system' being a 'logic'. Having to do that could cause considerable difficulty for the system.

The problem areas mentioned above constitute but some of the areas of difficulty that SMS faces. Although some of the problems do not appear to have easy solutions, if indeed some of them have solutions at all, it appears that SMS provides a promising environment within which to attempt to solve the problems. The long-term effort will reveal whether this is actually so.

## 12.3 Future Work and Concluding Remarks

Most of the features of SMS described in this book are still under development or are being enhanced to implement SMS theory more effectively. The intent in discussing the key aspects of the theory and system without presenting in-depth and fine-point descriptions of those aspects was to give the reader a view of the structure of this unified approach that is being employed to address a variety of problems. A natural language generation module is being built for the enhanced version of the system that will allow it to interact with the user in detailed discussions about inferencing, all this to be done in an environment that is friendly to the user. The scope of application of the system is being extended to include complex rule-based applications such as those found in the legal domain. A version of SL is being developed that when encoded will be indistinguishable in appearance from ordinary English. The hope is that when all the formalisms, expansions and relations that are to be used in the enhanced version have been specified, those components will be able to ground a sophisticated natural language understanding system.

# REFERENCES


Allen, J. F. (1984), "Toward a general theory of action and time," *Artificial Intelligence*, vol. 23, pp. 123-154.

Allen, J. F. (1981), "An interval--based representation of temporal knowledge," *Proceedings of the Seventh International Joint Conference on Artificial Intelligence*, Vancouver, Canada, 1981, pp. 221-226.

Bellman, R. E., and Zadeh, L. A. (1977), "Local and fuzzy logics," in [Dunn and Epstein] at pp. 105-165.

Belnap, N. D. (1977), "A useful four-valued logic," in [Dunn and Epstein] at pp. 8-37.

Bencivenga, E. (1986), "Free logics," in [Gabbay and Guenthner] at pp. 373-426.

Bledsoe, W. W. (1977), "Non-resolution theorem proving," *Artificial Intelligence*, vol 9(1), pp. 1-35.

Boy, G. A., and Kuss, P. M. (1986), "A fuzzy method for the modeling of human-computer interactions in information retrieval tasks," in [Karwowski and Mital, 1986] at pp. 117-133.

Brodie, M. L., Mylopoulos, J., and Schmidt, J. W. (eds) (1984), *On Conceptual Modelling*, Springer-Verlag, New York.

Bundy, A. (1983), *The Computer Modelling of Mathematical Reasoning*, Academic Press, London, England.

Charniak, E., (1981), "A common representation for problem-solving and language-comprehension information," *Artificial Intelligence*, vol. 16, pp. 225-255.

Charniak, E., Gavin, M. K., and Hendler, J. A. (1983), "The Frail/NASL reference manual," Technical Report CS-83-06, Department of Computer Science, Brown University, Providence, Rhode Island, February 1983.

Charniak, E., and McDermott, D. (1985), *Introduction to Artificial Intelligence*, Addison-Wesley Publishing Co., Reading, Mass.

Chen, S. (1988), "A new approach to handling fuzzy decision-making problems," *Proceedings of the 18th International Symposium on Multiple-Valued Logic*, pp. 72-76, May, 1988.

Cheeseman, P. (1985), "In defense of probability," in *Proceedings of the International Joint Conference on Artificial Intelligence*, Los Angeles, California, 1985, pp. 1002-1009.

Cocchiarella, N. B. (1966), "A logic of possible and actual objects," in abstracts for papers in *J. Symbolic Logic*, vol. 31, p. 688-689.

Copi, I. M. (1967), *Symbolic Logic*, The Macmillan Company, New York.

Copi, I. M., and Gould, J. A. (eds) (1967a), *Contemporary Readings in Logical Theory*, The Macmillan Company, New York.

Davidson, D. (1967), "The logical form of action sentences," in Rescher, N. (ed.), *The Logic of Action and Preference*, Pittsburg University Press, Pittsburg, Pa.

deBessonet, C. G., and Cross, G. (1985), "Representing some aspects of legal causality," in Charles Walter (ed.) *Computing Power and Legal Reasoning*, West Publishing Company, St. Paul, Minn.

deBessonet, C. G. and Cross, G. (1986), "An artificial intelligence application in law: CCLIPS, a computer program that processes legal information," *Berkeley High Tech Law Journal*, Univ. of Calif. at Berkeley, vol. 1, pp. 329-409.

deBessonet, C. G., and Cross, G. (1988), "Distinguishing legal language-types for conceptual retrieval," in Charles Walter (ed.) *Computer Power and Legal Language*, Greenwood Press, Westport, Connecticut.

Dubois, D., and Prade, H. (1980), *Fuzzy Sets and Systems: Theory and Applications*, Academic Press, New York.

Dubois, D., and Prade, H. (1988), "Default reasoning and possibility theory," *Artificial Intelligence*, vol. 35, pp. 145-286.

Dunn, J. M., and Epstein, G. (eds) (1977), *Modern Uses of Multiple-Valued Logic*, D. Reidel Publishing Company, Dordrecht, Holland.

Dyer, M. (1983), *In-Depth Understanding*, MIT Press, Cambridge, Mass.

Fahlman, S. E. (1979), *NETL: A System for Representing and Using Real-World Knowledge*, MIT Press, Cambridge, Mass.

Farreny, H., and Prade, H. (1986), "Dealing with the vagueness of natural languages in man-machine communication," in [Karwowski and Mital] at pp. 71-85.

Findler, N. V. (ed.) (1979), *Associative Networks: Representation and Use of Knowledge by Computers*, Academic Press, New York.

Fitting, M. (1986), "Notes on the mathematical aspects of Kripke's theory of truth," *Notre Dame Journal of Formal Logic*, vol. 27, pp. 75-88.

Gabbay, D., and Guenthner, F. (eds) (1986), *Handbook of Philosophical Logic, Volume III: Alternatives to Classical Logic*, D. Reidel Publishing Company, Dordrecht, Holland.

Gaines, B. R. (1977), "Foundations of fuzzy reasoning," in [Gupta *et al*, 1977], pp. 19-75.

Gaines, B. R., and Kohout, L. J. (1977), "The fuzzy decade: a bibliography of fuzzy systems and closely related topics," in [Gupta *et al*, 1977] at pp. 403-432.

Gallaire, H., Minker, J., and Nicolas, J. M. (eds.) (1977), *Logic and Data Bases*, Plenum Press, New York.

Gallaire, H., Minker, J., and Nicolas, J. M. (1977), "An overview and introduction to logic and data bases," in [Gallaire and Minker] at pp. 3-30.

Genesereth, M. R., and Nilsson, N. (1987), *Logical Foundations of Artificial intelligence*, Morgan Kaufmann, Los Altos, California..

Giles, R. (1985), "A resolution logic for fuzzy reasoning," *Proceedings of the 15th International Symposium on Multiple-Valued Logic*, pp. 60-67, 1985.

Gupta, M. M., Saridis, G. N. and Gaines, B. R. (eds.) (1977), *Fuzzy Automata and Decision Processes*, North-Holland, New York.

Haack, S. (1978), *Philosophy of Logics*, Cambridge University Press, Cambridge, England.

Hafner, C. (1985), "Semantics of temporal queries and temporal data," *Proceedings of the 23rd Annual Meeting of the Association of Computational Linguistics*, Chicago, Illinois, 1985, pp. 1-8.

Hart, H. L. A. (1958), "Positivism and the separation of law and morals," *Harvard Law Review*, vol. 71, pp. 593-629.

Hayes, P. (1974), "Some problems and non-problems in representation theory," in *ASIB Summer Conference, Univ. Sussex*, pp. 63-39.

Hayes, P. (1977), "In defense of logic," in *Proceedings of the International Joint Conference on Artificial Intelligence*, Cambridge, Mass., 1977, pp. 559-565.

Hendrix, G. G. (1979), "Encoding knowledge in partitioned networks," in [Findler, 1979] at pp. 51-92.

Hewitt, C., and de Jong, P. (1984), "Open systems," in [Brodie, Mylopoulos and Schmidt, 1984] at pp. 147-164.

Heyting, A. (1966), *Intuitionism*, North-Holland.

Hintikka, J. (1962), *Knowledge and Belief: An Introduction to the Logic of the Two Notions*, Cornell University Press, Ithaca, New York.

Hirst, G. (1987), *Semantic Interpretation and the Resolution of Ambiguity*, Cambridge University Press, Cambridge.

Hobbs, J. R. (1985), "Ontological Promiscuity," *Proceedings of the 23rd Annual Meeting of the Association of Computational Linguistics*, Chicago, Illinois, 1985, pp. 61-69.

Hobbs, J. R., and Moore, R. C. (eds.) (1985), *Formal Theories of the Commonsense World*, Ablex Publishing Corp, Norwood, New Jersey.

Hogger, C. J. (1984), *Introduction to Logic Programming*, Academic Press, London, England.

Israel, D. J., and Brachman, R. J. (1984), "Some remarks on the semantics of representation languages," in [Brodie, Mylopoulos and Schmidt, 1984] at pp. 119-142.

Karwowski, W., and Mital, A. (eds.) (1986), *Applications of Fuzzy Set Theory in Human Factors*, Elsevier Science Publishing Company, Amsterdam.

Kaufmann, A. (1977), "Progress in modeling of human reasoning by fuzzy logic," in [Gupta *et al*, 1977] at pp. 11-17.

Keenan, E. L., and Faltz, L. M. (1985), *Boolean Semantics for Natural Language*, D. Reidel Publishing Company, Dordrecht, Holland.

Kleene, S. C. (1967), *Mathematical Logic*, John Wiley & Sons, Inc., New York.

Kowalski, R., (1979), *Logic for Problem Solving*, North Holland, New York.

Leblanc, H., and Thomason, R. H. (1968), "Completeness theorems for some presupposition-free logics," *Fundamenta Math.*, vol. 62, pp. 125-164.

Levesque, H. J. (1984), "The logic of incomplete knowledge bases," in [Brodie, Mylopoulos and Schmidt, 1984], at pp. 165-186.

Levesque, H. J. (1986), "Knowledge representation and reasoning," in [Traub, Grosz, Lampson and Nilsson, 1987], at pp. 255-287.

Lewis, C. I. (1931), "Alternative systems of logic," *The Monist*, vol. 41, pp. 481-507.

Liu, X., and Xiao, H. (1985), "Operator fuzzy logic and fuzzy resolution," *Proceedings of the 15th International Symposium on Multiple-Valued Logic*, pp. 68-75, 1985.

Lukasiewicz, J. (1920), "O logice trojwartosciowej" (On 3-valued logic), *Ruch Filozoficzny*, vol. 5, [Tr. in McCall, S. (ed.), *Polish Logic: 1920-1939*,

Oxford University Press, (1967)].

Martin, J. N. (1987), *Elements of Formal Semantics*, Academic Press, Inc., Orlando, Florida.

McCarthy, J. (1980), "Circumscription-a form of non-monotonic reasoning," *Artificial Intelligence*, vol. 13, pp. 27-39.

McCarthy, J. (1986), "Applications of circumscription to formalizing commonsense knowledge," *Artificial Intelligence*, vol. 28, pp. 89-116.

McCawley, J. D. (1981), *Everything that Linguists Have Always Wanted to Know about Logic*, University of Chicago Press, Chicago, Illinois.

McDermott, D. V. (1978), "Tarskian semantics, or no notation without denotation!," *Cognitive Science*, vol. 2, pp. 277-282.

McDermott, D. V., and Doyle, J. (1980), "Non-monotonic logic I," *Artificial Intelligence*, vol. 13, pp. 41-72.

McDermott, D. V. (1987), "Logic, problem solving, and deduction," in [Taub, Grosz, Lampson and Nilsson, 1987] at pp. 187-229.

Mercier, C. (1912), *A New Logic*, The Open Court Publishing Company, Chicago, Illinois.

Minsky, M. (1975), "A framework for representing knowledge," in P. Winston (ed.), *The Psychology of Computer Vision*, McGraw-Hill, New York.

Moore, R. C. (1982), "The role of logic in knowledge representation and commonsense reasoning," in *Proceeding of the National Conference on Artificial intelligence, AAAI-82, Pittsburg, Pa.*, pp. 428-433.

Moore, R. C. (1985), "A formal theory of knowledge and action," in [Hobbs and Moore, 1985] at pp. 319-358.

Newell, A. (1980), "Physical symbol systems," *Cognitive Science*, vol. 4, pp. 135-183.

Nilsson, N. (1971), *Problem Solving Methods in Artificial Intelligence*, McGraw-Hill, Englewood Cliffs, New Jersey.

Nilsson, N. (1980), *Principles of Artificial Intelligence*, Tioga, Palo Alto, California.

Nute, D. (1981), *Essential Formal Semantics*, Rowman and Littlefield, Totowa, New Jersey.

Orenstein, A. (1978), *Existence and the Particular Quantifier*, Temple University Press, Philadelphia, Pa.

Patel-Schneider, P. F. (1985), "A decidable first-order logic for knowledge representation," in *Proceedings of the International Joint Conference on Artificial Intelligence*, Los Angeles, California, 1985, pp. 455-458.

Pearl, J. (1988a), "Embracing causality in default reasoning," *Artificial Intelligence*, vol. 35, pp. 259-271.

Popper, K. (1976), *Unended Quest*, Fontana/Collins, London.

Prade, H. (1982), "Possibility sets, fuzzy sets and their relation to Lukasiewicz logic," *Proceedings of the 12th Symposium on Multiple-Valued Logic*, Paris, May 24-27, pp. 223-227.

Putnam, H. (1976), Meaning and Truth, Sherman Lectures, February, University College, London.

Quine, W. V. (1980), *Elementary Logic*, rev. ed., Harvard University Press, Cambridge, Mass.

Quine, W. V. (1986), *Philosophy of Logic*, 2nd ed., Harvard University Press, Cambridge, Mass.

Reichenbach, H. (1947), *Elements of Symbolic Logic*, The Macmillan Company, New York.

Reiter, R. (1980), "A logic for default reasoning," *Artificial Intelligence*, vol. 13, pp. 81-132.

Reiter, R. (1984), "Toward a logical reconstruction of relational database theory," in [Brodie, Mylopoulos and Schmidt, 1984] at pp. 191-233.

Reiter, R. (1987), "Nonmonotonic reasoning," in [Taub, Grosz, Lampson and Nilsson, 1987] at pp. 147-186.

Rescher, N. (1969), *Many-Valued Logic*, McGraw-Hill, Inc.

Robinson, J. A. (1965), "A Machine Oriented Logic Based on the Resolution Principle," *Journal of the ACM* vol. 12, 25-41.

Schank, R. C., and Nash-Webber (eds.) (1975), *Theoretical Issues in Natural Language Processing*, Association for Computational Linguistics.

Schank, R. C., and Abelson, R. P. (1977), *Scripts, Plans, Goals, and Understanding*, Lawrence Erlbaum Associates, Hillsdale, New Jersey.

Schubert, L. K. (1976), "Extending the expressive power of semantic networks," *Artificial Intelligence*, vol. 7, pp.163-198.

Shapiro, S. (1979), "The SNePs semantic network processing system," in [Findler 1979] at pp. 179-203.

Shen, Z., Ding, L. and Mukaidono, M. (1988), "Fuzzy resolution principle," *Proceedings of the 18th International Symposium on Multiple-Valued Logic*, pp. 210-215, May, 1988.

Smets, P., Mamdani, A., Dubois, D. and Prade, H. (eds.) (1988), *Non-Standard Logics for Automated Reasoning*, Academic Press, London.

Smullyan, R. (1968), *First-Order Logic*, Springer-Verlag, Berlin.

Sowa, J. F. (1984), *Conceptual Structures: Information Processing in Mind and Machine*, Addison-Wesley, Reading, Mass.

Stickel, M.E. (1988), "Resolution theorem proving," in [Taub, Grosz, Lampson and Nilsson, 1988] at pp. 285-316.

Strawson, P. F. (1974), *Subject and Predicate in Logic and Grammar*, Methuen & Co. Ltd, London, England.

Tarnawsky, G. O. (1982), *Knowledge Semantics*, Dissertation, New York University.

Tarski, A. (1941), *Introduction to Logic and to the Methodology of the Deductive Sciences*, Oxford University Press, New York.

Thomas, J. A. (1977), *Symbolic Logic*, Charles E. Merrill Company, Columbus, Ohio.

Traub, J. F., Grosz, B. J., Lampson, B. W., and Nilsson, N. J. (eds.), (1986), *Annual Review of Computer Science*, vol 1, Annual Reviews Inc., Palo Alto, California.

Traub, J. F., Grosz, B. J., Lampson, B. W., and Nilsson, N. J. (eds.), (1987), *Annual Review of Computer Science*, vol 2, Annual Reviews Inc., Palo Alto, California.

Traub, J. F., Grosz, B. J., Lampson, B. W., and Nilsson, N. J. (eds.), (1988), *Annual Review of Computer Science*, vol 3, Annual Reviews Inc., Palo Alto, California.

Turksen, I. B. (1986), "Measurement of membership functions," in [Karwowski and Mital, 1986] at pp. 55-70.

Turner, R. (1984), *Logics for Artificial Intelligence*, Ellis Horwood Limited, Chichester, West Sussex, England.

Wallace, C. S., and Boulton, D. M. (1968), "An information measure for classification," *Computer Journal*, vol. 11, pp. 185-194.

Wang, H. (1967), "On formalization" in [Copi and Gould, 1967a].

Wilensky, R. (1983), *Planning and Understanding: A Computational Approach to Human Reasoning*, Addison-Wesley Publishing Company, Reading , Mass.

Winograd, T. (1983), *Language as a Cognitive Process: Volume 1: Syntax*, Addison-Wesley Publishing Company, Reading, Mass.

Wojcicki, R. (1988), *Theory of Logical Calculi*, Kluwer Academic Publishers, The Netherlands.

Woods, W. A. (1968), "Procedural semantics for a question-answering machine," *AFIPS Conference Proceedings (Fall Joint Computer Conference)* **33** pp. 457-471 (1968).

Wos, L., Overbeek, R., Lusk, E and Boyle, J. (1984), *Automated Reasoning*, Prentice-Hall, Englewood Cliffs, New Jersey.

Yager, R. (1980), "A foundation for a theory of possibility," *J. Cybernetics*, vol. 10, pp. 177-204.

Yager, R., (1986), "An introduction to fuzzy set theory," in [Karwowski and Mital] at pp. 29-39.

Yager, R. (1987a), "Using approximate reasoning to represent default knowledge," *Artificial Intelligence*, vol. 31, pp. 99-112.

Yager, R., Ovchinnikov, S., Tong, R., and Nguyen, H. (eds.) (1987b), *Fuzzy Sets and Applications: Selected Papers by L. A. Zadeh*, John Wiley & Sons, New York.

Zadeh, L. A. (1965), "Fuzzy sets," *Information and Control*, vol. 8, Academic Press, New York.

Zadeh, L. A. (1971), "Similarity relations and fuzzy orderings," *Information Sciences*, vol. 3, pp. 177-200.

Zadeh, L. A. (1975), "The concept of a linguistic variable and its application to approximate reasoning," *Information Sciences*, vol. 8, Parts 1 and 2, pp. 199-249, 301-357.

Zadeh, L. A. (1978), "Fuzzy sets as a basis for a theory of possibility," *Fuzzy Sets and Systems*, vol. 1, pp. 3-28.

Zadeh, L. A. (1979), "A theory of approximate reasoning," in Hayes, J., Michie, D., and Mikulich, L. I. (eds.), *Machine Intelligence*, vol. 9, Halstead Press, New York.

Zadeh, L. A. (1983a), "The role of fuzzy logic in the management of uncertainty in expert systems," *Fuzzy Sets and Systems*, vol. 11, pp. 199-227.

Zadeh, L. A. (1983b), "A computational approach to fuzzy quantifiers in natural language," in [Yager *et al*, 1987] at pp. 569-613.

Zadeh, L. A. (1985), Syllogistic reasoning in fuzzy logic and its applications to usuality and reasoning with dispositions," *IEEE Trans. Systems, Man, and Cybernetics*, SMC-15, pp. 754-763.

Zadeh, L. A. (1986), "Test-score semantics as a basis for a computational approach of the representation of meaning," *Literary and Linguistic Computing*, vol. 1, pp. 24-35.

# INDEX

9 780792 391388